Multiple Man:
Explorations in Possession and Multiple Personality

Multiple Man is a remarkable study of the phenomenon of multiple personality disorder and I am pleased that Adam Crabtree chose to include my life experience as a multiple personality patient in this fascinating work. His concepts of possession are not only intriguing and thought-provoking, but highly illuminating revelations of the innermost recesses of the mind.

—Chris Costner Sizemore,
subject of *The Three Faces of Eve*
and author of *I'm Eve*

Multiple Man:
Explorations
in
Possession
and
Multiple Personality

by
Adam Crabtree

HOLT, RINEHART AND WINSTON
London • New York • Sydney • Toronto

To Josephine, Edward and Andrew
for their understanding,
and to Frank A. Delsing for himself.

Holt, Rinehart and Winston Ltd: 1 St. Anne's Road,
Eastbourne, East Sussex BN21 3UN

British Library Cataloguing in Publication Data

Crabtree, Adam
  Multiple Man: Explorations in Possession and Multiple Personality
  1. Multiple personality
  I. Title
  616.85′236   RC569.5.M8
ISBN 0-03-910640-3

Printed and bound in Canada by John Deyell Company

Last digit is print no: 9 8 7 6 5 4 3 2 1

Contents

Introduction by Colin Wilson

A few years ago, I made a series of programs for BBC television about various aspects of the paranormal; one of them was a study of the classic case of 'multiple personality,' Christine Beauchamp, as described by her doctor, Morton Prince. Christine (whose real name was Clara Fowler) was a shy, quiet girl who would periodically lose her memory; during these periods of amnesia she was 'taken over' by a mischievous practical joker who called herself Sally, and who landed Christine in all kinds of embarrassing situations.

Each of our programs ended with a discussion among various experts, and the panel who analyzed the Beauchamp case included some distinguished psychologists. As the chairman, I naturally did my best to persuade them to advance theories to explain how two different people could apparently inhabit the same body. I expected, at the very least, some interesting speculations about the structure of human personality; but to my surprise, it was quite impossible to persuade any of the experts to stick out his neck that far. All they would say is that science has reached no agreement on the mysteries of the human personality—and then they moved on hastily to minor aspects of the case. Since then, I have raised this issue of multiple personality every time I met a professional psychologist; almost without exception, they tried to dismiss the whole problem as some kind of hysteria or semi-deliberate fraud: 'play acting'.

Now, anyone who has ever looked into the problem—even to the extent of reading *The Three Faces of Eve*—knows that this is nonsense. Multiple personality is perhaps the most baffling enigma in the whole realm of abnormal psychology, and the psychologist who finally solves it will be guaranteed an important place in science's hall of fame. In the nineteenth century, there were many remarkable cases, several of them discussed by William James in his *Principles of Psychology*. The early years of the twentieth century saw two of the most extraordinary of all such cases: Morton Prince's Christine Beauchamp, and Walter Franklin Prince's Doris Fischer.*

*I have discussed both in my book *Mysteries*.

Then came Freud and the sexual theory of neurosis. Suddenly, it was decided that multiple personality was just another kind of sexual hysteria: strange and incomprehensible, perhaps, but in the last analysis, not all that interesting. Most medical textbooks written between, say, 1910 and 1970, dismiss it in a few lines. Then in 1957, Thigpen and Cleckley's *Three Faces of Eve* aroused immense public interest in the mystery. But it was not until 'Eve' herself—real name Christine Sizemore—wrote a full account of the case (*I am Eve*, 1979) that some of its strangest aspects emerged. She describes how her little sister fell into the creek as a child, and how, that night, Jesus came to her in a dream and told her that her sister had diphtheria. She told her parents at breakfast; the doctor was sent for and confirmed that it *was* diphtheria; a serum was transported from a hundred miles away, and the child was saved. As an adult, Eve had a premonition that her husband would be electrocuted at work; she persuaded him to stay at home, and the man who took over his job was electrocuted. She gives many more examples of this kind of 'second sight'. And it becomes clear that the mystery of multiple personality is, in her case at least, inextricably mixed with problems of the 'paranormal'.

We find another hint of the same thing in *The Minds of Billy Milligan*, Daniel Keyes' remarkable study of a criminal suffering from multiple personality. One of Milligan's personalities was a Serbo-Croat named Ragen Vadascovinich, who could apparently write and speak fluent Serbo-Croat—a language Milligan himself had never had a chance to study. Keyes offers no hint of how Milligan acquired the language.

Now one of the most interesting and controversial of anthropologists, Max Freedom Long, suggested in his study of the Huna religion of Hawaii (*The Secret Science Behind Miracles*) that multiple personality may involve the phenomenon known as 'possession'. This is, of course, a view that would strike most psychologists as nonsensical. Yet it must be admitted that many of the phenomena of multiple personality *look* very much like what used to be called 'demonic possession'. This being so, there can be no harm in a doctor making a kind of provisional hypothesis that certain cases of multiple personality are of the 'possession type,' and using it as a convenient label.

This is what Adam Crabtree has done in this very remarkable book—for me one of the most exciting and disturbing books ever written on the subject of multiple personality. Crabtree, who has been a lecturer in philosophy, as well as in the psychology of religion, practices as a psychotherapist in Toronto. If he seems rather more broad-minded than most psychotherapists, this may be because he was at one time a Benedictine monk, and was ordained as a Catholic priest in 1964. In a letter to me he remarks: 'Becoming a psychotherapist was just one more step in the attempt to fathom the human psyche. In my clients I encountered experiences which were to all appearances truly paranormal, and this led me to the study of parapsychology'.

Yet he is first and foremost a scientist, and his first response to the mystery of multiple personality was to study its medical history in detail. The first part of the present book is as balanced an introduction to this bewildering topic as I have ever come across. But the most important section of the book is the one that begins with Chapter 10, describing Crabtree's own experience of such cases. It was, I think, just as well for Crabtree to offer his credentials as a scientific historian in the first part of the book, otherwise some of these cases—and I draw particular attention to those of 'The Confused Father' and 'The Complaining Mother'—would give rise to the suspicion that he is stretching his facts. While some psychologists will, no doubt, prefer to ignore Crabtree's findings, those who are open-minded enough to consider them without bias will find that they open strange and exciting perspectives.

—*Colin Wilson*
Cornwall, England
June, 1984.

Author's preface

It is characteristic of the human condition that each of us thinks of himself as a unity, all the while experiencing the greatest multiplicity. Possession and multiple personality, dramatizing as they do that baffling inner multiplicity which is the lot of human beings, probably fascinate the curious mind more than any other psychological phenomena. In possession, an individual is taken over by an entity which originates outside him. In multiple personality, he is taken over by some psychic fragment from within. *Multiple Man* will carry out a fresh examination of both phenomena in order to derive a new understanding of man's experience of himself.

The title, *Multiple Man*, says something about my view of human personality as revealed through my studies of possession and multiple personality. For me the existence of these phenomena as genuine facts of psychological experience indicates that human beings possess a mysterious inner malleability or plasticity. At some obscure depth of the psyche, a molding of discrete mental units can take place; these then manifest as separate personalities.

Whether this phenomenon is totally due to the creative power of the individual psyche, as seems the case in multiple personality, or results at times from the direct intervention of an outside agent, as possession literally implies, is for me an open question. The important thing is that both multiple personality and possession point to a remarkable inner versatility. Something which, at first glance, might be considered a negative thing: after all, in these—its extreme manifestations—nothing but misery is produced. But things are not always what they seem at first glance. In many contexts, states of possession are actually sought out. As for multiple personality, many psychiatric workers call it a *creative illness*—a condition that results from an ingenious attempt to cope with extreme difficulties while retaining the ability to function in daily life.

So perhaps a more appropriate way to view this remarkable human versatility is as something that can be used either way: to produce happiness or harm. To make this clear, consider for a moment the various personalities formed from the human psyche as *tools* needed to accomplish some task. We often speak of people having a "telephone personality," a "work personality" or a "social personality." Such personalities may be seen as instruments constructed for well-defined situations and specific tasks. How productively the personality-tool serves the individual depends on its quality and the nature of its task. If the task is a constructive one and the tool well made, the result will be positive. If the task is destructive or the tool inappropriate, the result can be disastrous.

As we examine the various cases of multiple personality and possession, we will see examples of both negative and positive results. It is my hope that the study of this extraordinary data of human experience will help illuminate more ordinary existence so as to improve our chances of releasing the tremendous potential of the human personality.

My approach is based on the premise that we have not yet as a species reached the stage of knowledge which makes possible a final pronouncement on the reality or unreality of possession and multiple personality. It is based upon the further premise that we can move toward a more complete understanding of human nature only by examining every aspect of human experience which becomes available to us, no matter how odd it may seem to be. *Multiple Man* is intended as a contribution in that direction.

Multiple Man is divided into four parts. The first is an examination of multiple consciousnesses within human beings. It includes some of the history of major discoveries made in this field over the last two hundred years and gives some examples of multiple personality cases.

The second part takes up the subject of possession, using cases from antiquity to the present to illustrate the many types of possession. It also examines the various remedies used to cure unwilling possession victims of their affliction.

Part three is drawn from my own therapeutic work with possession. It describes types of possession cases rarely mentioned in previous literature and details the therapeutic approach I use in dealing with these conditions.

The fourth part of the book details various attempts to explain the phenomena of possession and multiple personality.

The book concludes with a chapter on my own views of the nature of multiple man in light of the information so far available.

—*Adam Crabtree*
Toronto, May 1984.

Part One
The Multiple Self

It has long been known that popular thinking lags many decades behind scientific discovery. This is no less true in the area of human psychology than it is in that of physics. Thanks largely to the work of Freud, begun some ninety years ago, we now tend to think of ourselves as complex beings whose unconscious minds are capable of remarkably intelligent operations of which we have no awareness.

In the last ten years, work in the study of hypnosis and multiple personality indicates that there is not just one, but many "minds" operating simultaneously within each human being. But the first really significant scientific breakthrough concerning man's inner multiplicity of consciousness goes back at least two hundred years. By the time Freud began his work with patients, there had already been nearly a hundred years of experimentation directed at exploring man's hidden self.

This opening part of the book will bring together the findings of workers in the field of human multiplicity over the last two hundred years. I believe this is the best way to gain a clear picture of the richness of man's multidimensional nature.

1

Chapter 1

Mesmerism and the Discovery of Divided Consciousness

There are few men in modern history who can be truly said to have influenced all subsequent human thought. But Franz Anton Mesmer (1734–1815) is one. Much of what we know today about the mind's mysterious inner reaches can be traced back to his introduction of what he called "animal magnetism" and the subsequent discovery of "artificial somnambulism." Only since then has it been possible to initiate an orderly scientific study of mental illness in general and of multiplicity-type disturbances in particular.

Yet Mesmer is little understood and much maligned. Reading the stock encyclopedia articles and many accounts in medical histories, one would think him an occult fanatic or a medical charlatan. He was neither. Mesmer was from beginning to end a physician and a scientist, a man dedicated to promoting a theory which he believed to have a firm scientific basis in experience. He called it "animal magnetism" and whether or not one agrees with his conclusions, a close study of his writings and the events of his life shows that Mesmer believed he had made a discovery that would be of great benefit to mankind.

Mesmer, the son of a gamekeeper in a small German town, grew up showing no particular signs of genius. He was educated at a Jesuit college in Bavaria and attended the University of Ingolstadt, where he earned a doctorate in philosophy. He entered the University of Vienna in 1759 and in 1766 received his M.D. degree with a dissertation entitled, "A Physical-Medical Treatise on the Influence of the Planets."

In 1768 Mesmer married a well-to-do widow, ten years his senior, and settled into the pleasant social life of upper-class Vienna. He was a great lover of music. His garden became a frequent gathering place for such composers as Haydn, Gluck and, most frequently, Mozart.

In Mesmer's day the taming of electricity and the relatively new art of constructing iron magnets were subjects of intense interest among those with scientific inclinations. Mesmer was particularly interested in magnetism and its potential for use in healing. A leading expert on magnets, the astronomer Maximilian Hell, constructed some for Mesmer, who used them in experiments with his patients.

Mesmer soon became impatient with using iron magnets and left that technique behind for a system he believed to be an original discovery: that the universe is full of "magnetism" (he called it magnetic fluid; we might call it magnetic energy); that all living things function on a particular form of this magnetism which, by analogy with ferro-magnetism, he called "animal magnetism"; that the body itself is a magnet; and that a physician may use his own body to affect the magnetic balance of that of his patient, restoring the natural ebb and flow of vital "currents" in the body, and thereby curing certain ailments.

Mesmer did not claim that this method of treatment would cure *all* illness; rather, he emphasized that it could "cure nervous disorders directly and other disorders indirectly." He believed that the magnetizer, by directing "magnetic currents" into the patient's body, was basically affecting the nervous system. He claimed to be able in that way to cure functional illnesses, but not conditions caused by organic damage or lesion. For example, if a person was blind because the optic nerve had been destroyed by disease, there was no hope for restoration of sight. If, however, blindness was caused by some condition connected with the nervous system, for example hysteria, animal magnetism could effect a cure.

It is clear that Mesmer was, before all else, a physician and healer. He was preoccupied with the problem of human illness and its cures. He believed he had discovered a humane, effective way to defeat illness, and he devoted his life to promoting that message. Mesmer moved to Paris, the intellectual center of the Europe of his day, and quickly attracted attention, both favorable and adverse. The adverse attention came largely from the medical establishment. The positive interest was shown by aristocrats, intellectuals and the man in the street. Mesmer set up a clinic in Paris where he would treat both the poor and the powerful. Over the next few years, he reported thousands of cures of a great variety of illnesses.

3

But Mesmer was never a man of diplomacy and in his stubborn single-mindedness to promote animal magnetism, he often needlessly turned people against him. Marie Antoinette, for example, was at first fascinated with Mesmer and interested in his work, yet he managed to alienate her with an arrogant letter. This lack of tact finally forced him to leave Paris and attempt to promote his work elsewhere.

Although some practitioners had learned the techniques of animal magnetism from Mesmer in Paris (notably Charles Deslon, private physician to the Comte d'Artois), it was only as he traveled the French countryside that Mesmer began to contemplate teaching his methods systematically. In 1781 he returned to Paris and founded the first of his "Societies of Harmony," intended to initiate practitioners, for a substantial fee, into the ways of his art. These were like private clubs and were eventually set up in various locations in France.

It was through the agency of the parent Society of Harmony in Paris that one of Mesmer's most important pupils received his training. He was Armand Jacques Marc de Chastenet, Marquis de Puységur (1751–1825). Puységur, as he is ordinarily called, would take animal magnetism to a new stage, paving the way for vital discoveries about the human mind.

PUYSÉGUR AND THE PEASANT

The Marquis de Puységur was a member of an old and distinguished French family. After an impressive career as an artillery officer, which included participation in the siege of Gibraltar, Puységur retired to a relaxed life on his estate near Soissons, where he began to use the techniques of animal magnetism—or mesmerism, as it was coming to be called—to relieve suffering.

In May, 1784, a peasant named Victor was brought to Puységur for help with a bad inflammation of the lungs. Puységur applied the usual "magnetic passes" (repeated downward movements of the hands over the length of the body to balance the "magnetic fluid") in an attempt to relieve the condition and Victor soon fell into a peaceful sleep. This was not in itself unusual, but when Puységur went to awaken Victor, he found that he could not. Instead of waking up, Victor entered into a new state of consciousness in which he exhibited some unusual phenomena. He could hear Puységur's voice and would respond to all of his suggestions and commands without resistance. If told to stand, he would do so immediately. If told to sing, he would do so with great gusto. If Puységur suggested that he was hunting or at a dance, Victor would go through the appropriate gestures and movements for each situation.

Puységur was fascinated. His training in Paris had not prepared him for anything like this and he recognized that he had stumbled across something extremely important. He would call this newly discovered state "magnetic sleep."

Over the following days Puységur repeatedly put Victor back into the state of magnetic sleep. He tried a variety of tests with him and came to some remarkable conclusions. First of all, not only Victor's actions but also his thoughts and imagination were influenced by any suggestion Puységur made. In addition, Victor's intelligence and general mental alertness improved radically when in the magnetic state. And Puységur also came to believe that at the same time an immediate mental rapport was established between himself and Victor, the latter being aware of his thoughts without any words being spoken. The rapport was also such that when in the magnetic sleep, only Puységur could touch Victor without causing him great agitation.

Another remarkable property of magnetic sleep was that the separation between the two states of consciousness seemed complete. In his normal consciousness, Victor had no memory of what had taken place when he was "asleep." Each consciousness had its own chain of memories, one for the "sleeping" Victor and another for the waking Victor. It was as though Puységur were dealing with two different people. This was the first recognition of what came to be called "divided consciousness" or "double consciousness."

It was a startling concept. It meant that every human being was double, with what people had thought of as the "I" only a part of their whole self. There was another consciousness below the surface, one which could now, for the first time, be communicated with in a systematic way.

Word of Puységur's discovery quickly spread throughout Europe where it was soon compared to somnambulism or sleepwalking.

Sleepwalking has been recognized through the ages as an in-between state where someone who has fallen asleep appears to awaken but actually shifts into a kind of misty consciousness. A sleepwalker is not usually aware of his surroundings, even though

5

he will exhibit an uncanny alertness to obstacles and dangers. In the sleepwalking state individuals may be quite suggestible. If spoken to they may carry on a conversation, but their part of it is seldom logical. They often return naturally to their beds and resume normal sleep, awakening from it with no recollection of the sleepwalking episode.

The similarity of this well-known condition to magnetic sleep could not be overlooked, but because the one occurred through a natural process while the other was artificially induced, magnetic sleep came to be referred to as "artificial somnambulism."

As mesmerism and, in particular, artificial somnambulism became better known, men all over Europe began to try their hand at it. Though some were quacks and stage performers, many of these early "magnetizers" were men of solid reputation and high intellectual attainment who had read the major writings on animal magnetism, observed demonstrations and now began serious experimentation of their own.

FIVE ENGLISHMEN

Typical of these early magnetizers were five men who were working in England between 1840 and 1860.

The Reverend Chauncy Hare Townshend was an Anglican clergyman and a poet as well as a world traveler. He was considered by those who knew him to be a level-headed observer of facts, someone unlikely to be led astray by enthusiasm. Joseph Haddock was a physician in Bolton with a special interest in physiology. William Gregory was a professor of chemistry at the University of Edinburgh and a biochemist of international repute. James Esdaile, originally from Scotland, was a surgeon practicing in Calcutta. A physician of great skill, he was appointed Surgeon to the Government of India in 1847. Herbert Mayo was a senior surgeon of Middlesex Hospital and professor of anatomy at the Royal College of Surgeons.

All five of these early English magnetizers wrote about their experiences, providing a picture of the prevalent knowledge of artificial somnambulism and divided consciousness at the time.

The Method

These five men used very similar mesmeric techniques. Here, for example, is William Gregory's description:

> If you will try the experiment of drawing the points of the fingers of your right hand, without contact, but very near, over the hands of several persons, downwards from the wrist, the hands being held with the palm upwards, and your fingers either all abreast, or one following the other, and repeat this, slowly, several times, you will most probably find one or more who distinctly perceive a peculiar sensation, which is not always the same in different persons. Some will feel a slight warmth, others a slight coolness, others a pricking; some a tingling; others a numbness . . . You may now, having found a person susceptible . . . try the effect of passes, made slowly with both your hands downwards from the crown of the patient's head, over the face, to the pit of the stomach, or even down to the feet, always avoiding contact, but keeping as near as possible without contact. Or you may make the passes laterally, or go downwards over the arms. It is necessary to act with a cool, collected mind, and a firm will, while the patient is perfectly passive and undisturbed by noise or otherwise. He ought to look steadily at the eyes of the operator, who, in his turn ought to gaze firmly on his subject. The passes should be continued, patiently, for some time, and will generally excite the sensations above mentioned, warmth, coolness, pricking, tingling, creeping of the skin, or numbness, according to the individual operated on.

Gregory also speaks of another frequently used method where the magnetizer would sit facing the patient and take each of his thumbs between his own thumb and forefinger, gently pressing them. He would gaze intently into the patient's eyes, concentrating his mind upon him and upon the state he was trying to induce. This intense physical, visual and mental focusing could produce the same effects as the passes, without fatiguing the magnetizer in the same way as repeated physical movements.

The Magnetic Sleep

Although all of the authors mentioned used mesmerism to heal people, they were particularly interested in producing and experimenting with artificial somnambulism, here described by Gregory:

> The first [phenomenon] is a twitching of the eyelids, which begin

to droop, while, even when the eyelids remain open, there is in many cases, a veil, as it were, drawn before the eyes, concealing the operator's face and other objects. Now also comes on a drowsiness, and, after a time, consciousness is suddenly lost, and on awaking the patient has no idea whatever how long it is since he fell asleep, nor what has occurred during his sleep. The whole is a blank, but he generally wakes, with a deep sigh, rather suddenly, and says he has had a very pleasant sleep, without the least idea whether for five minutes or for five hours. He has been, more or less deeply in the mesmeric sleep.

As these men experimented with magnetic sleep, they were particularly intrigued by the alterations in consciousness that it produced and the resulting phenomena, commonly referred to as the "lower" and the "higher" phenomena. Put simply, the lower phenomena were those which, although unusual, did not defy belief. The higher phenomena were so extraordinary that they were difficult to accept as genuine, no matter how compelling the evidence. While the lower phenomena showed that the somnambulist was in a new state of consciousness which had profound effects upon the physical organism, the higher phenomena indicated that this new state awakened mental powers beyond the ordinary—powers that we would describe as paranormal.

Whether one accepts the more extraordinary phenomena as genuine or not, the fact remains that a second consciousness does exist and it can be reached. On that score the early experimenters acquired a mass of evidence which could not be refuted.

THE LOWER PHENOMENA

(a) A sleepwaking kind of consciousness. A person in the state of artificial somnambulism was called a "sleeper." "Sleepwaking" was the term used to describe the condition, involving, as it did, both consciousness and a kind of sleep state. As Gregory put it:

> I have just said that the sleeper wakes [from the somnambulistic state], . . . but we are not to suppose . . . that it has really been a mere torpid, insensible, unconscious slumber. It is only an unconscious state, in reference to the ordinary waking condition; for the sleeper may have been actively engaged in thinking, observing and speaking during the whole period of sleep. This it is which renders the sleep so interesting a phenomenon. . . . It is a sound, calm, undisturbed sleep; that is, it is not broken

8

by gleams of ordinary consciousness. But the sleeper answers when spoken to by the operator, and answers rationally and sensibly.

(b) Double consciousness and double memory. The waking state and the somnambulistic state are each a species of consciousness. But they are completely distinct, each with its own chain of memories, as Gregory and Haddock set out:

> The sleeper in the mesmeric state, has a consciousness quite separate and distinct from his ordinary consciousness. He is, in fact, if not a different individual, yet the same individual in a different and distinct phase of his being. . . . As a general rule, . . . the sleeper does not remember, after waking, what he may have seen, felt, tasted, smelled, heard, spoken or done during his sleep; but when next put to sleep he recollects perfectly all that has occurred, not only in the last sleep, but in all former sleeps, . . . usually very accurately indeed. He lives, in fact, a distinct life in the sleep, and has what is called a double or divided consciousness.

> That every man possesses *two memories*, an internal and an external, is sufficiently obvious from the general results of mesmeric investigation. . . . By some observers, the phenomenon has been called *double consciousness*. In the normal wakeful state, these two memories *act as one*, so that the impressions made on the common sensorium are also impressed on the inner memory. Hence, what is known in the wakeful state, can be remembered in the internal psychic state. But the impressions made on the inner sensorium of a subject in the psychic state, or state of mesmeric trance, are, as observed above, not remembered, and are in fact totally unknown when the subject returns to the normal state.

(c) Loss of sense of identity. In the mesmeric trance the individual often has trouble knowing who he is. This is reflected in a peculiar difficulty with names. As Gregory describes it:

> He often loses, in the mesmeric sleep, his sense of identity, so that he cannot tell his own name, or gives himself another, frequently that of the operator; while yet he will speak sensibly and accurately on all other points. He very often gives to his operator, and to other persons, wrong names, but always, so far as I have seen, the same name to the same person. . . .

(d) Suggestibility. This was an attribute of the mesmeric state that struck Puységur very forcibly in the case of Victor. The mesmerizer has the power to create any kind of illusion in the imagination of his patient. Gregory cites the example of a certain Mr. Lewis, a master mesmerizer:

> Mr. J.D. . . . put to sleep in my presence by Mr. Lewis, exhibited, in great perfection, all the effects of suggestion. Whatever Mr. Lewis told him, he acted on it with a perfect conviction. He was thus made to fish, to shoot, to sing, to imagine himself a general or a lecturer, to take a stick for a sword or a gun, a chair for a wild beast, to feel the pelting of a pitiless storm, to hear the thunder, to be drenched with rain or frozen with cold, to swim for his life in the flood, to taste water as beer, milk, lemonade, or whisky; and when he had taken a little under the last-named form, to be so utterly drunk that he could not stand without support. Indeed he continued so perseveringly drunk, that it took Mr. Lewis a quarter of an hour to sober him.

(e) Heightened memory. When in the state of artificial somnambulism, an individual's memory is frequently enhanced, as Townshend describes:

> The memory of Anna M. was much developed during mesmeric sleepwaking. All the reminiscences of her childish years seemed to recur to her mind; and thence she was enabled to show an acquaintance with the past histories of the inhabitants of her native town, which in primitive times would have been by no means to her advantage. Under James the First she would infallibly have been burned for a witch.

(f) Deadening of the senses. While in the state of magnetic sleep the patient often loses the ability to see, hear, smell and taste in the usual way. Townshend describes the phenomenon:

> [Mr. Berckmans] permitted me to see one of his sleepwakers, who, from a natural predisposition, often kept her eyes open during sleepwaking. During twenty minutes or half an hour that I saw her thus, I could most truly affirm that, though her eyes were open, their "sense was shut." A dull film seemed to overspread them; the pupil was dilated, and did not contract with light. A candle brought near, or a hand waved suddenly and quickly before the patient's eyes, produced no perceptible al-

teration or motion either in the lid or in the apparatus of vision. Altogether there seems to be every reason to conclude that the eye, in mesmeric sleepwaking, is either so disordered or so paralyzed in its functions as to cease to convey impressions to the mind, in any mode, at least, that can be termed ordinary.

(g) Insensibility to pain. One of the most remarkable qualities of the mesmeric state is that some individuals when deeply entranced will feel no physical pain, even of the most severe kind, a property potentially of great benefit for the surgeon. Mesmerism had been discovered and developed in the decades just before chemical anesthetics.

The first recorded use of magnetic sleep for painless surgery was on April 12, 1829. Madame Plantin, a sixty-four-year-old woman with "scirrhus of the breast," was the patient. She had been put into the somnambulistic state each day for a number of days prior to her operation, and although in her ordinary state the thought of having her breast removed terrified her, in the mesmeric state she lost all fear. When the day arrived she was placed in the magnetic state as usual. The operation, performed by Jules Cloquet, lasted about twelve minutes. Madame Plantin spoke calmly with the surgeon throughout and showed no signs of pain. Her breathing and pulse were not the least affected. The operation was considered a complete success.

The surgical use of mesmerism as an anesthetic came into prominence under the auspices of two British physicians: John Elliotson and James Esdaile. Elliotson promoted its use over stiff opposition from his medical colleagues. His *Numerous Cases of Surgical Operations without Pain in the Mesmeric State* (1843) became a classic, and Esdaile's *Mesmerism in India* (1846) was almost as well known.

But 1846 also saw the discovery of ether and this would have far-reaching effects upon the use of mesmerism as a surgical aid. Even with ether's unfortunate side-effects—and the fact that there were none with mesmerism—the chemical anesthetic was much more convenient to apply and worked in all cases. Somnambulism, on the other hand, could not be induced in every patient and this unpredictability was something most surgeons wanted to avoid.

Even after the discovery of ether, Esdaile believed mesmerism to be the best possible anesthesia because the patient always remained completely calm, even through the most radical amputations, and there was no incidence of shock after the operation. He developed his own mesmeric technique, using it successfully in hundreds of surgical operations. Mesmerism could also be applied repeatedly after the surgery to relax the patient and remove postoperative pain. Here is how Esdaile prepared his patients for surgery:

> Desire the patient to lie down, and compose himself to sleep, taking care, if you wish to operate, that he does not know your intention: this object may be gained by saying it is only a trial; for fear and expectation are destructive to the physical impression required. Bring the crown of the patient's head to the end of the bed, and seat yourself so as to be able to bring your face into contact with his, and extend your hands to the pit of the stomach, . . . make the room dark, enjoin quiet, and then shutting your patient's eyes, begin to pass both your hands, in the shape of claws, slowly, within an inch of the surface, from the back of the head to the pit of the stomach; dwelling for several minutes over the eyes, nose and mouth, and then passing down each side of the neck, go downwards to the pit of the stomach, keeping your hands suspended there for some time. Repeat this process steadily for a quarter of an hour, breathing gently on the head and eyes all the time. The longitudinal passes may then be advantageously terminated, by placing both hands gently, but firmly, on the pit of the stomach and sides. It is better not to test the patient's condition by speaking to him, but by gently trying [to see] if the cataleptic tendency exists in the arms. If the arms remain fixed in any position they are left in, and require some force to move them out of every new position, the process has been successful; the patient may soon after be called upon by name, and pricked, and if he does not awake, the operation may be proceeded with. It is impossible to say to what precise extent the insensibility will befriend us: the trance is sometimes completely broken by the knife, but it can occasionally be reproduced by continuing the process, and then the sleeper remembers nothing; he has only been disturbed by a nightmare, of which on waking he retains no recollection.

(h) Rapport: a special connection with the magnetizer. It was soon apparent that the operator, by inducing the somnambulistic state, established a singular kind of relationship with the patient who would be continually aware of him and often able to hear his voice alone. Suggestions would be accepted only from the operator. Only the operator might touch the patient without causing him great

disturbance. It was a connection that strengthened with each sitting.

At the same time, rapport could be deliberately transferred by the magnetizer to other persons present; as Gregory pointed out:

> The sleeper, if naturally insensible to the voice or to the actions of all but his mesmerist, may be put *en rapport* with any other person. This may be done by simply giving him the person's hand, in many cases. In others, the sleeper requires to be told to communicate with that person, and this having been done, he becomes as completely and exclusively *en rapport* with him as he before was with the mesmerist. It often happens, that the stranger thus placed *en rapport* with the subject, must again retransfer him to the mesmerist, before the latter can communicate with him. The transference from one to another, in such cases, is usually attended with a start on the part of the sleeper, but he does not awake.

The special connection between magnetizer and patient became a subject of great concern in some quarters, the fear being that a dependency which could prove harmful would be established. In this scenario, the magnetizer loomed as a figure of great power, ready to abuse the confidence of his innocent subjects. Fictionalized stories of such abuse, like that of Svengali in *Trilby* for example, led to the popular notion that mesmerizing was a sinister business, with a powerful "magnetic" personality reducing some naive victim to helplessness. However, any familiarity with the literature of the serious experimenters shows what a great distortion this was.

Though accounts like those given above were becoming more and more commonplace in the mid-nineteenth century, it was about another fifty years before the lower phenomena gained general acceptance in the scientific world.

The higher phenomena, on the other hand, border on the paranormal and for them acceptance was very slow in coming. As will be seen, the higher phenomena point to the existence of capacities within human beings which are strongly disputed even to this day.

The Higher Phenomena

These phenomena fall into the four general divisions given below.

13

1. Physical or Sensorial Rapport

(a) Community of sensation. Though this phenomenon was discovered early by the magnetists and attested in hundreds of cases, it long remained a subject of controversy. It amounts to a kind of physical continuity between mesmerist and patient, whereby the sensations experienced by the former are shared by the latter. If the mesmerist sniffs some ammonia, the patient winces and rubs his nose. If the mesmerist is jabbed in the left arm, the patient will clutch the corresponding spot on his own arm and complain of pain. To all appearances the mesmerist and patient are one sensing unit, as Haddock wrote:

> By transfer of state or feeling is meant that curious effect of *reflected action*, which is exhibited by good mesmeric subjects, in feeling whatever is done to the mesmerizer as *done to themselves.* This I have witnessed so often, and under such a variety of circumstances, as to admit of no doubt of its correctness. Thus, on one occasion, while lecturing, one of the audience, to test my assertions, came unawares and pricked my leg. I looked round for a moment with surprise, and some little indignation; but by the time I comprehended the motive . . . the mesmerised subject felt it, and screamed out loudly, saying, "that some one had pricked her leg," and pointing . . . to the part of her own leg, corresponding to that which had been pricked in mine. I have got individuals to tread on my toes, pull my hair, or pinch different parts of the body; and I invariably found that, with this subject, not many seconds would elapse before she would complain of exactly similar treatment . . .

(b) Community of muscular action. In this case the *movements* of the mesmerist's body were transmitted to the patient and though the phenomenon is much less noted than transfer of sensation, Townshend has described it thus:

> The patient's eyes closed as by a spell, and his head followed the mesmerizer's [the elder brother's] hand in the usual manner. Charles, the elder brother, now got up from his chair, when Edward rose also. The former raised his right arm, the latter immediately raised his; his left arm, the same result. Charles walked forward, Edward advanced also. Charles stopped, and Edward stood still on the instant; in short, all the gestures of the one were faithfully imitated by the other. But the mother

became now alarmed, and insisted upon the young mesmerizer awaking his patient. This was soon effected; and Edward, opening his eyes, and staring about like one just startled from slumber, expressed the greatest astonishment at finding himself standing in the middle of the room, declaring, at the same time, that his unconsciousness had been complete.

2. Mental Rapport

(a) Reading the operator's thoughts. Puységur noted this phenomenon with Victor who seemed able to sense his commands. Later mesmerists discovered that the patient could read the thoughts of anyone with whom he was put in rapport. In some cases the patient even seemed able to gather from the mind of his mesmerist information which had been consciously forgotten. Gregory said of this phenomenon:

> For example, the sleeper describes a room, at the request of the experimenter. . . . every statement is confirmed by the proprietor, who sees the whole in his mind's eye, as when he left it. But all at once, perhaps, the sleeper speaks of the hangings, or pictures, and says he sees the picture of a dog, a horse, or a man, in such or such a position, with reference to another object. This is denied; but the sleeper is firm. So is the other, and after a long dispute, each retains his opinion. But on returning home, the experimenter finds that he had been mistaken and the sleeper right. He now remembers that up to a certain period, the picture hung where he had said, but that he himself, or someone else, had changed its position to that described by the sleeper, as he himself formerly knew, but had forgotten. Similar occurrences are very common.

(b) Mesmerizing at a distance. Many magnetizers came to believe that once the operator had established rapport with a patient he could induce the somnambulistic state at a distance by means of a simple mental act. Here is Haddock's disconcerting account of how he once produced this phenomenon unintentionally:

> On another occasion, I was wishful to induce the mesmeric sleep on a lady, for the relief of a rheumatic affection from which she was suffering. Finding the continual *stare* very fatiguing to my eyes, and also, expecting to be called away by patients, it occurred to me, that if I directed her to look steadfastly at some-

thing, it might answer the same purpose, and allow me to leave her without interrupting the mesmeric action. I therefore arose, and took a small magnet and suspended it by a wire from a hook in the ceiling. Emma [a servant frequently mesmerized by Haddock] was in the kitchen, situated *under* the room where I was operating, and knew nothing of my movements. In a few minutes the smell of burning linen arrested my attention, and I desired my daughter to go down stairs and ascertain the cause. She called me quickly to come down, saying that Emma was on fire; I ran down, and found her with her eyes closed, and *mesmerized*, and on her knees before the kitchen fire, engaged in sweeping the hearth, and her apron on fire from contact with a burning coal that had fallen from the grate; but of the fire she was unconscious, or, at least, she took no notice of it, and her attention was wholly directed to a point in the kitchen ceiling, under where I had been sitting in the room above. Having asked her what she was doing or looking at, she replied, *"I want that magnet."* I pretended not to understand her, and said, "What magnet?" The reply was, "That magnet hanging up there,"—pointing accurately to its situation. I extinguished the fire without saying anything to her about it, and led her up stairs, and put her into connection with the lady by joining their hands. When she was aroused, she expressed great surprise at finding herself in my sitting room, and was quite unconscious how she came there or of the fire. Upon enquiry, I found that she was engaged as above stated in the room below me, and that she felt some strange sort of influence come over her, and that she knew nothing after that until I aroused her. The influence from myself, and I have reason to think, from the magnet also, passed through the floor and ceiling, and affected her unconsciously in the room below.

There were other magnetizers besides Haddock who believed they could induce the magnetic state at a distance. Although some produced strong evidence to substantiate their claims, this phenomenon remains in dispute to this day.

3. Clairvoyance

(a) A new order of vision. A minority of somnambulists showed what seemed to be the ability to see things happening at a distance without the use of the senses. This clairvoyant power seemed to awaken gradually. The patient, with eyes closed, would at first become aware of a "light," usually in one particular direction. After a while he would be able to see things placed close by in that light.

The amount of ordinary light present in the room was apparently irrelevant, total darkness being as good as broad daylight. Next, the range of vision increased to include objects at greater distances—the next room, farther away in the house, outside the building, until eventually, some subjects could see things at any distance. Herbert Mayo gives an example of the more ordinary type of clairvoyance:

> The following experiment, which is decisive, was made at my suggestion: A gentleman standing behind the entranced person held behind him a pack of cards, from which he drew several in succession, and, without seeing them himself, presented them to the new visual organ of the patient. In each case she named the card right.

(b) Medical clairvoyance. This included the ability to see into the body, diagnose disease and prescribe remedies. Sometimes it involved a prediction of the course the disease would take. Haddock cited this case:

> Madame Lagandre . . . possessed the faculty of clairvoyance . . . the surgeon, M. Cloquet, was desirous that she should be mesmerized in his presence, that he might hear her statement of her mother's case [which she had already made to his colleague, Dr. Chapelain] . . . [He asked], "Do you think that we can sustain the life of your mother?" "No: *she will sink early tomorrow morning, without agony, without suffering.*" "What are the diseased parts?" "The right lung is shrunken and compressed; it is surrounded by a pasty or gluey membrane; it floats in the midst of much water. But it is chiefly *here*," said the somnambule, pointing to the inferior angle of the shoulder blade, "that my mother suffers. The right lung aspires no longer. It is dead. The left lung is sound; it is by that my mother lives. There is a little water in the envelope of the heart." "How are the abdominal organs?" "The stomach and the intestines are sound, the liver is white and discolored at the surface." The physician tried all his powers to magnetize his patient that day, but could hardly induce sleep. When he again called about seven o'clock the next morning, she had just expired. . . . The following is abridged from the official report of the autopsy. ". . . Interior—on opening the chest we found the cavity of the right pleura filled with a thick serosity, about two pints in quantity. . . . The [right] lung is greatly pressed inward, etc. The pericardium contains

about three or four ounces of limpid serocity. The liver is of ordinary volume. The upper face is covered with whitish specks, which do not extend beyond the surface of the organ. . . ." From this report, it is seen, that Madame Lagandre was quite correct in her diagnosis of her mother's case, and could even foresee the time of death.

(c) Traveling clairvoyance. Here, the somnambulist seems to mentally travel over great distances, even around the world, and to view events taking place elsewhere, while resting comfortably under the magnetic influence. Many striking instances of this phenomenon are given in the literature. Here is one related by Gregory:

> Mr. Atkinson had mesmerized a young lady, the daughter of a medical man, who resided many miles from London, where the young lady was. She became clairvoyant, but her father, who came to see her, would not believe in her [clairvoyance.] Mr. A. then requested him, when he got home, to do anything he chose, not telling any one, at a certain hour and in a certain room. At the time appointed, Mr. A. mesmerized the young lady, and requested her to visit her father's diningroom. [It was at dinnertime.] She did so, and saw her father and the rest. But all at once she began laughing, and said, "What does my father mean? He has put a chair on the dinner-table, and the dog on top of the chair!" Mr. A. sent by the first post an account of what his patient had seen, which was received next morning, and in answer he was informed that she had seen correctly, for that her father, to the amazement of his family, had put the chair on the table, and the dog on the chair, at the time agreed on.

(d) Clairvoyance back through time (retrocognition). In these cases the somnambulist is able to view events unknown to him which took place at some period in the past. Esdaile writes of such a phenomenon in connection with the famous somnambulist Alexis:

> The following is an account of a trial of Alexis's clairvoyance, made in the presence of Lord Normanby, the English Ambassador at Paris, and Lord Frederick Fitzclarence, neither of whom believed in Mesmerism. . . . Lord Frederick had up to this moment been a mere spectator; but now broke silence, took the hand of Alexis, and, with his characteristic kindness of manner, asked the following question: "Can you tell me how I was em-

ployed the day before yesterday with that gentleman?" pointing to one of the company. "I see you both," replied Alexis, "going to the Rue Lazare in a carriage; there you take the train and travel to Versailles; you then get into another carriage, which conveys you to St. Cyr. You visit the military school, and it was the other gentleman who proposed this excursion, he having been educated there." "All this is admirable, Alexis," exclaimed his Lordship. "Go on, Alexis." "You return to Versailles; I see you both enter a pastry-cook's. Your companion eats three little cakes; you take something else." Lord Frederick, perfectly astonished, said, before Alexis had time to think: "You are right; I ate a small piece of bread." "You next take the train again and return to Paris. However, let us thoroughly understand each other. You started by the railroad on the right bank, but you returned by that on the left." The latter circumstance astonished his Lordship so much, that he not only congratulated us before the whole party, but offered us his high patronage on every occasion.

4. Ecstasy

This is a condition in which the patient seems to reach an elevated state of consciousness with an awareness of spiritual things. The individual may have visions of the afterlife and communicate with spirits of the departed. In this state, the individual is not always subject to the usual somnambulistic amnesia, but rather remembers all that he has seen when he returns to the normal waking state. Here is Gregory's description of the somnambulist Emma's experience of ecstasy:

> In the state of extasis she sometimes retained a recollection of the place she was in, and of the persons around her, but her mind was chiefly occupied with visions, apparently of another state of existence, and of what appeared to be spiritual beings. She always spoke of the state as of one to which she went away, or was taken away, and on returning to her usual mesmeric state, she would remember and describe what she had seen and felt. Her eyes were turned up, and she was entirely insensible to pain. At first her limbs were flexible, but subsequently her whole frame was rigid. She could, when asked, perceive any concealed object by clairvoyance, but was usually too much engrossed with her spiritual perceptions to attend to such matters.

The exploration of the lower and higher phenomena of magnetic sleep caused a great sensation in the first decades following the discovery of animal magnetism. Beyond the legitimate controversy which arose about certain of these phenomena there stands a solid, unshakable fact: a second consciousness had been discovered—a consciousness with properties very different from ordinary waking consciousness. Puységur had discovered it and the later magnetizers confirmed it. This second consciousness could be contacted and investigated. It was revealed to have its own sense of itself and its own chain of memories; it possessed its own personal characteristics; it could make its own independent judgments about things; and it viewed itself as quite distinct from the ordinary waking self. This was the "second self." Its discovery was a landmark in the history of human psychology. The implications of its existence were vast.

Chapter 2

The Second Self

Hypnotism and the Second Self

Although it was the practitioners of mesmerism who made the discovery of the second self an observable scientific fact, it was the promoters of the new discipline of hypnotism who took that discovery on to its next phase of investigation.

In 1842 James Braid, a surgeon from Manchester, England, wrote a little pamphlet entitled *Satanic Agency and Mesmerism Reviewed*. It heralded a radical shift in thought about mesmerism and affected the course of all future research into human consciousness.

On November 13, 1841, Braid had attended a mesmeric demonstration by the Frenchman Lafontaine, and thought the effects were produced by trickery. However, upon attending a second time, he noted what he believed to be a genuine phenomenon: the mesmerized individual could not open his eyes. Intrigued by this observation, Braid set out to find the explanation. He performed some experiments with friends and relatives and made his evaluation of the cause of the mesmeric sleep: a rapid exhaustion of the sensory and nervous systems producing a feeling of somnolency in the mind, which then "slips out of gear." News of these experiments reached a certain Reverend H. McNeile who preached a sermon against Braid on Sunday, April 10, 1842. This prompted Braid's pamphlet.

In his pamphlet Braid listed three common attitudes towards mesmeric phenomena and a fourth which was his own: first, that they are due to a system of collusion and delusion; second, that they are real but the products of imagination, sympathy and imitation; third, that they are caused by the influence of a magnetic fluid (the theory of animal magnetism); fourth, Braid's own view that they are attributable to a peculiar physiological state of the

21

brain and spinal cord. Braid thought a new word was needed for the phenomenon which had been called magnetic sleep, and proposed one which has stuck to the present: "neuro-hypnotism" (nervous sleep) or just "hypnotism."

In the following year Braid wrote a full treatise on the subject and elaborated his proposed vocabulary with words such as "dehypnotise," "hypnotic" and "hypnotist." He intended his terminology and theory to replace that of the animal magnetists and thus do away with the notion of a magnetic fluid as the agent which produces mesmeric phenomena. His own theory was that these phenomena were of subjective origin.

Braid's terminology did in the long run replace that of animal magnetism. And so did his theory. Though it, unfortunately, wiped out a whole dimension of animal magnetism: that of healing through the interaction between magnetizer and subject. Braid's theory had only to do with the altered state of consciousness produced. For this, he asserted, it was not even necessary to have a magnetizer or hypnotist. Since the hypnotic state was purely subjective in origin, it could even be self-induced. Once the notion of a magnetic fluid was removed, the whole phenomenon of artificial somnambulism became much more palatable to the academic world. Hypnotism had made animal magnetism respectable.

Once hypnotism was accepted as a genuine reality and its study considered to be legitimate, the way was open for scientists to freely experiment with the strange states of consciousness it produced, so that by the 1880s, we see the beginning of some very important research into the nature of the "second self."

THE HYPNOTIC SELF

Although those who began to use hypnotism to study the second self might not have accepted the validity of all the phenomena connected with artificial somnambulism, they believed one thing for certain: in the magnetic sleep or hypnotic somnambulism a consciousness showed itself which was hard to consider identical with the normal waking self.

There were signs that this hypnotic self possessed many of the characteristics of a separate personality. It had a completely distinct consciousness of its own which could reason and form conclusions and in some cases show great intuitive powers. Its personality traits could be quite different from those of the waking subject.

And, most importantly, it would often insist that it was not the same individual as the waking self, even speaking of it as foolish or stupid. Though it would be aware of all the waking personality did, because memory was not inhibited in that fashion, the hypnotic self would often see those actions as the deeds of someone else.

The waking personality would, in most cases, have no memory of what had occurred during the hypnotic trance, but through suggestion, the hypnotist could bring memories of it into the normal conscious state. In such cases, the subject would usually perceive these memories in the same way as those of a dream: one's own, but with a different "feel" from the remembrance of things done while in the normal state of consciousness.

The fact of divided consciousness, then, came to be even more firmly established as the practitioners of hypnotism explored their art. The division was clear and once it had been accepted, a crucial question had to be answered: did the hypnotic self continue to exist while the individual was in his normal state, or was it simply a phenomenon which came and went with each hypnotic session?

EVIDENCE FROM HYSTERIA AND DISTRACTION

Some of the first strong proofs of the persistence of the second self came from work done with individuals who were afflicted with a malady called "hysteria," a psychological condition which is not the same as the popular notion of being in a state of uncontrollable ranting or screaming. It is, rather, a state in which certain fragments of personal experience become split off from the consciousness of an individual, manifesting themselves in bodily symptoms such as paralysis of an arm, a leg, or one whole side of the body; blindness or deafness in one or both organs; numbness of the skin in various regions of the body and so on. Hysteria is a neurosis; one who suffers from it may have to endure a lot of misery, but he is not considered to be insane.

Two of the chief researchers in this area of experimentation were the Frenchmen Alfred Binet (1857–1911), director of the Psychophysiological Laboratory at the Sorbonne, and Pierre Janet (1859–1947), one of the most important and influential psychological researchers of modern times. Through their experiments with hysterics in the 1880s and 1890s they came up with conclusive evidence that the second self does indeed have a continuous existence parallel to that of normal waking consciousness, and just below its surface. Binet, for instance, discovered that the second self is directly involved in the physical symptoms of hysteria, as it takes over or "possesses" certain parts of the body from which it has forced the normal self to withdraw. Thus the paralyzed arm or the blind eye may become useless for the waking self while serving as a perfectly good instrument for the second self.

One of the techniques used to get the subwaking self to manifest while the subject was awake was called by Janet the "method of distraction." The experimenter would simply get the subject involved in some very engaging activity, such as a lively conversation with a third party. While the subject was thus occupied, the experimenter would whisper some command or question to him in a very low voice, but he would have no conscious awareness of the message and would continue his activity without interruption. Except that the subject *would* obey commands given in this fashion without realizing it; he might even answer questions quietly posed by the experimenter through unconscious signs or automatic writing. The subject could also be induced to go through a series of awkward bodily movements without any knowledge of what was happening. In this way Janet believed he conclusively demonstrated the active persistence of a second self in the subject while in the waking state.

In *The Psychology of Suggestion*, written in 1898, the American psychologist Boris Sidis amplified the work of Binet and Janet. From the practice of the latter he drew an interesting example of the use of distraction that well demonstrates the continuous existence of this second self:

> P., a man of forty, was received at the hospital at Havre for delirium tremens. He improved and became quite rational during the daytime. The hospital doctor observed that the patient was highly suggestible, and invited M. Janet to experiment on him. "While the doctor was talking to the patient on some interesting subject," writes M. Janet, "I placed myself behind P., and told him to raise his arm. On the first trial I had to touch his arm in order to provoke the desired act; afterward his unconscious obedience followed my order without difficulty. I made him walk, sit down, kneel—all without his knowing it. I even told him to lie down on his stomach and he fell down at once, but his head still raised itself to answer at once the doctor's questions. The doctor asked him, "In what position are you while I am talking to you?" "Why, I am standing by my bed; I am not moving."

The secondary self accepted motor suggestions of which the primary self was totally unaware.

On another occasion Janet was able to obtain from the second self a description of its mental processes in meeting a challenge. In this case he had presented the subject with a number of blank white cards and induced the hallucination of a portrait on one of them. He then mixed them up and asked the subject to pick out the one with the "portrait." She was always able to do so, no matter how they were shuffled.

By using the technique of distraction, Janet then placed himself in contact with the subject's second self and asked what it saw on the card in question. It pointed out a small black spot on the card which enabled it to distinguish that one from the others. So while the waking personality believed it was able to pick out the card because of the portrait on it, the second self revealed the real means of distinguishing.

Sidis quotes another example that not only confirms this conclusion, but also indicates that the second consciousness is the same as the hypnotic self. He writes:

> . . . Mr. Binet had been kind enough to show me one of [his] subjects . . . rendered unconscious by anesthesia, and I had asked his permission to produce on this subject the phenomenon of suggestion by distraction. Everything took place just as I expected. The subject (Hab.), fully awake, talked to Mr. Binet. Placing myself behind her, I caused her to move her hand unconsciously, to write a few words, to answer my questions by signs, etc. Suddenly Hab. ceased to speak to M. Binet, and turning toward me, continued correctly by *the voice* the conversation she had begun with me by unconscious signs. On the other hand, she no longer spoke to M. Binet, and could no longer hear him speak; in a word, she had fallen into elective somnambulism (rapport). . . . We had heard clear and direct proof as to the presence of a conscious agency lying buried below the upper stratum of personal life, and also as to the identity of this hidden, mysterious self with the hypnotic self.

EVIDENCE FROM HYPNOTISM

One important area of exploration for evidence of the second self was that of posthypnotic suggestion. It was discovered, for instance, that if someone placed in a state of somnambulism by a hypnotist was told at that time to make some gesture, once awake, after the hypnotist had clapped twenty times, he would invariably do so, no matter how occupied he was with other things or how randomly and quietly the hypnotist might clap. Yet the subject's waking consciousness was aware neither of the suggestion itself nor of the number of claps being made, and if asked why he was making such a gesture, he would not know. Even when experiments were devised which required calculations more complex than counting, the same results were obtained.

Another bit of evidence of the persistence of a second self while one is in the waking state came from investigations of *memory* carried on in connection with hypnotism. A person was placed in the hypnotic state and certain operations carried out; the suggestion was then made that he would remember nothing about them when he awoke but *would* be able to give an account of it all through automatic writing. This proved to be the case, again indicating the presence of an intelligent, continuously existing second self.

Given the opportunity, the second self can even give an account of the reasoning it uses in making judgments, as in Edmund Gurney's hypnotic experiment which required the subject to keep an accurate account of the passage of time. One March 26 he told a man who was in a hypnotic trance that on the one hundred and twenty-third day from then he was to put a blank sheet of paper in an envelope and send it to a friend of Gurney's at his home. Upon awakening the man remembered nothing of the suggestion, but since Gurney was doing regular hypnotic experiments with him, he used subsequent sessions to question him about it. Here is Gurney's account as given in the *Proceedings* of the Society for Psychical Research:

> The subject was not referred to again until April 18, when he was hypnotized. . . . He at once repeated the order, and said, "This is the twenty-third day; a hundred more."
>
> S: (the hypnotist) "How do you know? Have you noted each day?"
> P–11: (the subject) "No, it seemed natural."
> S: "Have you thought of it often?"
> P–11: "It generally strikes me in the morning, early. Something seems to say to me, 'You've got to count.' "
> S: "Does that happen every day?"
> P–11: "No, not every day—perhaps more like every other day.

It goes from my mind; I never think of it during the day.
I only know it's got to be done."

EVIDENCE FROM AUTOMATIC WRITING

For automatic writing to be produced the primary self must
remain in charge of the individual, so that the more he is mentally
involved elsewhere, the more freely and automatically the writing
will flow. But with the writing itself, the subwaking mind is at work.

The individual who wishes to engage in automatic writing sits
comfortably at a table, pen or pencil in hand, allows his hand to
rest upon the writing sheets and then proceeds to distract himself
by reading or conversing with someone. While it is usually some
time before legible writing is produced, after a period of experimentation, the subject may be rewarded with legible writing and
meaningful phrases.

From one point of view, automatic writing constitutes an inten-
tionally produced cleavage between the normal self and the second
self, as the latter comes forward to communicate. It may start by
bringing out latent memories. When questioned this second self
will respond, often with great cleverness. As the process continues, the second self will gather more intelligence and some degree
of self-consciousness. It may at times even reach the point of
eloquence, giving discourses on philosophical or religious issues.
And the views it expounds may not agree with those of the waking
personality. Here the cleavage between the normal self and the
second self is quite complete.

William James, in his *Principles of Psychology*, gave a very striking
illustration of this phenomenon. He writes of a Mr. Sidney Dean,
a "member of Congress from Connecticut from 1855 to 1859, who
had been all his life a robust and active journalist, author and man
of affairs." Dean practiced automatic writing for many years, ac-
cumulating a large collection of manuscripts. James quotes him:

> . . . The writing is in my own hand but the dictation [is] not of
> my own mind and will, . . . and I, myself, consciously criticise
> the thought, fact, mode of expressing it, etc., while the hand is
> recording the subject matter and even the words impressed to
> be written. If *I* refuse to write the sentence, or even the word,
> the impression instantly ceases, and my willingness must be

> mentally expressed before the work is resumed, and it is resumed at the point of cessation, . . . Sentences are commenced without knowledge of mine. . . . It is an intelligent *ego* which writes, or else the influence assumes individuality, which practically makes of the influences a personality. It is *not* myself; of that I am conscious at every step . . .

Dean's description had all the marks of a mild experience of possession, which is what seems to happen. The second self rises up and takes possession of the writing arm and communicates through it. As this happens, the waking self very often ceases to receive sensations from the arm; the second self is now in possession of those sense impressions. Experiments have shown that, as with hysterical anesthesia, the numb arm—or, more accurately, the second self—will be aware of jabs given it and that awareness will show up in the writing, but the waking self is aware of no sensation. At the end of the automatic-writing session, the second self relinquishes possession of the arm and the anesthesia ceases: further proof that the second self persists as an intelligent, semi-autonomous consciousness. The question then is: just what can be said about the mysterious second self?

TERMINOLOGY

Over the last one hundred years many different names have been given to this submerged consciousness: the subwaking self, the coconscious self, the hidden self and the under-mind. Terms used for our ordinary consciousness are the waking self, the primary self, upper consciousness, and the over-mind.

But three sets of terms must be specially mentioned: "subconscious self-conscious self" (first used by Pierre Janet in the 1880s and taken up by many researchers who followed him, it is still in common use today); "subliminal self-supraliminal self" (a term originated by F.W.H. Myers (1843–1901), the well-known British psychical researcher and psychologist, in referring to a self "below the threshold" of consciousness).

The third set of terms requires a bit of explanation and has become well known in our day: "unconscious mind—conscious mind." Although references to "the unconscious" go back long before Freud, it was he who gave that term a well-defined meaning.

Unconscious in this case does not mean "lacking in consciousness." The unconscious in Freud's meaning is quite capable of intelligent thought—even great cleverness—but he used the word to emphasize that what we call our normal self is not aware or is "unconscious" of what is going on in those hidden realms of the psyche which he took such pains to explore. Though the conscious mind is not in direct communication with the unconscious mind, the latter does have its own consciousness or thought activity.

All three sets of terms agree on one basic fact: below the stream of ordinary consciousness, there exists another consciousness with its own thoughts and attitudes, and that second self must be seriously studied if we are to gain a deep knowledge of the nature of man.

THE SECOND SELF: ONE OR MANY?

One of the first things that struck the early experimenters was that the hypnotic state seemed to have a number of different stages of "depth." The subject would move from ordinary consciousness, through light trance to somnambulism and then to complete unconsciousness. Opinions differed as to the number of states but there was general agreement that distinct levels of consciousness were produced as the trance was deepened.

Work by Edmund Gurney in the 1880s revealed that the hypnotist could create two distinct memory chains in the hypnotized individual, at two different levels of consciousness. Memories from either level were available to the subject only when he was at that level. They seemed to exist in airtight compartments. When Eleanor Sidgwick and Alice Johnson, two leading members of the Society for Psychical Research, repeated Gurney's experiments a few years later, they discovered in one subject eight distinct levels of memory, so that there seemed to be no specific limit to the numbers into which the hypnotic self could divide. Stronger proof of this came through research done on the creation of hallucinations in hypnotized subjects.

The mesmerizers had long known that an individual in the somnambulistic state was very suggestible. He could be made either to experience or to block out sense impressions, with the first type of illusion called a "positive hallucination," the second a "negative hallucination." It was research on the latter in particular that cast light upon the question of multiple levels of consciousness.

For example, a good hypnotic subject might be placed in a state of somnambulism and seated at one end of the room, with the hypnotist at the other. There is a table between them. The hypnotist gives the subject this posthypnotic suggestion: on awakening, he will perceive the room as devoid of furniture—a negative hallucination with regard to the table. When the subject is awakened, careful questioning reveals that he really believes there is no furniture in the room. The hypnotist next asks the subject to walk over to him and he does so, but instead of walking in a straight line, he moves in an arc, thus avoiding the table. When the hypnotist asks why, the subject says he does not know why or makes up some weak excuse, but when asked whether he was trying to avoid something, he will reply, "No, of course not." When further questioned about whether there is any furniture in the room, the subject will again answer no.

But in order that the subject *not see* something and act in the manner suggested by the hypnotist, something within him *had to see* the object and act upon that perception. In his little work, *On Double Consciousness*, Alfred Binet described the conundrum clearly:

> . . . In order to cease to see an object—to have that alone excluded from sight—a person must begin by perceiving and recognizing it, however that may be done, and the rejection of the perception can only take place after it has been established. . . . Now, who does this supervising? What is the intelligence that always decides that the subject shall perceive this and not that? It is not the normal ego, for that is not conscious of anything. It only accepts what it gets. It must be, therefore, a personality capable of *seeing the object*, . . . As to what this personality may be, I for one am completely in the dark . . .

The obvious answer to the question is: the hypnotic or subconscious self, but the answer is really not that simple, as the following will show.

Suppose the operator repeats his experiment, but with this important variation: he does not make the suggestions *posthypnotic*. Instead he has the negative hallucination take place immediately. Now the subject does not perceive the table *while still in the hypnotic state*. What is the result? Everything takes place as before. The subject still walks around the table of whose presence he is ignorant, and when the operator brings him out of hypnosis and questions him about the experiment, the subject knows nothing of what has happened.

Now the question about "the intelligence in the background" is very difficult to answer. It is not the waking self. He knows nothing at all about the matter. It is not the hypnotic self, for he operated under the influence of the negative hallucination. Who, then, is it?

The contemporary investigator of hypnotism, Ernest Hilgard, has done a great deal of investigation on this long-standing question. In his book, *Divided Consciousness*, (1977), Hilgard describes how a class demonstration led to a new slant on the problem broached earlier by Binet. In a demonstration of hypnotically induced deafness with a young blind man as a subject, the young man showed no sign of response to loud sounds made near him. Then a student in the class asked whether some part of the young man might be aware of what was happening. Hilgard decided to test this by addressing that "part" of the subject in a low voice, suggesting that if it could hear and understand him, it should cause the index finger of the subject to rise. The finger then rose. Realizing that his finger had just lifted, the subject asked to be restored to his waking state to find out why. This done, he was asked what he remembered of the events which had just taken place. He described the induction and ensuing deafness. He said he had felt bored sitting in the silence, and so had started to amuse himself with a statistical problem. Then he felt his finger lift.

This indicated to Hilgard that the waking man was ignorant of the noises, of the words Hilgard had spoken to him and of his meaningful response. Before explaining to him what had happened, Hilgard again induced hypnosis and spoke to the part that had made the man's finger rise. Here is what it said:

> After you counted to make me deaf you made noises with some blocks behind my head. Members of the class asked me questions to which I did not respond. Then one of them asked if I might not really be hearing, and you told me to raise my finger if I did. This part of me responded by raising my finger, so it's all clear now.

Upon returning to his *usual* hypnotic consciousness, the subject remembered nothing of what he had just said. When aroused from the state of hypnosis and told he would remember, he did.

Hilgard decided to call this behind-the-scenes source of awareness and knowledge the "hidden observer." His intention was to use the word metaphorically. He did not mean to indicate that he held the hidden observer to be a secondary personality with a life of its own. He did not believe the data justified going that far.

31

In later experiments Hilgard made use of his important discovery in the study of the hypnotic reduction of pain. Testing the levels of pain in subjects who submerged the hand and forearm in ice water, he made the surprising discovery that while the hypnotic subject might be experiencing no pain at all because of a posthypnotic suggestion of analgesia, the hidden observer was experiencing essentially normal levels of pain. In the process of this research many hypnotic subjects became familiar with their hidden observer and were willing to try to give their own personal impressions, as witness one young woman who gave a particularly intriguing description, which Hilgard called a clear statement of the phenomenology of the experience:

> The hidden observer is analytical, unemotional, businesslike. The part of me that was hypnotized was off on a tropical island. The hidden observer is a portion of Me. There's Me 1, Me 2 and Me 3. Me 1 is hypnotized, Me 2 is hypnotized and observing and Me 3 is when I'm awake. . . . The hidden observer is cognizant of everything that's going on; it's a little more narrow in its field of vision than Me 3, like being awake in a dream and fully aware of your actions. . . . The hidden observer sees more, he questions more, he's aware of what's going on all of the time but getting in touch is totally unnecessary. The first time [ice water pain] I thought maybe it was an artifact of the situation, but after the second time, with hearing, I don't think that's the case. He's like a guardian angel that guards you from doing anything that will mess you up. . . . The hidden observer is looking through the tunnel, and sees everything in the tunnel. . . . It's focused, doesn't pay attention to extraneous things. It's aware that the tones are coming through, aware that I was saying "zero," that the Me 1 was also busy floating. Me 2 is watching all of this. Unless someone tells me to get in touch with the hidden observer I'm not in contact. It's just there.

Hilgard's work provides important information about the multiplicity of consciousness within us. It also raises questions which can be answered only through further experimentation with the hidden observer phenomenon, such as whether there is only one level of hidden observerness. Or put another way, could the hidden observer itself be hypnotized or somehow made subject to negative hallucination? And if so, would we then find yet another hidden observer "behind" the first hidden observer who remains aware of what is going on through the whole procedure? To my knowledge such experiments have not yet been undertaken.

Be that as it may, recent research has discovered the presence of *multiple* hidden observers within individuals. It has shown that if a subject is placed in a number of distinct hypnotic states, each one will have its own hidden observer with distinguishable personality traits. In *Unity and Multiplicity* Oregon psychiatrist John Beahrs emphasizes the importance of this recent research. He says that all human beings have many coconscious selves residing within, and that there can be "an unlimited, potentially infinite number of hidden observers or 'personalities' within a single human individual." This is strong confirmation that we have an unlimited number of potential centers of consciousness within us. Not only does a second self exist, it seems able to generate any number of other selves. When it comes to consciousness, it seems we are all multiple.

INNER PERSONALITIES

One day Pierre Janet was working with Lucie, one of his hysterical patients. While her normal self was chatting with someone else, Janet spoke quietly to her subconscious self and received its response through automatic writing. The exchange is described in his *L'Automatisme Psychologique*:

> "Do you hear me?" asked Janet.
> "No," she answered (in writing).
> "But you have to hear in order to reply."
> "Yes, of course."
> "Then how do you do it?"
> "I don't know."
> "Must there not be someone who hears me?"
> "Yes."
> "Who is it?"
> "Someone other than Lucie."
> "Oh, indeed. Another person. Should we give this person a name?"
> "No."
> "Yes. It is more convenient."
> "All right, then—Adrienne."
> "Well, Adrienne, do you hear me?"
> "Yes."

You see here the spontaneous creation of a secondary personality. By giving the communicating consciousness a name, it took on the beginnings of individuality. By suggesting—or rather insisting—that it be given a name, Janet aided in its birth.

Once such a secondary personality has been spawned, it will tend to define itself more and more clearly as an individual. It may even become as much an individual as the normal personality of the subject. Indeed, such an inner personality will often speak of the normal ego in the third person, and pretend they have nothing in common.

Sometimes it fails to form a full personality, as in instances of automatic writing where the communication claims to be coming from some specific individual, but the content is inconsistent or insubstantial. At other times the personality formed is very complete indeed and may even exhibit greater emotional balance and keener intellectual ability than the primary self.

There does not seem to be any particular limit upon the number of inner personalities which may be created. Hypnotists have experimented with the creation of inner personalities and found them not difficult to produce, though they may be quite ephemeral—the temporary crystalizations of tendencies and submerged memories latent in the subject.

When it comes to the creation of multiple well-formed, semipermanent personalities, however, we are dealing with multiple personality properly speaking.

Chapter 3

Multiple Personality

Multiple personality is a condition in which two or more personalities manifest themselves in one human being. It is generally considered to be a neurotic condition rather than a psychosis or form of madness. The subject may, in *all* of his personalities, be perfectly sane and subject neither to paranoid delusions, hallucinatory fantasies nor irrational thought processes. How then, has multiple personality shown itself and how has it been treated?

FROM SOMNAMBULISM TO MULTIPLE PERSONALITY

In the form that we now know it, multiple personality seems to be a relatively modern phenomenon. Although there are a handful of previously noted cases, the first to be publicly recorded was that of Mary Reynolds, described by S.L. Mitchill, a New York City physician, in the year 1816. Her condition, which will later be described in detail, was termed "alternating" or "dual personality."

Since instances of multiple personality first gained public attention in the heyday of animal magnetism, it is not surprising that the phenomenon was soon related to magnetic sleep or somnambulism. It was thought to be simply an elaboration of the condition of double consciousness that had so effectively captured the imagination of the times. For once it was acknowledged that the second self was capable of forming personalities with varying degrees of stability, it was a short trip to seeing multiple personalities as identities formed subconsciously, incubated there for a time, and eventually brought into the light of day.

Certain aspects of the process of subconscious formation have been fairly well understood, with one of the clearest expositions given by William McDougall (1871–1938), professor of psychology at Harvard, in his remarkable book *Outline of Abnormal Psychology* (1926). He describes how an individual may have an experience which he wants to forget or a set of fantasies or drives which he does not want to acknowledge. He succeeds in getting rid of them by splitting them off from his conscious awareness. This is called dissociation. However, his success is only partial, for these things continue to exist in his subconscious mind as encapsulated units held back behind a barrier of amnesia. They continually threaten to push their way into consciousness and upset the individual's precariously constructed emotion edifice.

Now and again these dissociated units may overcome the amnesiac barrier and burst through in some striking dramatization, termed a "psychic automatism" by McDougall. He calls a brief episode of that kind a "hysterical fit" and it stands at one end of the spectrum. At the other is the longer lasting and much more complex phenomenon of multiple personality. In between is found a multitude of types of automatisms.

McDougall gives many illustrations of these uprushes of dissociated units. He starts at one end with an example of the hysterical fit, taken from his work during World War I when he served in the British Army Medical Corps and was in charge of shellshocked patients who needed skilled medical treatment. He writes:

> A game young soldier had fought very gallantly until wounded in one foot. When convalescing from the wound he began a long series of "attacks," each of which closely resembled the rest. Sometimes the "attack" came on in his sleep, sometimes during waking. He would suddenly fall to the ground, seem to be utterly unaware of his surroundings, and reenact, in the most dramatic way, a scene lived through in the trenches but forgotten: in this scene he took a very active part in repelling an attempt of the enemy to rush the trench; he worked a machine-gun, shouting in the utmost excitement to his comrades. As the excitement subsided, the dramatic actions gave place to mere spasmodic movements and contortions, which in turn would subside and leave him sleeping quietly.

The hysterical fit is a short episode, often lasting but a few minutes and ending in sleep.

As he moves on to more complex psychic automatism, McDougall discusses the "fugue," an episode in which a person suddenly disappears from the usual scene of his life to reappear at some distant place, astounded to find himself there and unable to give any account of what has happened in the interim. As an example, McDougall draws upon the rich casework of Pierre Janet:

> Rou was a poor boy who lived with his mother in a city where he was employed in the humdrum tasks of a small store. He had for years been in the habit of frequenting taverns, where he associated with sailors and listened avidly to their stories of adventure on the high seas. He longed for a life of such adventure. . . . One day (when in all probability Rou had been drinking with his acquaintances, as his habit was—and we have seen that alcohol favours dissociation) he disappeared. Subsequent investigation showed that he had worked his way towards the coast, at first on canal barges, enduring many hardships, later in the service of a traveling tinker. . . . Some months after Rou had left home, his master procured some wine, it being a feast day, and proposed a little festivity. Again we are not positively told whether alcohol was taken before the change; but only that, at the mention of the date, Rou cried out: "It is my mother's birthday!" and therewith was himself again, except that he could not recollect any event since the day of his departure from home.

The altered consciousness of the fugue state can reach the point where it not only stretches on for months, but becomes fairly competent at dealing with the practical affairs of daily life.

The fugue state contains in its very definition the notion of escape, deriving from the Latin "fugio" (to run away). If the escape were to involve simply a change of consciousness and not a change of venue, and if the episodes were repeated with the same altered consciousness returning again and again, we would have a case of multiple personality. As a matter of fact, some of the classical cases of multiple personality discussed in the literature are really instances of prolonged fugue.

Such, for example, is the famous case of Ansel Borne, a resident of Rhode Island, who in 1887 disappeared from the streets of Providence and two weeks later turned up at Norristown, Pennsylvania. There, under the name of A.J. Brown, he rented a room, using the front portion of it as a variety store and the rear part as living quarters. He led a quiet life with regular habits, paying his bills promptly and attending the Methodist church on Sundays. He would later report that one morning, six weeks after arriving in Norristown, he heard the sound of an explosion in his sleep. Awaking, he noticed that his bed did not feel like the one he was used to. He went to the window, pulled back the curtains, and looked into the street. To his great surprise he did not recognize the view and since the last thing he could remember was walking down a street in Providence, he spent two fearful hours trying to figure out where he was and what to do. Finally, he knocked on the door of a neighbor, who greeted him as "Mr. Brown." On learning that he was in Pennsylvania, and the date, Borne realized that he had lost two months of time.

Some time later Professor William James worked with Borne to see if he could recover the memory of the missing two-month period. In the hypnotic trance he became A.J. Brown and was able to describe in detail all that he had done in that identity. In the waking state, however, as Ansel Borne, he was never able to reclaim the memory of that period. At no point did one personality ever make contact with the other. The spontaneous alteration of personality which Borne suffered in 1887 was never again repeated.

CASES OF MULTIPLE PERSONALITY

MARY REYNOLDS

Mary Reynolds was the daughter of a Baptist minister living in backwoods Pennsylvania. She seemed to be of average intelligence and good physical constitution. In 1811, when Mary was eighteen, she began to have "fits" and the following year she suffered a particularly severe attack.

She had taken a book to the meadow to read one day and after some time, was discovered there, lying unconscious. On recovering consciousness she was found to be blind and deaf but five weeks later, her hearing suddenly returned. Her sight was restored more gradually.

Three months after her spell of unconsciousness in the meadow, when she was nearly back to normal, she was one morning discovered lying in bed in a state of deep sleep from which she could not be aroused. She remained that way for some eighteen hours and then awakened in a state of altered consciousness in which she was like someone newly born. She had lost all memory of her previous life, knew only a few words, and at first those seemed unconnected to any particular thoughts. She did not recognize anyone around her—parents, relatives or friends.

In this new or "second" state of consciousness Mary had to be taught everything anew, from the names of objects and their uses to who her family was and how they were related. But she learned quickly because her intellect was fully mature.

Then one morning, five weeks after her change in consciousness, she awoke her old self again. All memory of her "original" life had returned but she knew nothing about the events of the five weeks just gone. She went about her normal tasks as if nothing had happened, although she was surprised that so many things around her had changed in what seemed like one night.

Mary remained in her natural state for a few weeks and then again fell into a deep sleep from which she awoke in her second state, taking up her life again precisely where she had left it. She remembered all that had taken place during the five weeks of her existence in the second state and once more had no knowledge of her natural life.

In "Mary Reynolds: A Case of Double Consciousness" written for *Harper's New Monthly Magazine* in 1860, Reverend William S. Plumer, head of Western Theological Seminary in Pennsylvania, gives a good summary of Mary's condition. He remarks particularly on the profound difference in personal disposition between the two states:

> . . . Not only were the two lives entirely separate, but . . . in her first state she was quiet and sedate, sober and pensive, almost too melancholy, with an intellect sound though rather slow . . . and apparently singularly destitute of the imaginative faculty. In her second state she was gay and cheerful, extravagantly fond of society, of fun and practical jokes, with a lively fancy and a strong propensity for versification and rhyming, though some of her poetical productions appear to have possessed merit of a high order. The difference in her character in the two states was manifested in almost every act and habit. . . . In her natural state the strange double life which she led was the cause of great unhappiness. She looked upon it as a severe affliction from the hand of providence, . . . but in her abnormal state . . . she looked upon [changing back] as passing from a bright and joyous into a dull and stupid phase of life.

So it was that Mary Reynolds manifested two completely unconnected personalities. Neither knew anything of the other directly; all the information each had of the other was obtained from relatives and friends who experienced both. Mary's alterations from one state to the other continued for some sixteen or seventeen years and then ceased entirely, leaving her permanently in her second state—that livelier, more enterprising personality—for the final twenty-five years of her life.

FELIDA X

The case of Felida X was quite different, with the second personality possessing a complete knowledge of the life of the first, but the first totally ignorant of the second. For thirty years, beginning in 1858, this case was observed by Dr. Etienne Azam (1822–1899), who was professor of surgery at the Bordeaux Medical School. In his book *Hypnotisme, Double Conscience, et Altérations de la Personnalité* he gives a detailed account.

As a young girl, Felida was quiet, intelligent, self-preoccupied and melancholy to the point of moroseness. At thirteen she began to exhibit symptoms of hysteria: various pains and anesthesias. At fourteen and a half, she would sometimes fall into a deep sleep and awaken in a different state of consciousness which would last for an hour or two; she would then enter into another state of deep sleep and wake up in her normal consciousness. These episodes took place every five or six days.

In her "secondary state," as Azam called it, Felida was an entirely different person from her normal self; smiling and gay, she moved swiftly from one household task to another, seeming to possess enormous physical energy. Her hysterical symptoms were completely absent in the secondary state. Azam's view that Felida was in every way healthier and better balanced in her "abnormal"—or "morbid"—state led him and other researchers in the area to question what value the word "normal" has in such cases.

Because Felida remembered in her secondary state all that had happened previously in the same state, *and* all the events of her normal life, but had no memory whatsoever during the latter of events from her secondary condition, a great deal of confusion sometimes arose. She might, for instance, be on her way to a funeral in her secondary state and, suddenly switching to her primary condition, not have any idea who had died. The personality alterations sometimes also caused her great embarrassment with customers at her shop whose orders she might have taken in her secondary condition, but she eventually became skillful at covering

40

up the personality transitions to all but people who knew her intimately.

As time went on, Felida was more and more subject to the secondary state. In the early years, that personality had taken up approximately one tenth of her life, but by the time Azam wrote about her case—thirty years after its onset—her secondary state was in almost complete charge of her life (as with Mary Reynolds), her primary state appearing only briefly and infrequently. This gradual pushing out of the neurotic personality by the healthy one had all the appearances of a self-cure.

SPANISH MARIA

In 1919 Charles Cory, professor of philosophy at Washington University, described a case of alternating personality that was important to the study of the phenomenon. This summary is taken from his account in the *Journal of Abnormal Psychology.*

Maria, a young woman of twenty-nine at the time, had begun to manifest a second self three years earlier. While her original personality, called "A" by Cory, was timid, frail, and easily exhausted, the new one, "B," was vivacious and aggressive.

The new personality had emerged as the result of a traumatic shock: news of her father's tragic death had prompted her physical collapse. She was unable to walk normally; she began to experience hallucinations; then she started to evince strange habits—attacks of extreme vanity and sudden urges to jump out of bed and dance. Finally, the second personality, which had been responsible for these things, began to come forward.

According to A's own description, the first full appearance of B occurred one evening when she was alone at home, seated at the piano. Suddenly it was as if someone said to her, "Take a deep breath." Then the sound of singing came from her, a singing unlike any she knew, and she became frightened. She said that just before the singing she had shuddered "as if something had possession of me." That "something" was the personality B who then began to assert herself in A's consciousness as the departed soul of a Spanish woman. Since she could not account for what was happening in any other way, A accepted this as true.

The interplay between the two personalities in this case is particularly interesting. At any moment, either A or B would be dominant. Nevertheless, each, if interested, could remain conscious of

41

the other. The difference between the two was that when B was forward, A would play the role of onlooker—powerless to do anything to determine B's conduct, but when A was forward, B was quite capable of profoundly influencing what A did. And since they were often conscious simultaneously, the two personalities could carry on direct conversations with each other; whichever was to the fore would speak aloud and the other would communicate by an inner voice. (This phenomenon of simultaneous consciousness had come to be called "coconsciousness" by workers in the field and has its counterpart in the possession experience in what is termed "lucid possession," which will be discussed later.)

Cory described the B personality as older than A and more serious and dignified. She helped Cory in his therapeutic work with her case and could read difficult treatises on the unconscious and multiple personality with ease, expressing her thoughts with great clarity. Yet, despite this, she remained convinced that she was not a dissociated part of A but the spirit of a long-dead Spanish woman.

A striking aspect of the case was B's speech. She spoke English with a marked Spanish accent but, according to Cory, had neither been instructed in a foreign language, nor exposed to Spanish-speaking people, except for a brief period in classes with some Spanish-speaking girls. Yet not only did B speak English with a foreign accent, she also at times spoke in and could write automatically a "tongue" made up entirely of fragments of Spanish with apparent traces of Italian.

What added to Cory's puzzlement was that B's whole character, all her tastes and preferences, were molded by the Spanish idea. He writes that, like a magnet, B seemed to have absorbed vast quantities of material relating to Spanish life and culture. In Cory's view, after due incubation in the subconscious, there evolved out of this mass of material the fabrications which then entered B's consciousness as memories.

Cory finally traced the origin of B's Spanish interest to a relationship Maria had begun shortly after her father's death with a Mr. X, a man many years her senior. Although at this time the B personality was already forming, she had not yet come forward to manifest. Nonetheless, it seems that B became fascinated with Mr. X, whose mother was Spanish and who was himself very Spanish in appearance. Cory believed that it was during this period that B's preoccupation with things Spanish developed.

B even insisted that Maria's involvement with Mr. X was her affair, indeed, *B*'s sexual feelings were a dominant aspect, as she believed that in her former lifetime she had been a large, powerful woman whose passionate nature had got her involved in many stormy love affairs. She could not get adjusted to *A*'s small physical frame and spoke of herself as a "lion in a bird cage."

Another peculiar aspect of the Spanish Maria case was the singing ability manifested by *B*. *A* sang poorly but *B* had a magnificent voice. Professionals who heard her judged that with training, she could have made her living as a singer, and *B* claimed that in her Spanish life she had often sung to great crowds of people, so that now she could perform with complete confidence and abandon—a source of continual wonder to *A*.

In the course of her therapy, *B* described the experience of "getting out." Before she emerged, she said, it was like viewing things through a window. When she got out, she could see people close up but they appeared to be in a "glare" and she would squint her eyes protectively. After *A* and *B* began to alternate dominance, further peculiarities were noted: when *A* was forward, *B* would often see things that escaped *A*'s notice; when reading a book, *B* was faster and would try to turn the page before *A* was ready, but if both were strongly interested in it, the lines would actually appear double.

B and *A* might be completely aware of each other, or *B* might be more submerged, only indirectly making her presence felt, for example, by influencing *A*'s feelings, sometimes quite against her wishes.

B had much better memory recall than *A* and could remember many incidents of *A*'s early life which *A* herself had forgotten. *B* also claimed that she never slept and was often conscious when *A* was asleep.

The two personalities were quite ready to criticize each other harshly, sometimes entering into prolonged arguments. *B* would accuse *A* of being lightheaded and without ambition, and she deplored *A*'s preoccupation with her health. *A*, on the other hand, thought *B* egotistical and arrogant but even so, she acknowledged *B*'s many good qualities. She said that she would truly miss *B*, should she disappear.

Though we do not find here the element of amnesia so common to multiple personality cases, there was this peculiarity: the inner thought behind any action was known only to the personality that performed it, each thus cognizant of only as much of that inner life as the other chose to reveal. In that way the two related much like two friends who knew each other well.

Cory apparently was unable to bring about any significant change in Maria's dual personality through the therapy he applied. In fact, Cory's main function seems to have been to draw them out about their experience and help them understand it, at the same time recording one of the more interesting cases in the annals of multiple personality.

CHRIS COSTNER SIZEMORE

The best known multiple personality case of modern times is that first reported in the book *The Three Faces of Eve*, which describes the work of two psychiatrists with a young woman whose three personalities were named "Eve Black," "Eve White" and "Jane." "Eve White" was a quiet housewife and mother. "Eve Black" was a coarse, seductive woman who loved the night life. "Jane" was a mature person who knew the other two and with whose cooperation, it seemed, the integration of the whole personality could take place. In one therapeutic session, at the point of recovery of some particularly traumatic memory material, Jane let out a scream. At that moment the three personalities merged into a fourth which was different again and called itself "Evelyn White." As Eve's psychiatrists were writing their book, two years after this dramatic event, they admitted their uncertainty about the stability of the new personality. This proved to be well founded.

Many years after the appearance of *The Three Faces of Eve*, the subject, Chris Costner Sizemore, published her own book with the assistance of her cousin, Elen Pittillo. Entitled *I'm Eve* (1977), it is the source for this summary of the case.

Christine was born in 1927 and grew up in a rural area of the Carolinas, the daughter of a struggling couple with the uniquely colorful names of Zuline and Acie Costner. She was early exposed both to death and to the trials of poverty.

Her first experience of a split-off personality that she unconsciously created occurred at two years of age, soon after she witnessed a horrifying scene at the sawmill where her father worked. A man had been killed by the machinery and was lying in a pile of sawdust. Zuline had rushed to the scene with her little girl and screamed when she saw the man's severed arm lying near his body. Later that day, Christine was at home alone with her mother, when Zuline accidentally broke a glass jar and sliced her wrist badly. Seeing the blood, Christine thought her mother's arm had been cut off like that of the dead man at the sawmill. Zuline told her urgently to run and get her father but Christine, paralyzed with fear, backed away to the feather bed in the corner and hid under the pillow. Then the first split happened, as Sizemore describes:

> Through the watery haze [of tears], Christine saw a small red-haired girl standing near the fireplace watching the terrible red blood spill over her mother's arm and onto the stones. She was dressed in a yellow checked apron-dress with white knee stockings, and her dry blue eyes were calm and unafraid, and at the urging to "go for Daddy," she turned and quietly hurried from the room.
>
> Christine watched as the other child stood near and observed her father tightly bind her mother's arm with torn strips of white cloth. The bright blood stained the white cloth, but it no longer dripped onto the floor. She heard her mother say, "Acie I thought you would never get here. The baby didn't seem to understand me. . . . Christine, where are you?"
>
> As the child lifted her head from against the bed, the first thing she noticed was that the small red-haired girl was gone.

The second incident of splitting took place some time later, when Christine had been playing by an irrigation ditch near the Costner's house. Her mother had warned her often not to go near it, and fortified her warning with the threat of a monster that lived in the ditch. But Christine had a mind of her own.

On this occasion her play was interrupted by her uncle Amos's calling her father to "come quick" to the ditch. When she moved toward the voice, she saw her father and uncle near a small footbridge, struggling to pull the body of a neighbor from the water. Amos said, "I think he's dead." At the word "dead," her breath stopped. She had seen enough in her short life to know how upset people became in the face of this "death." As the men brought the body up into sight, its grotesque features were visible to Christine. She became rigid and terrified. Again the splitting occurred:

> She wanted to move back, to run, to cry; but she was frozen. Her head swam and her sight blurred, her chest hurt, she could not breathe. She could feel the warm sun on her face, she could feel the sharp prick and jab of the bushes, she could even smell

45

the sweet scent of the tub roses. But her mind and being were filled only with the face and consciousness of death.

Almost against her will, she opened her eyes. The scene had changed little. The two men were slowly dragging the awkward body through the water to the bank beside the road. But there was someone else in the picture now, someone who had not been there when Christine closed her eyes. On the bridge looking directly down upon the scene in the water stood a little girl. Her dark red hair shone brightly in the morning sun, and the first thing Christine noticed was that her bright eyes were calm and unafraid.

The next thing Christine was aware of was her mother's voice calling her from nearby and she thought to herself, "I'm going to get whipped, but they will have to whip that other little girl, too." Zuline asked Christine what she was doing near the ditch but even before she got an answer Acie told her to get the child away. She grabbed Christine and pushed her towards the house, giving her a couple of swats as they went. Christine began to wail that it was the little girl on the bridge who should be punished. But when she looked there, the girl was gone. At this point, Zuline became really angry at what she believed was a lie and began slapping the child harder and dragging her towards the house.

From then on, in times of stress, Christine would often see the little girl with red hair doing what she could not. Often such bold actions were things Zuline had forbidden and when caught in the act, Christine would innocently blame the little girl—who would by that time have disappeared. In this way Christine gained a reputation for lying. As she was to realize much later in life,

> . . . [the] creative intelligence of the child could not be contained, and its overflow was interpreted, at its best, as unrestrained curiosity, and at its worst, as uncontrolled naughtiness. Her self-image was daily buffeted by damaging traumas, but her intelligence would not let her sensitivities perish. Paradoxically, to survive intact, she splintered; she created other selves to endure what she could not absorb, to view what she could not comprehend, to do what she had been forbidden, to have what she had been denied.

As Christine was growing up, more personalities were formed. In one incident which took place when she was entering that awkward phase of growth connected with adolescence, her mother had just made her a new dress. Christine thought it very beautiful and was trying it on in front of a mirror with her two sisters looking on. While admiring the dress, she noticed her own freckled face in the mirror and it seemed particularly ugly to her. She felt nauseated, closed her eyes, and when she opened them again, she was another person. Her face contorted with fury. The new personality was enraged with that freckle-faced girl for having got such a beautiful dress, and in her envious fury she ripped it to shreds.

Her horrified sisters ran to get their mother who immediately grabbed Christine, inducing a change back to her usual personality. She grew calm and looked around, puzzled. She asked her mother what had happened, then realized that one of those inexplicable episodes must have taken place.

There were by now at least three personalities: the vain girl who had ripped the dress, a red-haired girl who was unafraid and the freckled girl from whom they both came. Later in her teens she developed "the blind girl" personality, completely deprived of sight. Shortly after that she started to suffer from severe headaches.

At nineteen Christine married Ralph White, a young man just returned home from military service. In 1948, a child, Taffy, was born to the young couple. But Christine was unhappy in the marriage which did not seem to provide her with enough emotional nourishment. This and her difficulties with new motherhood caused Christine to form new personalities. This is the period in which she created Eve Black who hated her life with Ralph and Taffy and who just wanted to have fun, and Eve White, the dutiful wife and mother. The latter knew nothing about the former, but thought she was only a voice in her head. But Eve Black knew all about Eve White and could use that knowledge to her advantage.

It was at this point that Christine's personal unhappiness and the confusion brought about by the coming and going of the personalities led her to seek therapeutic help. Her search led her to the university medical center at Augusta, Georgia, only a short distance from her South Carolina home, and she was able to make the regular trips without too much hardship. She began to be treated by Drs. Thigpen and Cleckley who were associated with the University of Georgia Medical School and would write *The Three Faces of Eve*. In the course of her therapy a third personality called Jane was formed. She assisted in the treatment and helped

47

to bring about a temporary coalescence of all three at the end of Christine's treatment.

During the treatment, Chris separated from her husband, then divorced him and married a man named Sizemore. The resolution of the three personalities nevertheless proved to be very shaky and eventually more were developed, with names like the Strawberry Girl, the Purple Lady and the Bell Lady. They showed some peculiar interrelationships, as in the matter of an allergy, which would come and go instantaneously with the switch in personalities. For example, Chris's skin could at one moment be covered with red blotches from contact with fur, and at the next, after a personality switch, the blotches were gone and she could wear the furs with no trouble.

The relationship of memory was interesting, too. On occasion a number of personalities would emerge from Chris, one after the other—though always in groups of three—and it was as if each personality came through the previous one. When this happened amnesia was present in one direction, but not the other, as Sizemore writes:

> The manifested personalities were so clearly defined that they seldom interfered with each other's activities, and they were also able to view the others' activities only in the order in which they first emerged; the first one out in a group of three could not view the activities of those who followed, but those who followed could view the activities of the ones who had come before them. . . . The first one to emerge in any group became the pivot through which all the others must come and go. This intricate design was as stringently adhered to as if it had been a natural physical characteristic rather than a subconscious mental phenomenon; and when these cardinal rules were, on rare occasion, violated excruciating repercussions followed.

Many years after her therapy with Thigpen and Cleckley, Chris again sought help, over a period of time receiving psychotherapy from Drs. Tibor Ham and Tony Tsitos. Through this therapy it emerged that Chris had developed a multitude of personalities over the years and that her work with Thigpen and Cleckley had been very incomplete. Her new therapists helped her to understand the condition of multiplicity from which she suffered and she came to realize that her personalities were formed as defenses against painful feelings. If she was willing to endure the discomfort of those feelings herself, she would no longer need their services.

The doctors worked with her as she faced more traumatic experiences from her early life and came to terms with the splitting those experiences had induced. Eventually, after a confusing life in which she had existed as twenty-two different personalities, she was able to leave behind her long-used defense against emotional strain. She realized that she was in fact all her personalities, that she embodied all of their characteristics. Now she felt ready to accept this and remain consistently herself—Christine Costner Sizemore.

BILLY MILLIGAN

In the fall of 1977 a young man named Billy Milligan was arrested in Columbus, Ohio. He was indicted on three counts of kidnapping, three counts of aggravated robbery and four counts of rape. The police had finally caught the much feared Campus Rapist who had been terrifying women on the Ohio State University campus for weeks. The following account of this unusual case is taken from *The Minds of Billy Milligan*, by Daniel Keyes.

During lengthy police interrogation sessions, Milligan showed certain mental peculiarities which prompted the authorities to call for medical opinion on his condition. Because he seemed to exhibit characteristics associated with multiple personality, Dr. Cornelia Wilbur, an expert in that field, was called in to give her opinion.

Up to this point those who spoke with Milligan had encountered a number of personalities with different names, very distinct characteristics and varying degrees of willingness to cooperate. Dr. Wilbur, however, got Milligan to relax to the point where he could allow his stronger personalities to recede and the original core personality, called "Billy," to come forward. Billy was at first in a state of extreme terror, fearing punishment for some misdeed of which he had no knowledge but Dr. Wilbur reassured him, saying that he needed help to understand what was happening. Then she told him he could go back to where he had been and rest for a while. With that, Billy was replaced by another personality.

Before this interview many of the authorities involved had been skeptical about Milligan. They thought he was putting on an act, trying to escape the responsibility for his crimes by pretending to be crazy. After the interview, many began to believe his story, among them the prosecuting attorney, who was present at the interview.

Through a series of preliminary judgments, Milligan was able to be further observed before being brought to trial. By the time the case came to court the terms of the judgment had been clearly defined and there was no question that Milligan had committed the crimes. The only matter in dispute was his responsibility for them. On that score the judge found Milligan not guilty by reason of insanity—the first time in the history of American law that a man had been acquitted of major crimes because of insanity due to multiple personality.

But Billy Milligan was still in danger of being sent to prison. He had been on parole when arrested for the Campus Rapist crimes and was in violation of that parole on a number of counts. Billy's attorneys managed to obtain his release to the custody of an approved institution, the Athens Medical Center. He would be under the care of the medical director there, Dr. David Caul, who had been recommended to the court by Dr. Wilbur and Dr. Ralph Allison, a California psychiatrist noted for his work with multiple personality.

The material uncovered in Milligan's therapy presents a striking and unusually revealing account of the subjective experience of multiple personality. In his case, a total of twenty-four personalities were revealed. They were of both sexes and all ages from young children to adults in their mid-twenties. They included the original Billy, who could not stand the strain of acute emotional pressure, nine more that were revealed to the authorities and psychiatrists up to the time of the trial and another thirteen that were discovered during his treatment at Athens, along with a final personality,— the Teacher—representing the other twenty-three fused into one.

Among the ten initially revealed, two dominated and coordinated Milligan's activities. The first was Arthur, an Englishman who spoke with a pronounced British accent and considered himself to be a capitalist and an atheist. He had an extensive knowledge of physics, chemistry and medicine, could read and write fluent Arabic and was the first of all the personalities to become aware of the existence of the others. He was the one to decide which other personality should "come out" and interact with the world.

Arthur first sensed there were "others" when he realized he was "losing time," a phenomenon to which all the personalities were subjected. One of them, Allen, described it:

> You're someplace doing something. Then suddenly you're some-
> place else, and you can tell that time has passed, but you don't
> know what happened.

When Arthur realized that there were others operating through Billy's body, he began asking questions and gradually got to know the others. He then began to take charge of the situation, controlling access to the consciousness. However, he soon had to share this function with one other personality: Ragen Vadascovinich.

Ragen was the "keeper of hate." This personality was Yugoslavian, speaking English with a thick Slavic accent. He could read, write and speak Serbo-Croatian. In contrast to Arthur, his political leanings were communist. Ragen's expertise included karate, demolitions and weapons. He could summon remarkable physical strength by controlling the flow of adrenaline in his body, and was capable of inflicting serious physical harm to anyone he considered dangerous. His physical feats included tearing a toilet fixture from the wall of a jail cell and throwing it across the room.

Whereas Arthur was dominant in safe situations, Ragen dominated the consciousness in dangerous ones. Whenever there was any sign of threat to the "family" of personalities, Ragen would immediately come forward, maintaining control of the consciousness until the threat had passed. He was especially concerned to look after the "children," as the "younger" personalities were called. He had committed the thefts with which Billy was charged in order to look after the "family." Ragen sometimes dominated Billy for long periods, either holding the consciousness himself or giving it to one of the personalities he thought could handle a tough situation.

The original core personality, Billy, had not been allowed to control the consciousness for the six years before Dr. Wilbur brought him out in her interview. This was because he had been on the verge of committing suicide and so destroying all of the family. Billy, who had never been able to take a great deal of stress, was still in school in 1971 when things had come to a head. Frequently the butt of his classmates's teasing, he was dragged into a lavatory one day by a group of girls who humiliated him by removing his pants. Afterwards he walked to the roof of the school and would have thrown himself off but for Ragen who came forward and slammed him down. At that point Ragen and Arthur held an emer-

51

gency conference to determine the rules for the whole family from that time on. Here is part of the exchange:

> *Arthur:* "He is a danger to all of us. In his depressed state, he might succeed in killing himself."
>
> *Ragen:* "Vat is solution?"
>
> *Arthur:* "Keep him asleep."
>
> *Ragen:* "How?"
>
> *Arthur:* "From this moment forward, Billy is not to hold the consciousness again."
>
> *Ragen:* "Who can control it?"
>
> *Arthur:* "You or I. We'll share the responsibility. I'll spread the word to the others that no one is to allow him to take the consciousness under any circumstances. When things are . . . in relative safety, I'll control things. If we find ourselves in a dangerous environment, you take over. Between us we will determine who may or may not hold the consciousness."

After Ragen and Arthur had agreed on how to handle things, Arthur set out to explain the situation to the children. The image he used to put across of how they would all work together is one of the most interesting in the literature of multiple personality:

> "Think of it," he said, "as if all of us—a lot of people, including many you have never met—are in a dark room. In the center of this room is a bright spot of light on the floor. Whoever steps into this light, onto the spot, is out in the real world and holds the consciousness. That's the person other people see and hear and react to. The rest of us can go about our regular interests, study or talk or play. But whoever is out must be very careful he or she doesn't reveal the existence of the others. It is a family secret."
>
> The children understood.

So being on "the spot" meant holding the position visible to the world. Arthur and Ragen were in control of the spot. All of the others were allowed there only with the permission of one of them. The personality named Adlana had a unique ability in this regard: she could wish any of them off the spot at will.

Adlana was a lesbian, and one of Billy's first group of personalities to be known. Shy and lonely, she had a strong desire for physical contact with women; strangely enough, it was she who was responsible for the rapes with which Billy was charged.

Each personality had its own particular talent and strength and Arthur encouraged all to spend time studying and practicing the skill for which they were specially suited.

Each personality had its own characteristic kind of emotion, too. They had, after all, been created precisely to handle emotions which Billy could not, so that one was the keeper of fear, another of pain, another of anger and so forth. This special parceling out of emotion inevitably led to a fragmentary emotional life; for example, until Billy began trying to fuse all his personalities, he had never experienced what is called "mixed emotions." Yet this experience was absolutely necessary for his recovery. If he was ever to be a unified personality, he had to learn to tolerate the whole spectrum of emotions which situations evoke without switching to each of the separate personalities constructed to handle each emotion.

Billy Milligan's therapy was undertaken by two doctors at two different stages. Up to the trial he was treated by Dr. George Harding, Jr., of Harding Hospital in Worthington, Ohio. After the trial, by Dr. David Caul. They agreed on the nature of Billy's condition and the general methods to be used, with the key to the treatment being an understanding of the role of amnesia. As the barrier which separated the personalities from each other, amnesia was the perfect defense against the pain of life experiences. It affected the various personalities differently but Billy, the core personality, was the one most in need of protection and so he was given total amnesia for the actions of the others.

If the subject was to come to a full realization of how he became a multiple personality in the first place, this amnesia had to be broken down in therapeutic treatment. And it was of two kinds: the principal and most obvious was that operating in the *present* between the personalities—horizontal amnesia; but there was also vertical amnesia, the blotting out of memory of *past* events. The core personality could not begin to control the splitting until he could face the traumatic material.

Dr. Caul had to present some principles of treatment to the court at a hearing that was held after Milligan had behaved violently again, this time while in detention. He mentioned six main points and these give a good summary of the rationale of Billy's therapy: First, all of the personalities making up the multiple must be identified. Second, the therapist must discover the reason for their existence. Third, he must do therapy with all of them to bring about change. Fourth, the therapist must concentrate on positive qualities wherever they might be found, trying to effect some compromise among the alter personalities, especially those that were in some way dangerous. Fifth, the patient must be made fully aware of the situation and actively contribute to its positive resolution. Sixth, since antipsychotic medication may produce fragmentation and other harmful side effects, its use should be avoided.

Within this therapeutic framework, both of Billy's doctors worked for "fusion," the term experts in multiple personality use to describe the amalgamation of the alter personalities into a new integral personality. Keyes, author of *The Minds of Billy Milligan*, writes that under Dr. Harding's therapy, the core Billy was encouraged to acknowledge the existence of his alter personalities, listen to them and get to know them. Suggestion was used to allow him to remain on the spot longer and longer. The fusing itself was to be done in logical sequence, in pairs, with those alter personalities that had similar qualities being fused first. The results would in turn be fused, the final step being the merging of them all into the core Billy.

The fusion process was carried out through intensive suggestion. At this time, Arthur explained the concept to the younger children by means of an analogy. He compared it to Kool-Aid, where the powder is made up of many separate crystals. When you add water, the individual crystals dissolve. If you let the mixture stand, the water evaporates, leaving a solid substance. Nothing has been lost; it has only changed. After this explanation, the children understood.

Dr. Harding's treatment went ahead in fits and starts until he finally achieved the fusion of seven personalities into one. However, he could not get Arthur, Ragen and Billy to fuse. They had first to know that Billy would not go to prison.

At the trial Billy was acquitted and afterwards began a new phase of his treatment with Dr. Caul. It was now that the "Teacher," the sum of all twenty-three alter personalities, emerged.

Caul first learned of the Teacher's presence in a conversation one day with Ragen. At this point, Billy had revealed twenty-three separate personalities: besides the ten first known, there was a group of thirteen "undesirables" who had long before been banished from taking the spot because they had always caused trouble for the family. Now Ragen revealed that there was someone else.

He began by telling Dr. Caul that while the uncovering of the personalities had put Billy's defenses in disarray, it had also made his complete unification possible. At that point, Ragen said, the only dominant personality would be the Teacher. He went on to explain that in contrast to the various alter personalities, the Teacher's emotions changed according to circumstances. Ragen said that Dr. Caul had met parts of the Teacher, who had taught all the other personalities what they knew. In fact, said Ragen, the Teacher was Billy, all in one piece.

Dr. Caul decided to reveal this startling information to Billy and did so by having him come forward and watch the just related video-tape recording of the conversation with Ragen. Keyes described in some detail Billy's reflections afterwards.

Billy began to see how his core personality had split into many parts with an unnamed presence—the Teacher—behind them. It was he who had created all the others. And he was also responsible for what they had done, including their crimes. If all those personalities fused with the Teacher, that would be the whole Billy. Now an inner transformation took place as all of the personalities took the spot at once and the Teacher came forward for the first time, and spoke to Dr. Caul. This was the beginning of the lengthy task whereby Dr. Caul and the Teacher cooperated to piece together the complete history of Billy Milligan's life.

Though Billy was progressing toward complete fusion, there were setbacks, sometimes due to the inevitable hazards of work with multiples, at other times provoked by unfortunate outside interference. Then an unhappy series of events alarmed the authorities who held Milligan's fate in their hands. An incident led to the leveling of unsubstantiated charges of rape of a female inmate of the treatment center. The accusations terrified Billy who feared he would be removed from the center and its beneficial treatment. The result was a series of violent outbursts.

Billy was finally taken from his treatment center and imprisoned under changed conditions. Keyes ends his book with the unhappy comment that under the strain of his new environment Billy's fusion broke down. He says that at time of writing, no one can predict the final outcome of Billy's case.

TREATMENT

From the first identification of the condition called "dual personality" or "multiple personality," there have been those who consider it a deliberate deception on the part of the subject. Even Billy Milligan was thought to be a clever deceiver by some of his caretakers. However, the evidence gathered from clinical work and psychological testing over the last one hundred years only serves to confirm that the phenomenon is genuine. Most recently, research done at the U.S. government's National Institute of Mental Health at Rockville, Maryland, has provided further proof in that direction.

Writing in the October, 1982, issue of *Psychology Today*, Frank Putnam, a staff psychiatrist with the Institute, describes brain wave measurements performed upon individuals suffering from "multiple personality disorder" and upon healthy individuals who deliberately created and rehearsed imaginary alternate personalities. While the former showed significant differences in their brain wave configurations from one personality to another, the latter, tested as they switched from role to role, showed no change. Such evidence is extremely significant.

Therapy for multiple personality cases has gone through a considerable evolution. Before the turn of the century, a great deal of attention was given to observing the phenomenon and less to its treatment, the impression being that very few workers believed anything substantial could be done for someone suffering from it. Most researchers seem to have concentrated on gathering information and speculating on causes, rather than exploring possible treatment.

One early researcher who went more deeply into the therapy of multiple personality was Dr. Morton Prince (1854–1929), renowned author and for many years editor of the *Journal for Abnormal Psychology*. His work with the multiple personality Christine Beauchamp, which was begun in 1898, provides an example of an early attempt at treatment and also gives some indications about what *not* to do when dealing with this condition.

Miss Beauchamp (a pseudonymn) developed four different personalities as a result of certain emotional shocks. The personality (BI) who came to Prince for help was twenty-three and a student in a New England college. She suffered constantly from symptoms of hysterical origin: headaches, insomnia and bodily pains; Prince described her as a physical wreck. She was very reserved and also beset by an exaggerated concern about the effects of her actions. The second of the four personalities (BII) was Miss Beauchamp's hypnotized self. The fourth (BIV) was irritable and quick-tempered. The third personality (BIII) was by far the most interesting. She called herself "Sally" and wrote an autobiography of her life back to Miss Beauchamp's infancy, claiming to have total recall and insisting that she never slept. Neither did she suffer from any of Miss Beauchamp's physical complaints. In fact, she insisted all the way through that she was a "spirit" and not Miss Beauchamp at all. Sally spoke with a stutter, and had great vitality. She loved fun and practical jokes, usually at the expense of Miss Beauchamp (BI) whom she detested.

Dr. Prince described his therapy with Miss Beauchamp in great detail in his book, *The Dissociation of a Personality* (1905). Let us consider how he went about it, starting with his assumption that one of the four personalities was the "real" Miss Beauchamp.

Prince states his problem clearly:

> In the hunt for the real self the greatest difficulty lay in deciding between BI and BIV. Sally, whoever she might be, was clearly not the original Miss Beauchamp, and not a normal person. All the evidence pointed conclusively to the view that Sally, by all odds the most interesting of the personalities, was some sort of a dissociated group of conscious states, and therefore the psychological explanation of this young lady was, to this extent at least, comparatively simple.

Prince eventually decided upon BIV as the real Miss Beauchamp, making BI an interloper who had to go:

> . . . [This] Miss Beauchamp was not, properly speaking a real person, but a dissociated personality, a quasi-somnambulist rightfully distinguished as BI. She must be made to disappear, to go back into the unknown whence she came. This, under the hypothesis, seemed to be the hard logic of events.
>
> The situation was a dramatic one. If one pauses to think over all that this meant, and to apply it to oneself (for each one of these personalities is as individual as any one of us), one can realize the full meaning of the verdict that a self, with all its memories, feelings and sentiments, must be annihilated. It was the annihilation of the individual.
>
> The evidence seemed to be sufficiently strong to justify the hypothesis being accepted, provisionally at least, and BI was condemned to be sacrificed. So all therapeutic effort was directed toward extinguishing BI and keeping BIV in existence.

In this passage I believe Prince was saying more than he intended, thereby formulating a dilemma which anyone doing therapy with multiple personalities must face: can a therapist intervene and make a decision about what should survive in the personality of his client? Where the therapist comes to the conclusion that one or the other of his patient's personalities must be annihilated, is he not assuming a more than human authority? And even if he wants to, can he actually do so without the explicit permission of his client? And which of the personalities could give such permission?

Later in his book, Prince shows that he was himself dissatisfied with using either BI or BIV as the real Miss Beauchamp and decided upon a new tack: she would be an amalgamation of BI and BIV. But a personality—this time Sally—would still be annihilated:

> My idea was that if BI and BIV could be fused into . . . one character, the resurrection of the original Miss Beauchamp and the restoration of the original mental relations, Sally would disappear into her original subconscious abode, if she had one. To dispose of Sally in this way after our long friendship seemed cold-blooded, and I confess to certain qualms. But what was to be done? All three could not live. The choice had to be made, and the law of psychology condemned Sally.

So Dr. Prince undertook, with the connivance of the other two personalities, to "squeeze" Sally out of existence. This was not easy, especially when Sally resisted with all her might. However, she reluctantly gave in at last and was squeezed out. Prince stated at the end of his book: "The resurrection of the real Miss Beauchamp is through the death of Sally."

Things have changed since the days when therapists were ready to make life and death decisions for their clients. Today, those most experienced in dealing successfully with multiple personality cases no longer look for the "real" person among the alter personalities, then eliminate the others. Prince's notion of "integration" or "fusion," does remain, though, as we saw with work on the Billy Milligan case.

In Billy's case, termination of Dr. Caul's method of treatment halted his progress toward fusion and led to some degree of breakdown of the amalgamation already achieved. In this connection, however, there are some multiple personality therapists who doubt that complete and permanent fusion is possible or even desirable. John Beahrs writes in *Unity and Multiplicity* that we should not take it for granted that fusion is the thing to aim for. After all, he asserts (taking a page from Morton Prince's description of the annihilation of a personality), a kind of death is involved in the very notion of fusion:

> Furthermore, if or when fusion does occur, we cannot rationalize away the fact that alter personalities do die, in exactly the sense in which currently alive human beings look upon death. Death does not mean any loss of spiritual-material substance, but a dissolution of one's experience of an individual self as an entity separate from other entities in time or place. Since a true alter personality experiences himself as a separate self, he will fight that dissolution with the full force of the self-preservation instinct common to all life.

He therefore suggests that a cooperation of the coexisting parts in a harmonious functioning whole may be the more feasible resolution to multiple personality, a conclusion further supported, he says, by evidence that at a deeper level no part-self ever dies. Does it not seem better, he says, to allow the various personalities to arrive at an accommodation in which they work harmoniously together under the direction of that personality best suited for the job.

CONCLUSION

For two hundred years there has been strong evidence that every human being has a second consciousness within, a second self different in memory chain and personality characteristics from the normal self.

For one hundred years there has been strong evidence that human beings have not just one but many such inner consciousnesses, all operating simultaneously.

Now, recent research strongly indicates that the creative power of man's inner being is such that he may be able to produce an unlimited number of independent consciousnesses, each differing from the rest, all functioning at the same time within that mysterious unity we call a human being.

The phenomenon of multiple personality is now well-authenticated. Most recently, work done in administering psychological tests and EEG's (electroencephalograms) to the various personalities of multiples has removed whatever serious doubts may have remained.

When examining the data of multiple personality, one cannot overlook a phenomenon which exhibits certain striking similarities: "possession." Here, too, the subject exhibits a duality or even multiplicity of personalities which disclaim any identity with each other. Also, in both the multiple personality and the possession experience, amnesias of various kinds may be present. What, then, does the possession experience tell us about multiple man?

Part Two
The Possession Experience

Chapter 4

Possession: What It Looks Like

From the earliest known times, human beings have undergone the experience called "possession," which, broadly defined, is the invasion of an individual by some alien thinking entity. In its most dramatic form possession means the sudden and complete disappearance of the personality ordinarily inhabiting the body and its replacement by a totally different one. In some cases this transformation involves a violent struggle between the intruding entity and the unwilling victim; in others, it is sought as a religious experience, where the individual willingly gives up his body to be used by a "spirit" for some higher purpose. But whether possession is voluntary or involuntary, there is often a shift in personality so radical that family or friends of the victim can no longer recognize him.

In many cases the victim is unconscious while the possessing entity is in control, a state called "trance possession"; however, sometimes the victim does not lose consciousness of his usual personality at all. Rather, he will be a passive spectator during this "lucid possession."

Ordinary language indicates that this experience, which can occur so dramatically at times, has its everyday counterpart. Anyone who has said or done something totally out of character might say, "I don't know what possessed me." Or he might express this feeling of inner discontinuity with: "I was beside myself" or "I was not myself." Conversely, someone who displays great stability of character is called "self-possessed."

Between these extremes—the dramatic and the commonplace— lies a vast and complex array of human experience.

A great body of literature on possession has accumulated over the centuries. While it tends to emphasize the dramatic side, it does provide helpful information about the essential nature of every type of possession experience and about both possessor and possessed.

THE POSSESSING ENTITIES

The entities which possess people may be personal or nonpersonal, human or nonhuman.

Personal entities are those which have an existence in their own right and are not the productions of anyone or anything else. Because they have a "spirit" core, they can initiate action and make free choices. In most traditions, personal entities are considered to be immortal.

The nonhuman possessing entities include in their ranks not only demons, devils, and Satan himself, but their opposite: gods, muses and the Holy Spirit of Christian tradition.

Human possessing entities may be living or "dead" in the sense of no longer having their own body. The "dead" are more accurately called "discarnates."

Nonpersonal entities are produced either by intelligent beings or by "nature" itself. Though they may appear to behave intelligently, they do not have independently existing minds as such. "Thought entities" are an example. These are the product of concentrated thought that illustrate the occult principle that "thoughts are things." Their strength and lasting power depend upon how much energy has been focused upon them by their creators.

"Group-minds" are entities formed by groups of people whenever they gather to concentrate upon some idea or endeavor. It is believed that, to some degree, a group-mind takes possession of all members of the group which forms it.

Finally, there are instances of individuals being possessed by fragments of their own psyches, as an entity emerges from the darkness of the unconscious to take possession of the waking self.

THE POSSESSED

Willing hosts see themselves as intermediates between this world and the world of spiritual beings and are appropriately named "mediums"; they may be controlled or possessed by discarnate human spirits or other intelligent entities.

In the rituals of the occult tradition, participants may give themselves over freely to be possessed by a "god." This is called "magical invocation" and is practiced to gain knowledge or power or to promote personal growth.

Creative inspiration is another form of voluntary possession experience, one involving muses, inspirational spirit controls and various creative "little people."

Finally, there is the Christian tradition of possession by the Holy Spirit where those possessed willingly give themselves up to be the instrument of "the Spirit of God" or "the Spirit of Jesus."

Unwilling hosts may be the victims of diabolical possession, the most graphic and best known type of involuntary possession, with Satan or a lesser devil being the forcible invader.

However, in other cases of unwilling possession, the possessor is the spirit of a discarnate human being, often with evil intentions, though it may sometimes be simply bewildered and disoriented.

There exist also in the literature of possession instances of possession by the living but these cases are rare.

The last kind of involuntary possession to be examined involves psychic creations which may be produced by others, in such things as negative thought forms, or by oneself, as when one is taken over by one's own destructive intra-psychic creations.

An important note: when referring to possession as "involuntary," it is meant that the host is unwilling as far as his *conscious mind* is concerned. It has been my experience that in a great many cases of apparent involuntary possession the host was *unconsciously* willing to be possessed. More will be said about this in Part III.

LOOKING AT THE POSSESSION EXPERIENCE

The next three chapters attempt to draw the broad outlines of possession as it has been portrayed for us in the literature of those traditions which accept its existence. Descriptions from the casework of those who write about the phenomenon in order to show that it is not at all what it appears to be are not included here, but such material will be discussed in a later section of the book.

The approach to the cases given here is phenomenological, set down as experienced by the victims and witnesses, along with their own interpretations. Every effort has been made to present as accurate an account as possible of the cases used. And where some religious or philosophical interpretation is made, I have reported it in the spirit of the tradition involved. This does not mean, however, that I personally espouse the views of that tradition. Those who wish to probe more deeply into the circumstances of these cases will find useful points of departure in the bibliography at the end of the book.

Chapter 5

Willing Victims

COMMUNICATION WITH THE DEAD: MEDIUMSHIP

Spiritism is the belief that the living can communicate with the dead, a conviction that has had its place at some point in every culture. And there are certain individuals—mediums—specially suited to be the intermediaries.

The exercise of mediumship involves the creation of a state of possession, as the spirit of the dead—or "discarnate" human being—takes over the medium's body and uses it for communication. Messages may be given through voice or writing and signs of the spirit's presence may be manifested in startling physical effects around the medium: objects moving without contact; sounds, smells or lights unaccountably produced; human forms materializing.

General references to spiritistic seances appear in the most ancient of human documents, with detailed accounts of messages and paranormal physical phenomena going back at least to the fourth century A.D. Current anthropological literature is full of references to the exercise of mediumship among so called primitive peoples. But it is the modern religious movement called Spiritualism that provides the most enlightening illustrations of mediumship.

THE RISE OF SPIRITUALISM

Spiritualism as a religious movement has its roots in the practice of mesmerism. In France in the 1830s mesmerists were already throwing clairvoyantly gifted individuals into the magnetic trance state and discovering that they would sometimes have visions of heaven, communing with the spirits of the departed there. At the same time, followers of the Swedish seer Swedenborg were using mesmerism to carry on the tradition of ecstatic visions of their revered leader. But it was especially in America that this aspect of mesmeric practice prospered. From the late 1830s on, itinerant mesmerists traveled the countryside with their "medical clairvoyant" sidekicks, prescribing remedies for people's ills. In the early 1840s, Andrew Jackson Davis, often called the John the Baptist of Spiritualism, was magnetized by one of these wanderers and discovered in himself remarkable visionary powers. While in the trance state, he dictated numerous books, all of which dealt with matters that would become central concerns for the Spiritualist movement.

The movement itself can rightly be considered to have started at a particular place and a particular time, and its origin makes a fascinating story.

On the night of March 31, 1848, near Hydesville, New York, the tiny farmhouse of a certain John Fox was disturbed by strange knocking sounds. Maggie and Kate, the family's two teenage daughters, thought these sounds were coming from the walls and floor and were initially terrified. But soon they were making a game of the whole business as Slater Brown, in his fine history, *The Heyday of Spiritualism*, describes:

> In a playful mood Kate, the younger one, snapped her fingers and asked the raps to answer. The sounds, to everyone's astonishment, immediately obliged. Maggie then clapped her hands, asking the raps to reply, and again they did so. Not to be outdone by her daughters, Mrs. Fox asked the sounds to rap ten times. When the sounds at once responded, Mrs. Fox asked that they rap the ages of her six children in succession. To the family's increasing astonishment the raps rolled off the ages with complete accuracy.
>
> Convinced by this demonstration that some sort of intelligence lay behind the knockings, Mrs. Fox continued her questioning. According to a deposition made on April 4, she proceeded to interrogate the invisible spirit as follows: "I then asked if it was a human being that was making the noise, and if it was, to manifest by the same noise. There was no noise. I then asked if it was a spirit? and if it was, to manifest it by two sounds. I heard two sounds as soon as the words were spoken. I then asked, if it was an injured spirit? to give me the sound, and I heard the rapping distinctly. I then asked if it was injured in this house? and it manifested it by the noise. If the person was living that injured it? and got the same answer. I then ascertained by the same method that its remains were buried under the dwelling, and how old it was."

The Foxes immediately began calling in their neighbors so that over the next few days dozens of people swarmed through the small dwelling and heard the "spirit" answer their questions through simple raps. They examined the house from top to bottom and could find no natural source of the sounds.

The disturbances in the farmhouse caused such commotion that the Fox family moved in with their son David. But soon they discovered that the sounds had followed them. Up to that point, everyone had believed the raps were associated with the house, the manifestation of a spirit haunting the place of its demise. Now they realized that the knockings had to do with Maggie and Kate, occurring only in their presence. This connection quickly led to accusations of fraud, with elaborate theories of how the sisters perpetrated the deception.

When the Fox family realized that their daughters were at the center of the disturbing noises, they decided to try to get things back to normal by separating them. However, this seems to have accomplished nothing, for the sounds not only continued, but new phenomena were added. Now blankets were ripped off beds, objects floated through the air and the sounds of groans and shouts were added to the others.

At this point an important new element was introduced. As Brown describes it:

> We learn that the disturbances . . . finally quieted down when Isaac Post, a Quaker friend of the Fox family, suggested a method whereby the spirits could express themselves in a less exuberant manner. Learning that Duesler in Hydesville had obtained the [spirit's] initials by repeating the alphabet . . . Post suggested that verbal messages might also be procured by this means. When he inquired of the spirits if this were possible, they immediately responded with a shower of raps. The alphabet was then slowly recited, a rap designating each letter. To everyone's astonished delight the following cordial message was spelled out: "We are all your dear friends and relatives."

The Fox sisters took up this alphabetical method of communicating with the spirits and established themselves as mediums. Within a short time they were able to produce the physical phenomena at will: as soon as they seated themselves in a room, raps would resound from furniture and walls and objects would move about. They began to tour and give exhibitions, also holding seances to which they charged admission and as a result, a tremendous excitement began to sweep the country. The prospect of communicating with those who had left this life meant that practically overnight, people all through the United States began trying their hand at talking with the spirits.

Typically, a family would gather in the evening in their living room, sit in a circle around a table in low light, join hands, and then ask for some message from a spirit. A phenomenal number of these impromptu seances apparently proved successful, as a table produced knocking sounds or partial levitations in which one leg would rise and fall, rapping out an alphabetical code on the floor. Such experiences became so commonplace that within four years of the "Hydesville knockings," thousands of families were holding regular spiritualist sittings.

In these amateur circles some member would often emerge as being a particularly gifted medium. That person might, for example, spontaneously fall into a trance state, speaking or writing while in trance, conveying messages from the dead in that way. Such people were often encouraged to develop their gifts and give "sittings" for those in need of solace and guidance.

MEDIUMSHIP

As more and more people became involved in these experiments, Spiritualism developed into a full-fledged religious movement. Its heroes and heroines were the great mediums who could manifest the presence of spirits by producing extraordinary psychic phenomena. They were the ones who maintained a high profile before the public—who proved for anyone willing to see that the dead live on.

Almost without exception, these were *trance* mediums: they had the ability to put themselves into an unusual state of consciousness, one which has been described as a state of "dissociation." As we saw earlier, dissociation was considered to be the splitting off of a group of ideas and emotions which then proceed to carry on a life of their own in the subject's subconscious, sometimes to re-emerge in his consciousness in automatic actions of some sort. In the Spiritualist use of the term, however, a discarnate is believed to take control of the medium's body, the normal consciousness having left it. Spiritualists consider trance mediumship to be a state of voluntary possession, enabling the consciousness of a spirit to communicate messages from "the other side."

Mediums' descriptions of their experience of entering into and leaving the trance vary greatly. However, that of Mrs. Leonore Piper (1859–1950), one of the great *mental* mediums (those who convey their messages by speaking or writing) of the Spiritualist movement, may be of interest:

> I feel as if something were passing over my brain, making it numb; a sensation similar to that experienced when I was etherised, . . . I feel a little cold, too, . . . as if a cold breeze passed over me, and people and objects become smaller until they finally disappear; then, I know nothing more until I wake up, when the first thing I am conscious of is . . . a very bright light, and then darkness, such darkness. My hands and arms begin to tingle just as one's foot tingles after it has been "asleep," and I see, as if from a great distance, objects and people in the room; but they are very small and very black.

When trance mediums return to consciousness, they ordinarily remember nothing of what has taken place during the trance period. Aftereffects vary. Some will feel dazed; others experience a bone-weary exhaustion. Aches and pains are not uncommon. For the majority, it seems, *some* unpleasant symptoms result.

The Spiritualist movement has produced thousands of trance mediums over the last 130 years, both mental mediums, like Mrs. Piper, and physical mediums—those adept at producing paranormal phenomena.

Daniel Dunglas Home. Even in the extraordinary world of Spiritualist mediums, Daniel Dunglas Home (1833–1886) stands out as a rarity. Nandor Fodor (1895–1964), a well-known American psychoanalyst and psychical researcher, called Home "the greatest physical medium in the history of modern Spiritualism." While other mediums tended to have their "specialities," Home could produce *all* the physical phenomena known to occur, some with his own added touches. Besides bringing about the levitation and movement of objects at a distance, Home produced partial and full materialization of human forms, caused a pencil to write messages by itself, played the accordion while passively holding the end without the keys and—with no contact at all—produced lights and sounds. On at least a hundred recorded occasions, Home levitated and he is also credited with two phenomena extremely rare among modern mediums: elongation of the body and fire immunity.

Throughout his more than thirty years of mediumship (1852 until his death in 1886), no one ever provided serious evidence of trickery or fraud by Home. His ability to produce inexplicable physical effects was studied at length in a specially constructed laboratory by Sir William Crookes, the most eminent physicist of the day. Under stringent conditions, Crookes verified to his complete satisfaction that Home could apply force to an object at a distance *and* play the accordion without contact—actions which could not be explained by any known physical laws. Giving his personal impressions of Home, Crookes said:

> During the whole of my knowledge of D.D. Home, extending for several years, I never once saw the slightest occurrence that would make me suspicious that he was attempting to play tricks. He was scrupulously sensitive on this point, and never felt hurt at anyone taking precautions against deception. To those who knew him Home was one of the most lovable of men and his perfect genuineness and uprightness were beyond suspicion.

Home began his career as a medium in the United States. In *Heyday of a Wizard*, Jean Burton quotes a description of one of his early seances in Connecticut:

> One Sunday afternoon . . . Mr. Burr saw a table "*in broad daylight, and no one near enough to touch it,*" begin to rock and roll like a ship in distress. Next "creaks as of straining masts and timbers, and even the plunging sound of big waves striking the doomed vessel, could be distinctly heard." The alphabet was called for and a name spelled out. "Then arose a man on the other side of the room—a person from Hartford, James Mc-Chester—and made this statement: 'That is the name of one who was my near and dear friend. He was drowned at sea, in a gale in the Gulf of Mexico.' "

On his doctor's advice Home left America for England, and began a truly remarkable career which would take him from British drawing rooms to the private chambers of the emperor of Russia. Unlike many mediums of his time, he did not hire halls and give public demonstrations for fees. Rather he lived the life of a genteel man of the world, being invited as a house guest from home to home, refusing to take money for his mediumistic exhibitions.

Typically, Home would arrive at a place and spend the day conversing with the members of the household. After dinner, everyone would retire to the living room, be seated and continue to converse. Home would relax in his chair. Sometimes the physical phenomena such as raps would start before Home had even finished his conversation; at others he would grow quiet and quickly enter a light trance. Then, some more striking phenomena might occur: the movement of objects; the materialization of a detached hand which would perhaps present a flower to one of the women guests.

For the most spectacular of feats, however, Home would go into a deep trance where he would be possessed by one or more spirits who would refer to him in the third person as "Dan" and describe the phenomena as they were about to be produced. Home never remembered what had taken place in deep trance; his "controls" or spirit guides (who never revealed their identities) established a possession so complete that Home's personality was entirely absent. While in possession of his body, these guides would sometimes speak about spiritual matters like the nature of the afterlife.

Deep trance seemed essential for Home to accomplish elongations, fire immunity and levitations. There is a famous levitation incident described by his friend Lord Adare (1841–1926) in 1860 in his *Experiences in Spiritualism with Mr. D.D. Home* in which, to the horror of a group of watching friends, Home floated out one third-storey window and in another. On this occasion the spirits gave careful instructions about how to handle Home when he came out of trance:

> Home came in again directly, sat down and said, "Dan must awake now, he will be very nervous; but you must bear with him, it will pass off." . . . When Home awoke, he was much agitated; he said he felt as if he had gone through some fearful peril, and that he had a most horrible desire to throw himself out of a window; he remained in a very nervous condition for a short time, then gradually became quiet. Having been ordered [by the spirits] not to tell him, we said nothing of what had happened.

As regards the three kinds of feats mentioned, if Home had been aware of what was about to happen to him in trance, he would have been too frightened to allow it. His possessing controls thus kept him ignorant of their intentions.

Home never claimed any part in the production of these phenomena. He once said:

> I have not and never have had, the slightest power over these manifestations, either to bring them on, or to send them away, or to increase, or to lessen them. What may be the peculiar laws under which they have become developed in my person, I know no more than others. Some of the phenomena in question are noble and elevated, others appear to be grotesque. For this I am not responsible. I solemnly swear that I do not produce the phenomena aforesaid, or in any way whatever aid in producing them.

How little Home did control his phenomena was shown when the spirits took his powers away from him right in the midst of a dazzling tour. Though they told him his powers would be restored in exactly one year, they gave no explanation; but during that year, not one paranormal occurrence took place around Home. To his great relief, however, just one year to the day later, his ability returned.

Gladys Osborne Leonard was a Spiritualist who exhibited *mental mediumship*. During the fifty years before her death in 1968 she was the subject of many investigations by members of the Society for Psychical Research in England who sought conclusive evidence that the "discarnate spirits" who purported to speak through her were genuine. Certainly, while in trance she evinced knowledge of persons, things and events that she could not possibly have gained by conventional means. The case of Mrs. Leonard is also unique for its detailed descriptions of how possession operates in trance mediums.

Gladys Osborne was born in 1882. As a little girl she frequently had visions of what she called her "Happy Valleys"—beautiful natural scenes where she saw couples and groups of people walking around looking radiantly happy. Knowledge of these visions made her family—her father in particular—extremely uneasy. So with some difficulty, the girl suppressed the visions and eventually they ceased completely.

Gladys had hoped for a professional singing career, but a bout of diphtheria made this impossible, so she began to study acting. At twenty-four, she had an experience that made a deep impression upon her.

One day, she visited her mother, whose health was poor, and that night she suddenly awoke to see a large circular patch of light about four feet in diameter some five feet above her body. In the light she saw her mother very distinctly. She looked several years younger, healthy, her eyes were clear and she was smiling happily. She gazed down at Gladys for a moment, conveying to her a feeling of intense relief and a sense of safety and well-being. Then the vision faded. The time was 2:00 A.M. The next day Gladys learned that her mother had passed away at precisely that time.

This experience convinced Gladys that her mother still existed and could affect the living. She then began to accept some Spiritualist beliefs: for example, that when one dies, the old physical body is left behind and a new, different kind of body is taken on as the vehicle for the new phase of existence. Soon Gladys began to show her aptitude for the mediumship which would make her so famous. She and some theater friends began by experimenting with "table tipping" (a phenomenon in which a table rises and falls, tapping out an alphabetical code) and in the process she received a message from a spirit communicator who called herself "Feda." Feda claimed to be Gladys' great-great-grandmother, a Hindu by birth, who died around 1800 at the age of thirteen. She said that Gladys was destined to be a great medium and must develop her abilities. In just eighteen months, Gladys began to show signs of living up to Feda's predictions.

From the first, she proved to be a natural subject for trance. Once she had slipped into a state of unconsciousness, Feda would take over, relaying messages from discarnate spirits who were present and generally controlling the trance sessions. Other spirits would sometimes temporarily take possession, but Feda did most of the talking. When the sitting was over, she would disappear and Gladys' own consciousness return.

Gladys had by now married and her husband proved to be very supportive of all this. When she first met him, he knew nothing about Spiritualism, but was open to hearing about it. It appealed to him as a reasonable belief and his interest gradually deepened so that he became very involved in Spiritualism in his own right.

Over the years Feda and a few other spirits would provide a fascinating record via Gladys Leonard of what it was like for them to communicate through her. Their descriptions were an unusual attempt to reveal the *possessing* entity's experience of voluntary possession.

Along with Feda there were two spirit communicators in particular who undertook this task. They were "Etta" and "John," the deceased sister and father of the Reverend Charles Drayton Thomas (188?–1953), a clergyman who studied Mrs. Leonard's mediumship for many years. Accepting for the moment the claims of Feda, John and Etta to be possessing entities, let us take a look at their accounts.

Feda was always the first to control Mrs. Leonard when she fell into the trance state. When she was in control and about to relay a message from some other spirit to those present at the sitting, she "saw" that spirit occupying a position in the physical area in front of the medium. Feda said that spirit communicators were present in their "etheric bodies," and they communicated to her by sight, sound, smell or touch. The medium's eyes were always closed, and none of this "sensible" experience was accessible to the sitters, so the perception being described was something other than physical.

Feda's mode of perception was investigated in great detail by Lady Troubridge, a part-time psychical researcher, and described in an article in the *Proceedings* of the Society for Psychical Research in 1922. Lady Troubridge's view was that the spirit communicators conveyed their messages telepathically to Feda, with the result that clarity depended to a large extent on their ability to focus their thoughts. She gives an amusing description of the confusion that could result from this state of affairs:

> It would appear that, so long as the communicator can keep his mind exclusively on one fact or event . . . Feda's description will be relatively clear. . . . Should, . . . the communicator's mind wander ever so little, his irrelevant thought will be just as likely to reach Feda, and when it does it will appear in some form in her narrative. Feda apparently cannot always disentangle relevant from irrelevant impressions. . . . Supposing, for instance, I, being deceased, wished to describe through Feda my country residence and its garden with ornamental pond, and I should allow the thought to cross my mind that upon some particular occasion friends . . . had admired the pond and particularly enjoyed a good supper of lobster salad. I might easily appear in Feda's utterances as a demented spirit who asserted that I had owned an ornamental pond in which I kept lobsters and grew salad! I have known an improbability of this kind followed by indications denoting excitement on the part of the communicator.
>
> I have known this excitement either to bewilder Feda, or to be interpreted by her as denoting the spirit's eagerness to em-

phasize that the unlikely statement is correct, and I have been unable to resist picturing myself as an unfortunate communicator fully able to gauge the extent to which my communication had gone wrong, and making matters worse by conveying telepathically an unintelligible chaos of excitement and dismay.

In *The Mediumship of Mrs. Leonard,* Susy Smith, author of a number of books on parapsychology, provides more information about the process of communicating. Here, she quotes John on Feda's difficulties as a possessing entity:

> When I speak, Feda is frequently puzzled as to my meaning and fails to catch it either quickly or accurately. That is when I am unable to make my meaning reach her in the form of words. If I then project a thought of some concrete object, Feda may remark, "I see so-and-so," but though she may seem to be *seeing* the object, it is really *my thought* of it which has reached her.

Feda described how this kind of communication could be particularly difficult because on one occasion she might be able to "see," on another "see" and "hear" and on another only "sense." Etta elaborated on the problem in this way:

> [John] says it is something like finding all windows and doors locked except one; on entering the house through that one others can be unlocked from within. They may have to walk round and round trying one place and another first; it is that which gives people occasion to conclude that they are fishing, fumbling at it.

But sometimes the communicator could literally dictate words to Feda and in that way get across a very clear message. Smith quotes Charles Drayton Thomas on this:

> It is a noteworthy fact that for a period, rarely more than twenty minutes in any one sitting, Feda will speak as if . . . from dictation. I can often . . . catch each softly whispered sentence before hearing it repeated in the clear Feda voice. This dictation method always reaches a high degree of accuracy, and I realize that I am receiving, not merely the communicator's thoughts, but also the characteristic diction. When, however, Feda relapses into what appears to be her own phrasing of the message, the precision and accuracy become markedly less.

It should be noted that Thomas's reference to hearing the words "whispered" is an allusion to a phenomenon of *physical* mediumship called "direct voice" which is rare for Mrs. Leonard. In this case the sitters and Feda all heard the words being dictated at the same time, the voice coming from the air in front of both Mrs. Leonard and the sitters. According to Feda, the production of direct voice in Mrs. Leonard's presence happened only when the "power" was very strong, that is, when medium and sitters all projected a great deal of energy into the session.

Most of what Feda, John and Etta said about mediumistic communication concerned the tremendous difficulties which both the main control and the communicating spirits had to overcome. From Etta:

> It seems that no one yet understands the unique character of a sitting. . . . It is a no man's land between the two conditions, yours and ours. It is considered that communication concerns earth people and spirit people, whereas there is also the peculiar bridgeway which has to be used and which belongs neither to one nor to the other, yet has some of the characteristics of each. Here lies all the difficulty. Mediums and sitters are in part working in a condition which is not entirely theirs, and we work in one which is not entirely ours. It is a pooling of resources which creates the bridge. One gets out of one's depth sometimes on both sides.

Smith quotes the reflections of the well-known British philosopher C.D. Broad (1887–1971), after studying communications coming via Mrs. Leonard:

> The communicators allege that there are two main difficulties in trying to communicate directly by means of the medium's organism. One is their own failure to remember, due to the limitations imposed on them by their possession of a foreign organism. The other is their imperfect control over the brain and nervous system of the medium, which often prevents them from getting her to utter words which will express the ideas they want to convey. Any specific effort by a communicator to get the medium to utter a particular thought of his is liable to be unsuccessful at first. The medium's brain seems to stick. It is best then for the communicator to turn to some other topic. If he does so, the process which he started in the medium's brain by his original attempt may eventually work out to a successful conclusion. He

77

must then be ready to pounce on it and to revert to the original topic. These remarks may be compared with the experience which one has when one tries in vain to remember a name, and has it (as we say) "on the tip of one's tongue" and yet cannot utter it. Often if one turns to other things, the name will suddenly come to one.

As a concluding remark, Broad reminds us:

> I think it is worth while to remark that none of us has the slightest idea of how in detail his body comes to express by speech or writing the ideas that he wishes to express. The process is voluntary and deliberate in the sense that one would not be saying or writing what one does unless at the time one wished to express certain ideas. But it is certainly neither voluntary nor conscious in the sense that one deliberately does something to the appropriate parts of one's brain, as one deliberately and consciously strikes the appropriate keys of a typewriter. It is therefore hardly surprising that the Feda-persona should give a confused and confusing description of what she does when she tries to make Mrs. Leonard's organism express a certain idea.

The notion of communication with spirits is an ancient one. The Spiritualist movement focused upon communication with the departed. While this kind of mediumship goes back beyond written record, so, too, does that tradition that concentrates upon getting in touch with divine spirits.

POSSESSION BY THE GODS

From ancient times to the present, human beings have sought out ways to gain *knowledge* of the unknown and the future and so the countless methods of "divination" have arisen. Foremost among these techniques was that of the oracles where a god was thought to communicate with human beings through the mouth of someone specially prepared for that purpose. The oracle invariably spoke "automatically" from a state of trance, its personal consciousness in no way involved in the formulation of its words. The oracle was thus possessed by the god. The possession state was accepted voluntarily by the oracle and it was usually considered an honour to be chosen.

One of the best known examples of this kind of possession is that of the oracle of Delphi, in Greece. In the mists of antiquity there was discovered near the town of Delphi a chasm which emitted fumes capable of throwing an individual into a state of ecstasy. However, as one of its by-products was apparently the urge to throw oneself into the abyss, the chasm was closed up except for a small hole which allowed the fumes to escape. Delphi was consecrated to Apollo and the tradition arose that he would speak through those who were under the influence of the fumes. Since these divine utterances were considered sacred, as well as valuable sources of information about hidden matters, a young girl was eventually chosen to serve as "official" medium, and a temple was erected on the spot.

But the oracle of Delphi was only one of many ancient oracular traditions established in Greece. The tradition of oracular utterances in the possession state has been found all through history and in many cultures. It seems, for instance, that many of the original Indian tribes of North and South America had their oracles. Today, there are still trance-possession traditions in some Caribbean islands whereby individuals act as god-possessed and speak messages with an oracular quality.

Another goal of the ancient traditions was to gain *power* over the events of life through god-possession. Here, the shaman, witch or magician uses the tools of imagination and identification to effect possession by a god, that he may acquire that god's power.

In the Western occult tradition, for example, magic is considered to be the science and art of causing change in accordance with one's will. The procedure is to use powerful images formed by the imagination to control events. The magician's aim is self-realization: to become more and more one with his higher self, transforming his character and his life. Possession by the gods is one of his more powerful tools.

In ancient practice, god-possession frequently meant the pushing aside of the subject's ordinary personality so that the god could speak and act through him; however, in today's occult practice, the possession experience is often more subtle: the magician takes on the special qualities of the possessing god and so strengthens those qualities in his own being. Also, while possessed, he has, through identification, that god's powers and may use them to control the course of some set of events in his life. The object of god-possession is always to participate in the power of the god.

This possession is brought about by "invocation"—calling up the god to manifest within the magician's being, as opposed to "evocation," which has the god manifest objectively *outside* his being. One method of invocation is "assumption of the god-form." J.H. Brennan, author of a number of books on the occult, wrote in 1972 a work called *Experimental Magic,* in which he describes this. Brennan suggests the individual make his choice from among the ancient Egyptian gods; they are traditionally used and so their "astral" images are already half formed with energy. Suppose, says Brennan, you chose to assume the god-form of the Sun God, Ra. You must first find out all you can about him, his characteristics, mythology and the physical forms in which he has been portrayed. Then for the actual invocation, Brennan advises:

> You should see the Sun God as a gigantic form standing before you, radiating light and heat . . . [Attempt] to insert clarity and color into your vision. Try to see the golden hue of the skin, the glowing nimbus around the head. Bring your other imaginary senses into play, so that you seem to feel the heat, seem to hear the lordly voice.

By using his imagination in this way, the magician is helping the god Ra to manifest. He is creating a *form* in the "astral" plane which the god can animate and when this has happened, the magician seeks to be possessed. As Brennan says:

> When the form has been established in the Astral Light to the greatest degree your talent allows, assume physically the traditional posture and gestures of the god. Then, by an act of imagination, have the Astral god-form coincide with your body. What you are, in fact, doing here is blending it with your own astral body, providing points of contact for the god-force to flow into you. As the form coincides (something which may take a little practice) invoke the god verbally.

Brennan describes the immediate result of the operation as a "staggering inflow of sheer energy." At the end, the state of possession must be terminated:

> Complete the operation by separating the god-form from your body, projecting it before you and gradually allowing it to fade away through an act of imagination. It is also no bad thing to complete proceedings with a ritual gesture, giving a clear demarcation line between your magical experiments and your life in the mundane world.

To the modern reader, the whole tradition of possession by the gods and its rituals may seem very foreign. Yet this approach to life has been conspicuous throughout human history and remains today in the Wiccan religion, for instance. From this tradition, the popular notion of "witchcraft" first arose, though it has been largely misunderstood as centering in black magic. In fact Wicca was essentially an old form of paganism involving a whole variety of rituals and spells to cure disease and otherwise help people.

Along with the world's so-called primitive cultures, the groups like the Hermetic Order of the Golden Dawn present a contemporary example of the continued presence of the ritual magic mentality in the world. This latter group in fact counted among its members some of the more sophisticated intellectuals of modern Western culture.

CREATIVE INSPIRATION

In the literature of possession there are many instances of individuals who have been taken over by a spirit in order to express some art form. The degree of control runs the gamut from full trance possession to mere inner influence.

INSPIRATIONAL POSSESSION

Jesse Francis Grierson Shepard (1849–1927) provides one of the most dramatic examples of this type of possession. At seances which included such sitters as royalty and famous musicians, he used the piano but did not always play it himself, the music at times coming through the shut keyboards. Shepard would also occasionally sing with two voices, rendering songs in both bass and soprano at the same time.

In 1894 an account of one of his seances written by a certain Prince Adam Wisniewski appeared in the Spiritualist periodical *Light*:

> After having secured the most complete obscurity we placed ourselves in a circle around the medium, seated before the piano. Hardly were the first chords struck when we saw lights appearing at every corner of the room. . . . The first piece played through Shepard was a fantasie of Thalberg's on the air from "Semiramide." This is unpublished, as is all the music which is played by the spirits through Shepard. The second was a rhapsody for four hands played by Liszt and Thalberg with astounding fire, a

81

sonority truly grand, and a masterly interpretation. Notwithstanding this extraordinarily complex technique, the harmony was admirable, and such as no one present had ever known paralleled, even by Liszt himself, whom I personally knew, and in whom passion and delicacy were united. In the circle were musicians who, like me, had heard the greatest pianists of Europe; but we can say that we never heard such truly supernatural execution.

Twenty years before his death in 1927, Shepard ended his career as a musical medium and took up literary pursuits. Taking the name of Francis Grierson he enjoyed considerable literary acclaim for his writings which included *The Valley of Shadows, The Celtic Temperament* and *The Humour of the Underman.*

Rosemary Brown represents a less pyrotechnical version of inspirational possession. From early childhood Mrs. Brown believed she saw discarnate spirits around the family and at age seven, Franz Liszt began to appear to her. Here is her description of his first visit:

> I was not in the least scared when I saw him standing at my bedside. I had been accustomed to seeing discarnate beings— or spirits as most people call them—since I was a tiny child, . . . he never said who he was that morning. . . . But there is no mistaking Liszt . . . especially when he was [as he now appeared] an elderly man with long white hair and those sombre robes. All he said that morning, speaking slowly because I was a child, was that when he had been in this world he had been a composer and a pianist. He then said: "When you grow up I will come back and give you music."

Liszt kept his word and eventually came back—along with composers like Chopin, Beethoven and Monteverdi—to communicate new music to the world through Mrs. Brown. A spokesman for the group stated:

> We are not transmitting music to Rosemary Brown simply for the sake of offering possible pleasure in listening thereto; it is the implications relevant to this phenomenon which we hope will stimulate sensible and sensitive interest and stir many who are intelligent and impartial to consider and explore the unknown regions of man's mind and psyche.

This aspect of Mrs. Brown's mediumship falls into the category of inspirational influence. But there was also a certain kind of physical possession by the discarnate Liszt. Mrs. Brown, a British housewife, had had only a year of piano lessons as a child and a year and a half as an adult, but under Liszt's control she gave excellent piano performances of difficult compositions.

Her initiation into this mediumship came in her adult life. From the time of her husband's death in 1961, Mrs. Brown started to become more and more aware of Liszt's presence around her. Here is one of her accounts:

> Instead of my finding a piece of music and playing it for myself, I found he was guiding my hands at the piano. Music was being played without any effort on my part, and it was music that I had never heard before. The odd thing was that I was so curiously unsurprised by the whole episode. . . . Liszt had not spoken. He had just been there. I was not in any sort of trance—I had seen him in fullest consciousness. After that he kept coming back and giving me more and more music.

The possession experience seemed, according to Mrs. Brown's own description, to be partial:

> The only way I can describe his method then is to say that he took over my hands like a pair of gloves. Without astral assistance I could not play the piano at all well at that time.

The music first played in these partial possession states was apparently Liszt's initial attempt to communicate new compositions and it soon evolved into musical dictation in which Mrs. Brown learned to write down the notes.

The investigation of Rosemary Brown's mediumship has centered around the evidential nature of the communications from the departed and the authenticity of the music dictated by the various deceased composers; but her subjective experience of inspirational possession is a phenomenon equally worthy of study.

Patience Worth is the name given by a spirit entity who communicated through a St. Louis woman named Pearl Curran. Patience Worth claimed to have been a seventeenth-century Englishwoman who was born in Dorset and lived in America, meeting a violent death at the hands of Indians. With Mrs. Curran as medium, she wrote prose in late-medieval English, remarkable for an almost exclusively Anglo-Saxon vocabulary. Pearl Curran's own scanty education and meager exposure to English literature make the production of these works one of the great puzzles of psychical research.

As an instance of inspirational possession, this case falls into the category of "automatic" productions, the instrument of the automatism being the ouija board. The whole episode began on July 8, 1913, while Mrs. Curran and two friends were idly experimenting with the board and this puzzling message appeared:

> Many moons ago I lived. Again I come—Patience Worth my name. . . . Wait, I would speak with thee. If thou shalt live, then so shall I. I make my bread by thy hearth. Good friends, let us be merrie. The time for work is past. Let the tabby drowse and blink her wisdom to the fire log.

For some time after that the three friends met regularly over the ouija board. Short poetic statements and aphorisms started to come through from Patience Worth in the same archaic style. Eventually Mrs. Curran worked the board alone and the literary productions increased in length until finally she continued entirely through "automatic speech."

Over the following twenty-four years Patience Worth dictated more than four thousand pages of literary works. A very long poem and five novels were published including one on the life and times of Jesus Christ entitled *A Sorry Tale*, which was highly thought of at the time.

Matthew Manning was the focus of an outbreak of "poltergeist" phenomena that occurred at his father's home in Shellford, England in 1967. Objects were mysteriously moved and knockings heard. This ceased after only a few weeks but returned four years later, and now included the disappearance and reappearance of household items, the turning on of lights and faucets, childlike scribbles on the walls and the appearance of pools of water on the floor.

Matthew, then fifteen, went off to boarding school at the height of this second outbreak, and the phenomena switched their scene of operation, clearly indicating their connection with the boy. After beds in the dormitory moved mysteriously, showers of pebbles fell within the buildings, knives were seen flying through the air and warm, illuminated spots appeared on walls, the headmaster became alarmed. Efforts to control the phenomena proved fruitless, and it seemed that Matthew would not be allowed to stay in school. Fortunately, Dr. George Owen, an expert investigator of such phenomena, who had observed the family during the first outbreak, was able to assure the headmaster that Matthew was in no way to blame for what was happening. Now the phenomena declined somewhat.

At this time Matthew discovered "automatic writing," producing messages which purported to be from various people long deceased. After a session of this, Matthew would experience a period completely free of poltergeist activity. In his book *The Link*, Manning describes how he perceived the connection:

> Automatic writing appeared to be the most successful method of controlling or preventing the poltergeist phenomena, and if it looked as though disturbances were imminent, I would sit down and write. Later, it became clear to me the writing was the controlling factor. It appeared that the energy I used for writing had previously been used for causing poltergeist disturbances.

Matthew soon began to realize that he was the repository for an unusual variety of psychic abilities: he could see "auras," anticipate people's conversations, bend spoons paranormally and produce unusual Kirlian photography effects. Extensive laboratory tests on Manning while performing psychic feats have not only confirmed them as genuine but also revealed that he produces unique brain wave patterns at the moment when he "switches on his energy."

Manning became a subject of inspirational possession when he took up "automatic drawing." An extremely poor artist himself, he used the same procedure as with automatic writing, but now mentally requested a drawing. The quality of the first one was not good, but at its center was a horse, which he knew he could never have drawn. From that day, Matthew began requesting famous artists to draw through him; Albrecht Dürer, Picasso, Leonardo da Vinci, Aubrey Beardsley, Paul Klee and Beatrix Potter have all apparently obliged, drawing in their own characteristic styles. In *The Link*, Manning comments:

> I must here add two observations which, I believe, are important. First, I did quite frequently seek the cooperation of certain artists, and although I sincerely believe that the subsequent drawings originated from a source outside myself, I am sure that my subconscious may on occasions have caused me to embellish or

add to some drawings. This, however, I have never done voluntarily or consciously. The second point is that while the work is unmistakably in the distinctive style of the artist who purports to execute the drawings, a certain proportion of the automatic drawings, usually those I do first when an artist comes through, are merely reproductions or near copies of works executed by the artist when he was still alive. In most cases I am absolutely certain that I have never seen the original drawing before, and I am quite disappointed when it is recognized by experts.

Expressing his puzzlement with the whole thing, Manning continues:

Under the initial of Albrecht Dürer, I produced a series of portraits, all of which are named after the subject. The names include "Matthaus Lang von Wellenburg", "Bilibaldi Pirkeymheri", "Hans Tucher", "Lucas von Leydon", and "Ulrich Stark". None of these names, with the exception of Lucas von Leydon, the engraver (contemporary of Dürer), were known to me. However, little research was needed to discover that Bilibaldi Pirkeymheri was a close friend and patron of Dürer. . . . Most remarkable about these drawings is the speed with which they are drawn. They are usually started in the middle of the paper and then worked out toward the perimeter. They are always drawn straight onto the paper in ink, with no preliminary work or pencil outlines. . . . Although, I might spend one or two hours to produce a drawing, it would normally take an artist perhaps six to eight hours to draw the same picture.

INSPIRATIONAL INFLUENCE

Those who experience inner inspirational influence in artistic endeavors stand squarely in the tradition embodied in the Greek notion of the *muse*.

A surprising number of the world's most talented artists ascribe some of their greatest creative productions to a mysterious source external to themselves which is somehow able to use them as channels for its expression. Often the poem, the musical composition, or the story has seemed to come to the artist fully formed, as though out of nowhere, and he has felt so little involved in its production as to be loath to take credit for it.

Many writers experience certain characters as independent beings, who, by carrying on in their apparently autonomous lives, seem to be as much responsible for the development of the story as the writer himself. Charles Dickens, for example, alludes to this in his letters: one of his greatest creations, Mrs. Gamp, would often speak to him (usually in church) "with an inward monetary voice."

Another author, the nineteenth-century French dramatist de Curel, describes how his dramatic characters, after a period of incubation, seemed to become independent of him. He would passively watch whole sections of the play unfold before his mind's eye. Sometimes, while carrying on some unrelated activity, bits of conversation between characters would come to him and he would later discover that they were from a part of the play which he had not yet reached.

For some the source of the inspiration remained a mystery. But for others it was made known to them. The two cases given here fall into the latter category. But even though these two men have a sense of who their benefactors were, the mystery of the process remains.

Robert Louis Stevenson experienced this kind of inner inspiration in a most remarkable way. In "A Chapter on Dreams" in *Across the Plains*, he describes his awareness of "little people" or "brownies," as he calls them, who seemed to exist within him somewhere and who provided him with much of his literary output. Stevenson encountered these little people in his dreams and tells how he and his father before him could invent very interesting tales during their sleep. The stories would develop spontaneously, "told for the teller's pleasure" and seldom brought to completion.

But when Stevenson set out upon a literary career, his little people joined in with the undertaking. Writing of himself in the third person, Stevenson says:

> But presently my dreamer began to turn his former amusement of story-telling to (what is called) account; by which I mean that he began to write and sell his tales. Here was he, and here were the little people who did that part of his business, in quite new conditions. . . . When he lay down to prepare himself for sleep, he no longer sought amusement, but printable and profitable tales; and after he had dozed off . . . his little people continued their evolutions with the same mercantile designs. . . . For the most part, whether awake or asleep, he is simply occupied—he or his little people—in consciously making stories for the market.

Stevenson tells about how it would often happen to him that when in grave need of money, when "the bank begins to send letters and the butcher to linger at the back gate," he would push himself to write a story. As he put his mind to the task he would notice that his little people were stirring themselves to the same endeavor. Once they were mobilized, he would be able to relax, because they proved themselves again and again to be capable of excellent work. Here he refers to a story which they threaded skillfully along to a brilliant surprise ending:

> To the end they had kept their secret. I will go bail for the dreamer . . . that he had no guess whatever at the motive of the woman [the story's central figure]—the hinge of the whole well-invented plot—until the instant of the highly dramatic dec- laration. It was not his tale; it was the little people's!

From this assertion of the separate existence of his little people, Stevenson goes on to question more deeply who they are and how they collaborate with him. He continues:

> Who are the Little People? . . . What shall I say they are but just my Brownies, God bless them! who do one-half my work for me while I am fast asleep and in all human likelihood, do the rest for me as well, when I am wide awake and fondly suppose I do it myself. . . . For myself . . . I am sometimes tempted to suppose [I am] no story-teller at all, but a creature as matter of fact as any cheesemonger or any cheese, and a realist bemired up to the ears in actuality; so that, by that account, the whole of my published fiction should be the single-handed product of some Brownie, some Familiar, some unseen collaborator, whom I keep locked in a back garret, while I get all the praise and he but a share (which I cannot prevent him getting) of the pudding.

So Stevenson concludes his remarkable admission with a rather self-deprecating evaluation of his part in the creative process as he experiences it. Although not all creative people are conscious of a separation between themselves and the source of their inspi- ration—and few as starkly as Stevenson—it is more common than ordinarily thought, with writers and musicians especially prone to feeling their productions are handed to them fully formed from some intelligence other than what they think of as their own. What- ever can be made of this experience, it must be taken into account in any investigation of man's multiplicity.

Otto Erdesz grew up in prewar Hungary. From his early years he showed signs of great artistic talent, eventually becoming a graphic artist. But he was a man of many competences and interests, one of them music, so that he also received musical training, specializing in the violin.

As time went on, Otto's interest in violins themselves deepened. He began collecting them and became something of an expert at recognizing the origin and training of their makers. Otto would hover over the workbench as craftsmen repaired his instruments, noting the fine details of the inner structure. One day, when he was twenty-six, Otto was challenged by one of those repairmen to try his hand at making a violin himself. He could not pass up the challenge and in a relatively short time, working at home, produced two. They were judged by objective critics to be good specimens.

Otto's interest in violin-making grew and he now began reading the instructions of the old Italian violin-makers. However, he did not find their teachings very helpful, judging that they seemed to conceal as much as they revealed. Although there were instructors in the craft of violin-making in his own country, Otto deliberately avoided being trained by any, stating that he "did not want to be misled."

Among the old Italian master violin-makers, Otto was intrigued by Guarneri del Gesu—in his own words, "madly interested in him." He considered Guarneri to be the master of masters, an even greater violin-maker than the renowned Stradivari. The work of Guarneri del Gesu became Otto's "bible."

One day, in his twenty-seventh year, Otto was working on a violin when he suddenly heard a voice saying, "Make it thinner." Looking up, he confirmed what he already knew: there was no one else in the shop. As for the voice, it had a "ghostly" tone that gave Otto an eerie feeling.

After a short, rather stunned, pause he continued working on the violin. Again the voice came, instructing him "Do it this way. . . . Now it's fine. . . . Stop that . . ." and so on. Otto stopped, completely perplexed, but soon returned to his work. Each time he took up the violin the voice continued its instructing. At first, Otto thought that perhaps he was going mad.

Whenever he went to his shop to work on violins, the voice came in the same way as before. Eventually he began to accept the voice and follow its instructions, deciding that if he could not get rid of it, he might as well pay attention to what it was saying.

The voice instructed Otto for a whole year, during which his ability as a violin-maker developed remarkably. Then the whole thing stopped, but Otto kept working on his violins, wondering what had happened.

Shortly thereafter he had a dream in which he saw Guarneri del Gesu. Guarneri spoke to Otto and revealed that it was he who had been instructing him for the past year. Otto asked Guarneri why he had ceased his instructions. Guarneri gave the brief reply, "You don't need me anymore," and was gone.

Otto continued to make violins and also began producing violas, using the same fine skills. As the years went by, he concentrated more and more on violas, making them his specialty.

Experts in the field of violin and viola crafting often remark on the similarity in style and quality between Otto's work and that of Guarneri del Gesu. Otto's instruments have even been mistaken for those of that master. Today Otto Erdesz is regarded as the finest viola-maker in the world, his instruments prized above all by those who perform in the field.

Otto says of his experience: "I'm sure that it seems strange to claim that Guarneri became my teacher after being dead for three hundred years. I know it happened, but it would not be easy for others to accept."

In Otto's experience we have an example of explicit inner guidance seeming to come from a deceased person. Though it would not be considered possession in the sense of taking over the subject's physical organism, the apparent intervention into Otto's consciousness from outside justifies its inclusion here.

THE HOLY SPIRIT

According to Christian tradition, after the death and resurrection of Jesus Christ, his disciples gathered and waited expectantly for what was to come. It was the time of Pentecost. Suddenly, the room they were in was filled with a sound as of a mighty rushing wind, and tongues of fire rested on all of them. Filled with some powerful new energy, they burst out with strange, uncontrollable speech. This experience was immediately interpreted as the coming of the "Holy Spirit" spoken about in the Old Testament. It was the primitive Christian church's first exposure to this form of possession.

In Jewish tradition, the coming of the Holy Spirit was linked with the dawn of a new Messianic age. After the first descent of the Spirit upon the Apostles, the experience of possession by the Holy Spirit became a regular part of the life of the newly burgeoning church. It was a sign that God was intervening marvelously to save mankind from its misery.

The view of human nature prevalent among the Jews at the time saw such a forcible intervention as absolutely necessary. Mankind was viewed as a battleground for a war between the demonic forces of evil and the power of God. Human beings were helpless in the face of this battle of cosmic dimensions. They could easily be taken over by demons and become the helpless pawns of the powers of evil. Fear of possession by evil spirits was very intense at the time of Jesus and one of the signs that he was the Messiah was his ability to cast them out: "He commands even the unclean spirits and they obey him."

This view of human personality as so readily accessible to invasion by supernatural influences set the stage for the new age of the Spirit of God. Human beings were given new hope in the preaching of Jesus: instead of being invaded by evil spirits, men would be possessed by the invincible power of God's own Spirit.

Possession by the Holy Spirit had far-reaching effects. The Spirit-possessed could heal the sick and perform other physical wonders; they could "speak in tongues" and interpret this unusual speech; they were also endowed with courage, faith and extraordinary wisdom. Possessed by the Holy Spirit, the Christian was seen as a channel for the direct action of that Spirit.

Over the centuries since those first manifestations of the Spirit there have been cycles of pentecostal-type phenomena. In the face of growing conservatism in the early church, the rebel Montanus in the second century was possessed by an outpouring of the Spirit. In the early seventeenth century, many of the Protestants of Languedoc, under the pressure of persecution, were seized by an ecstasy of the Spirit. They spoke in tongues, gave prophecies in purest French and performed other marvels. Around 1830 members of the Catholic Apostolic Church, commonly known as the Irvingites, began to manifest the gift of tongues. The Reverend Edward Irving had been lecturing on the gifts of the Spirit when some members of his London congregation started speaking in an unknown language. This was interpreted as the Holy Spirit "using the tongue of man in a manner which neither his own intellect could dictate, nor that of any other man comprehend."

The Shakers and the Mormons are examples of nineteenth-century American religious groups that regularly gave exhibitions of possession by the Holy Spirit—especially through the gift of tongues. With the development of the modern pentecostal churches in the last century the stage was set for today's resurgence of Spirit-possession in the "charismatic movement." This movement has touched every major Christian denomination with the result that today we see in many Christian gatherings all of the symptoms of possession by the Holy Spirit observed in the primitive Christian church, especially those of healing and speaking with tongues.

There is likewise in the charismatic movement a strong emphasis on man as a battleground between good and evil forces and on the notion that an individual must be possessed by one or the other. *Confrontations with the Devil* by Robert Pelton provides a quotation that well sums this up:

> The devil is the exact opposite of the Holy Ghost. Both spirits cannot stay in the same person at the same time. . . . An individual can either be possessed by God's Spirit or possessed by the Devil's Spirit. God's Spirit is one of love. Satan's spiritual forces are of hatred, destruction and violence.

Chapter 6

Unwilling Victims

This chapter is concerned with possession that takes place without the consent of the host. Here the possessed person has not sought out the possessor. Rather, he or she fervently desires to be rid of it, and outside help may be called in to terminate the possession.

Involuntary possession may be diabolical—that is, possession by the devil—or may be by the spirit of some discarnate human being. Less frequently the possessor turns out not to be a person at all but a psychic creation—an entity formed by another mind or minds.

THE DEVIL AND HIS HENCHMEN

In the literature of possession, "devils" are frequently mentioned. The term denotes nonhuman wicked spirits, usually fallen angels of God. When the expression "the devil" is used, one of the leaders of the fallen angels is meant, often given the names Satan, Beelzebub or Lucifer. Lesser nonhuman spirits are normally not named and are simply referred to as "devils" or "demons"; the latter word has now come to signify "evil spirits" in general and so can include the spirits of wicked discarnate human beings.

THE ILLFURT BOYS

In the 1860s a case of diabolical possession occurred at Illfurt in Alsace that well illustrates the typical phenomena. A detailed account of this case is given in Montague Summers's *The History of Witchcraft and Demonology*. I have taken the following description from that source.

Joseph Burner, a Catholic, had two sons: Thiebaut, born in 1855, and Joseph born in 1857. They were considered quiet boys of average ability up to the date of September 25, 1865, when they began to behave in a most unusual way. Sometimes, while lying down, they would spin around with amazing speed. Sometimes they would be seized by convulsions which produced extraordinary contortions in every limb. At other times they became totally rigid, lying motionless for hours their joints immovable. Often these attacks would end with violent fits of vomiting.

Their hearing was sometimes affected, leaving them for whole periods deaf to the loudest sound. But their speech more than anything displayed great abnormalities: at times they could not speak at all; at other times they shouted continually in the voices of rough men, not schoolchildren. They would curse, swear and blaspheme for hours, terrifying the neighbors.

The Illfurt boys eventually displayed most of what the Catholic Church considers to be the classical signs of diabolical possession: paranormal knowledge, for example, describing in detail events happening at a distance; fluency in unfamiliar languages, in this case, English and Latin along with various dialects of Spanish and Italian although they had never even briefly been exposed to the latter. Another symptom considered to be a sure sign of the devil's presence was the boys' violent reaction to seeing any holy object, such as holy water, medals, rosaries or relics of the saints. The blessed sacrament was an object of particular horror and any pictures of the Virgin Mary—or even the mention of her name—would send them into a frenzy.

The parish priest quickly diagnosed diabolical possession but his bishop was not easy to convince. When he finally sent a committee to investigate, they decided, after a two-hour interview, that the boys were indeed under the control of the devil. The bishop then commissioned a Father Souquat to carry out an exorcism and he began the ancient ritual on October 3, 1869.

The boys were exorcized separately. The elder, Thiebaut, was first and he had to be forced to enter the chapel where the exorcism was to take place. Three strong men were needed to hold him during the whole ceremony as he stood before the tabernacle, eyes closed, face beet-red, lips swollen, drooling a continuous stream of thick yellow froth. The first day of prayer and ritual met with no success.

On the second day Thiebaut was strapped in a straightjacket and seated in an arm chair. As the rites began, the boy roared in a deep bass voice and struggled against his bonds. Later when the priest called upon the Blessed Virgin, a horrible scream of agony came from Thiebaut's lips, his body gave a sharp convulsion and he fell forward in a deep sleep. He came to an hour later with no memory of the previous two days. Although he was dazed, he was completely himself again; the exorcism had done its job.

Meanwhile, Joseph's condition had been deteriorating. He remained separated from his brother as preparations were made for his exorcism, to be performed by the parish priest, the abbé Charles Brey. The ritual was begun on October 27, immediately after the celebration of mass; but in this case it took only three hours to obtain the boy's release. After struggling and screaming frantically, he gave out a loud roar and collapsed. In a moment he awoke and was amazed to find himself in a church surrounded by strangers. Like his older brother, Joseph had no memory of the exorcism.

ANNA ECKLUND

The case of the possession of Anna Ecklund is one of the most sensational ever recorded and is useful as an example of possession by the devil and his henchmen, containing as it does almost all of the elements found here and there in the literature of diabolic possession.

Anna was born around 1882, apparently in the midwestern United States. At fourteen, she began to suffer from some unusual symptoms. Although she had been raised a Catholic and was very pious, Anna now found herself incapable of entering the church building, as though prevented by some invisible force. At the same time she was plagued with disturbing thoughts of committing what she considered to be unspeakable sexual acts, and her shame about this led her to near despair. Anna also started to be seized by powerful impulses to attack holy objects.

The first state of full possession Anna experienced took place in 1908. Help was sought from the church but there was a considerable delay because of the authorities' skepticism. Finally in 1912 an exorcism was performed by Father Theophilus Riesinger, a Capuchin monk from the community of St. Anthony at Marathon, Wisconsin. Though the exorcism was successful, it seems that Anna's father heaped malicious curses on her and she was soon thrown back into a state of possession which would last for many years.

In 1928 Father Theophilus decided to try it again. With his bishop's permission, he elected to carry out the exorcism in the little Iowa town of Earling whose pastor was a personal friend of his. There was a convent of Franciscan Sisters there and Father Theophilus chose their chapel as the setting for the rite which he began on August 18, 1928. There would be three periods of exorcism, totaling twenty-three days, and before it was finished a number of nuns would have to be transferred to another convent and the pastor, Father Joseph Steiger, would be exhausted, what with nocturnal disturbances in his room, a strange car accident and the general strain of having his parishioners upset and frightened.

When the ceremonies were about to begin, Anna was carried into a previously prepared room in the convent and placed upon the mattress of an iron bed. Knowing the violence that can erupt, Father Theophilus had a number of the strongest nuns hold on to Anna, pressing her firmly down on the bed. What happened next is well described in *Begone Satan*, the principal account of this case, written in German by the Reverend Carl Vogel and translated by Reverend Celestine Kapsner, O.S.B.:

> Hardly had Father begun the formula of exorcism in the name of the Blessed Trinity, when a terrible scene followed. With lightning speed the possessed dislodged herself from her bed and the hands of the protectors, her body, carried through the air, landed high above the door of the room and clung to the wall with catlike grips. All present were struck with a trembling fear. Father alone kept his peace. "Pull her down, she must be brought back to her place upon the bed!" Real force had to be applied to her feet to bring her down from the high position on the wall. The mystery was that she could have clung to the wall at all!

This spectacular occurrence was only the first of many extraordinary events to take place over the next few months.

After the terrified nuns had pulled Anna down from the wall, Father Theophilus continued the rite, his words being met with shrill howls and screeches from the possessed woman. The sounds were so loud that they brought the townspeople rushing to the convent to see what was going on. He concluded the ceremonies that first day without success.

The events which would take place over the course of the exorcism were of the kind one expects to find only in books of fiction or on the movie screen. Yet such things had been known before the Anna Ecklund case and have been reported since.

There were, for instance, many extraordinary physical phenomena besides the levitation already described. For example, Anna produced a variety of voices—itself unusual enough, but the manner of production seemed truly mystifying. Here is Reverend Vogel's description:

> Let it be noted that Satan in his speeches and answers did not use the tongue of the poor possessed girl to make himself understood. The helpless creature had been unconscious for the greater period of the trial, her mouth was closed tight. Even when it was open there was not the slightest sign that the lips moved or that there were any changes of the position of the mouth. It was possible for these evil spirits to speak in an audible manner from somewhere within the girl, possibly they used some inner organ of the body.

Anna was also subjected to terrible distortions of her body and some kind of inexplicable increase in weight:

> The woman's face . . . became so twisted and distorted that no one would recognize its features . . . her whole body became so horribly disfigured that the appearance of her human shape vanished. Her pale deathlike and emaciated head often extended to the size of an inverted water pitcher, became fiery red and again like glowing embers. Her eyes would protrude, her lips would swell up actually to the size of hands, and her thin emaciated body would bloat up to such enormous size that at the first occurrence the pastor and some of the sisters drew back out of fright, thinking that she would be torn to pieces and burst open. At times her abdominal regions and extremities became hard like iron and stone and were pressed into the bedstead so that the iron beams bent to the floor.

These physical anomalies, along with the vomiting of large quantities of foul matter from a woman who could take in only a small amount of liquid as nourishment each day, frightened those who were looking after her and placed a great strain on the situation.

Anna exhibited other strange phenomena. Her horror of holy items would at times show itself in an uncanny ability to know if something had been blessed. Before the exorcism started, Anna was eating normally in the convent, but she would never touch food that had been surreptitiously sprinkled with holy water. The nuns were never able to deceive her in this matter.

Like the Illfurt boys, she showed a knowledge of languages that could not be accounted for, so that when Father Theophilus was reciting sections from the rite of exorcism in English, German and Latin, the devil in Anna would reply correctly in the same tongue. The devil also evinced a detailed knowledge of childhood sins committed by those attending the exorcism.

As the exorcism proceeded, Father Theophilus began to extract information that shed light on Anna's condition. She was being possessed principally by four evil spirits, chief among them Beelzebub!

Exorcist: Why are you called Beelzebub if you are not the prince of devils?

Devil: Enough, my name is Beelzebub.

Exorcist: From the point of influence and dignity you must rank near Lucifer, or do you hail from the lower choir of angels?

Devil: I once belonged to the Seraphic choir.

Exorcist: What would you do, if God made it possible for you to atone for your injustice to Him?

Devil (demoniacal sneering): Are you a competent theologian?

Exorcist: How long have you been torturing the poor girl?

Devil: Already since her fourteenth year.

Exorcist: How dare you enter into that innocent girl and torture her like that?

Devil (sneeringly): Ha, did not her father curse us into her?

Exorcist: But that just you, Beelzebub, took possession of her? Who gave you that permission?

Devil: Don't ask so foolishly. Don't I have to render obedience to Satan?

Exorcist: Then you are here at the direction and command of Lucifer?

Devil: Well, how could it be otherwise?

The information about Anna's father cursing the devils into her was the first clue Father Theophilus had about how Anna's present condition had arisen. On asking Beelzebub if Anna's father, now long dead, was in her also as one of the possessing demons, he was told: "What a foolish question. He has been with us ever since he was damned."

Father Theophilus then tried to get Anna's father, Jacob, to speak, commanding him to come forward. But a rough voice announced instead the presence of Judas Iscariot, the former apostle of Jesus. After a fit of defiant spitting and vomiting Judas allowed himself a brief exchange with the exorcist on the subject of suicide, and then withdrew.

Father Theophilus's second attempt to summon Jacob was successful and he sensed at once that this demon, like Judas, had been human. *Begone Satan* tells what Jacob revealed:

> He now admitted that he had repeatedly tried to force his own daughter to commit incest with him. She however resisted him with her utmost strength. Therefore he had cursed her and wished in an inhuman manner that the devils should enter into her and ruin her body and soul and should entice her to every possible sin against chastity. He also admitted that . . . he was permitted to receive the sacrament of extreme unction. But this was of no avail as he, even in his last moments, scoffed at and ridiculed the priest ministering to him. In the judgment after death even all that was pardoned him, but [because] he had . . . cursed his own daughter . . . that ultimately was the guilt of his eternal damnation. And so he was still scheming in hell how he could torture and molest his child. This Lucifer gladly permitted him to do. With him in hell was likewise his concubine. Now that he was in his own daughter he would not, despite all the solemn prayers of the Church, be in the least disposed to give her up or leave her.

The next possessing demon to appear was Mina, Jacob's "concubine." Her conduct during the exorcism showed she was every bit his equal in malice and spite. She had been damned for her immoral life with Jacob and her murder of children. She had lived as Jacob's mistress while his wife was still alive. As to the child murders, she admitted to killing four, a probable reference to multiple abortions.

The author of *Begone Satan* comments:

> This Mina showed herself especially hateful. Her replies were filled with such bitter hatred and spite that they far surpassed all that had happened so far. Her demeanor towards the Blessed Sacrament surpasses description . . .

Beelzebub, Judas Iscariot, Jacob and Mina—these were the principal possessing demons. But various lesser devils were there too at times:

99

> Among these especially the so-called dumb devils and avenging
> spirits made themselves prominent. The number of silent devils
> was countless . . . apparently they were from the lower classes.
> They could put up little resistance against the powerful exorcism.
> It seemed as though they came and left in hordes to be relieved
> again by other crowds. They reminded one of the travelers' plight
> when suddenly overtaken by a swarm of mosquitoes. A few puffs
> of tobacco drive them away, only shortly to be pestered again
> with a similar swarm. Something altogether different were the
> avenging spirits. These were wild and violent fellows, of rough
> and ill-mannered character. They were filled with hatred and
> anger against all human beings made to the image of God.

It was a long time before Father Theophilus saw any signs of
progress in his exorcism but considering the tremendous physical
abuse her body was undergoing, Anna held up quite well. She had
lucid periods when she would talk with those present about the
progress of the exorcism. But as soon as the ritual prayers were
begun she would lose consciousness and move completely out of
reach. When the ceremonies of the day were finished she would
regain consciousness. During the whole period she took no solid
food, only small doses of liquid nourishment. Her mental disposition
remained strong throughout:

> What was most surprising was that such a wicked and blasphe-
> mous father was blessed with such a virtuous child. Her sincere
> piety, her pure and innocent disposition, her diligent application
> was very apparent. Even during the period of possession the
> devil could not disturb her inner basic disposition because the
> devil has no power over the free will of a human being.

Through the tireless efforts of Father Theophilus and those
assisting him, the resistance of the possessing entities began to
weaken:

> They seemed to become more docile. Their bold, bitter de-
> meanor gave way to mere moaning despairing tones. They could
> not bear the tortures of exorcism any longer. With great uneasi-
> ness they explained that they would finally return to hell.

The exorcist demanded that at the moment of their departure
they should call out their names as a sign of each one's leaving.
They agreed to do this.

The end came in dramatic form:

> With a sudden jerk the possessed loosened the grip of her pro-
> tectors with lightning speed and stood erect before them. It was
> only with her heels that she touched the bed. At first sight it
> appeared as if she were to be hurled up to the ceiling. "Pull her
> down, tear her down" called the pastor whilst Father blessed
> her with the relic of the cross: "Depart ye fiends of hell! Begone
> Satan, the Lion of Juda reigns!" At that very moment the stiffness
> of her body gave way and she broke down reclining on the bed
> upon her knees. Such a terrible sound rent the air at that very
> moment that would have made your body shiver with trembling
> anxiety: "Beelzebub, Judas, Jacob, Mina." And this was repeated
> again and again till it faded far away in the distance: "Beelzebub—
> Judas—Jacob—Mina." To these were added: "Hell—hell—
> hell!" . . . The girl opened her eyes and mouth for the first time,
> something that never took place during the whole process of
> exorcism. A kind smile rolled over her countenance. . . . Tears
> of joy rolled out of her eyes, as also out of all those present.
> During the first thrills of joy they were not even aware of the
> terrible odor that filled the room. All the windows had to be
> opened, the stench was something unearthly, simply unbearable.
> It was the last souvenir of the infernal devils for those they had
> to abandon upon the Earth.

Karen Kingston

In April, 1974, during a three-day exorcism of a teenage girl named
Karen Kingston, thirteen demons manifested their presence
and were expelled. They were all nonhuman spirits, hostile to
God, and may rightly be called devils. Here is a brief account of
this case, as described in Robert Pelton's *The Devil and Karen
Kingston.*

Karen was born on September 9, 1960. Her father was an alcoholic. When the girl was seven, her mother murdered him with
a butcher knife. Karen witnessed the brutal slaying and went into
a state of shock from which she did not recover. Placed in a foster
home, she began manifesting severe disturbances. She became
withdrawn and morose, stopped learning and threw violent fits
which were too much for her new guardians. On January 4, 1969,
she was turned over to the North Carolina state authorities and
placed in a home for retarded children.

By the time Karen was nine, later that year, she had deteriorated

101

to the point of complete helplessness. She could not feed or care for herself; she could not read or write. Her IQ was considered to be below fifty. Changes in her body also occurred. Her healthy, long reddish-brown hair suddenly turned coarse and dull. She became extremely pale and her body gave off a stench. Her face broke out in pimples and her skin developed running sores which would not heal.

On April 11, 1971, Karen's eyes suddenly crossed. They seemed to be coated with a dull film. Her gums were also affected, receding and leaving her teeth looking longer . . . and widely spaced. Late in 1971 she started to become stooped, and by the fall of 1972 she was in a completely hunched position. Her left leg began to be painful and was later found to be two inches shorter than her right. Medical doctors could not fathom what was happening to the girl who now looked more like an old hag than a young adolescent.

The idea of attempting an exorcism to try and help Karen was initiated by Robert Pelton, an investigative writer on possession. It was undertaken by Reverend Richard Rogers, a Holiness minister, with the assistance of his wife, Ruth, Father John Tyson, a Catholic priest, and Reverend Donald Sutter, a Baptist evangelist. Observing were Dr. W. Manley Fromme, a clinical psychologist, Dr. Clarence Emory, a psychiatrist, Dr. Julian Pershing, a general practitioner, and three nurses: Peggy Welch, Carol Petersen and Joyce Donaldson. Pelton was also present.

The procedure was begun at 7:00 A.M. on April 13, 1974. Reverend Rogers believed that Karen's physical symptoms were caused by demonic possession. He and his wife, Ruth, were eager to get on with the thing and make this case a proof of the power of God working among men. Reverend Sutter apparently thought possession was involved but the rest of those present were skeptical, although willing to see what would happen.

Reverend Rogers began with some readings from Scripture. He followed this with quiet prayer. He then addressed the evil spirits directly:

> "Come out of this innocent child. Come out of her in the name of Jesus Christ!"
>
> At that moment, a mocking voice responded, "This girl is mine! Go away! Go away! She belongs only to me! Leave us alone!"
>
> I [Pelton] quickly glanced around at the others in the room. The immediate reaction was one of stunned silence. . . . He

[Rogers] immediately began to converse with the spirit, "What is your name, you creature of death and destruction?"

"I don't have to tell you anything! You can't make me tell you anything!" responded the deep male voice. And then more sarcastically, "You are too weak to make me do anything! I own this girl! She is mine! *Only mine!*"

The exorcist then attempted to make the demon write something on a piece of paper and after refusing at first, it finally wrote a paragraph in good longhand script which was then passed around the room. The staff members of the home were astonished; they knew Karen could not write.

Next the exorcist forced the demon to reveal his name—an essential step in preparing to cast him out. He said his name was "Williams," and revealed that there were many demons residing in the girl.

Now Reverend Rogers began to apply pressure:

"In the name of Jesus, on His blood, demon come forth! Leave! Leave!"

"I'll come, but I'll kill this bitch first," screamed the demon. . . .

A faint tinge of bluish-green color appeared to emit from Karen. It enveloped her completely like a cloud. There no longer was any doubt about it—the aquamarine haze slowly changed to a dynamic red-orange followed by a brilliant flash of blinding light.

Karen tensed, screamed, and catapulted from her chair. . . . Williams . . . came forth with a roar like a wounded bull. The sound was deafening. And then he left on Rogers's command to return to where he had originally come from. Karen ceased to quiver. The room was quiet.

At this point Ruth cried out to her husband to look at the girl's hair. He reached out and touched it. Its coarse and stringy texture had changed completely; it was shiny and soft. The demon had gone after just an hour and forty-five minutes.

Over the three-day period there were twelve such exorcism sessions, each lasting from an hour and forty-five minutes to just over four hours. In the course of these sessions thirteen demons were expelled and remarkable changes brought about in Karen's condition.

Each demon had a characteristic personality: Hugh who spoke

in a cockney accent; Mockery who lived up to his name; Mariana, a sensual temptress; Jeanne, a spirit of lustfulness who loved sex and violence and who, although she hated women, wanted to possess them so she could go after men; Envy wanted to gossip about members of Reverend Rogers's congregation and about the personal lives of those present; King of the House was a slow-witted illiterate who could neither write nor draw. Prudence was a demon of illness and pain; Elizabeth, a two-faced demon who would alternate between syrupy cajoling and vicious attack. Linus was a macho demon who continuously spouted locker-room sexual talk. And so it went. In each instance there was a good deal of conversation in which the demon would show itself to be possessed of considerable knowledge peculiar to its personality.

As in the case of the first possessing demon, others were responsible for certain of Karen's physical maladies; when a particular demon had been cast out, the infirmity was gone.

The exorcism sessions were studded with startling paranormal occurrences. Karen was twice levitated off the ground for considerable periods of time. The first instance was most remarkable. The third demon, Elizabeth, had been carrying on with her vicious side so that Father Tyson and Reverend Sutter had to sit on Karen and hold her down lest she harm someone in the room. Then:

> . . . Her face became grotesquely contorted and her eyes flashed with spite. "So, you god-damned imbeciles want to play a game, huh? Well, hold on tight . . . I'm going to show you a thing or two."
>
> With this outburst, Karen's body tensed and became rigid. She slowly raised herself up into mid-air. There she stayed, suspended, with Tyson and Sutter still in position, approximately five feet off the floor. Tyson just sat there gasping. He looked rather ridiculous with his long legs dangling . . . Sutter looked like a captive who had been shot, then draped across a horse. . . .
>
> The nine of us stood by, astounded, . . . as a frail, sixty-three pound child, pinned to the floor by the combined weight of two huge men, suddenly began levitating while carrying this bulk— *a total of five hundred and thirty-five pounds.* And the diminutive child passively floated there for seven full minutes, while Tyson and Sutter, their eyes like saucers, grabbed and hung on for dear life.

On another occasion, Karen's body suddenly swelled to three times its normal size. Her skin broke in four places from the pressure, but there was no bleeding. At the end of that particular exorcism, she returned to normal in seconds with no aftereffects but some stretch marks.

The second demon, Linus, seemed to be particularly adept at producing paranormal phenomena. He made a vase sail across the room and land in Father Tyson's arms. Then it hovered in mid-air for a while and began to spin, ending its antics by smashing to pieces against a wall. A little later two pictures fell down one after the other. Then a couch began to move about as three large cushions floated in the air, drifting back and forth before settling on the carpet. Right after this Karen's skin turned pink and then red; blisters appeared on her arms and legs, some as large as quarters. When Father Tyson began to sprinkle holy water on the girl's forehead, the drops sizzled, turned to steam and disappeared before touching her skin. This was followed by a blast of heat from Karen's body which stifled those present, and the whole thing was capped when Father Tyson pulled out a sheaf of papers containing an exorcism formula and began reading it. As he did so, smoke rose in a black cloud that choked the man and he dropped the papers. They burst into flame and were soon a pile of ashes.

A total of eight handwriting samples were obtained from the demons, each with a very distinct style. A well-known handwriting expert, George D. Steinert, reached these conclusions about them:

> Different specimens of handwriting from a single individual are known to be highly consistent in both gross features and the smallest recognizable characteristics. It is this fact that allows handwriting to be known as a stable graphic expression of personality. . . . Based on the evidence from the handwritings and drawings of Karen Kingston, . . . it is an impossibility that all these specimens of writing could be the product of a single personality, that they differ in such a degree that cannot be accounted for by a more reasonable explanation, I am convinced that the handwritings of Karen Kingston examined here are unequivocally the result of a multiplicity of personalities which have their existence in and through her.

The day following the conclusion of the exorcism, Karen seemed like any other adolescent girl. She was alert and had regained her muscular control. Her legs were of identical length and she no longer limped. Her hair was now healthy and she had lively green eyes. Before the exorcism her IQ was rated at 45, where it had been for a number of years. A week after the exorcism it was measured at 74; a year later at 88 and two years after the exorcism, it had moved up to 110. At the time Pelton's book was written, the doctors who had been working with Karen estimated that by age sixteen she would have caught up with her contemporaries.

This case is one of the most dramatic on record in terms of the events of the exorcism and most significant in terms of the ensuing results. How one interprets the case will influence the way one views the mysterious multiplicity of human personality.

THE DEMONIC DISCARNATE

Instances of possession by a demonic spirit which is the soul of some discarnate human being can be discovered far back in the records of human history and still occur today. It has long been believed that the dead may take over the living to carry out some purpose against the wishes of their host. Two modern-day examples will help illustrate the scope of this phenomenon.

THE DISCARNATE HUSBAND

In *Psychic Self Defence* (1981), the modern occultist Dion Fortune gives the account of a woman who had just lost her husband to a lingering disease which resulted from his alcoholism. He was disliked by most who knew him, and his widow's friends thought she was well rid of this man whom Fortune describes as "of intensely malignant and selfish disposition [who] died unrepentant."

During his last illness, however, when he was bedridden and helpless, his wife had spun a fantasy about him, in which he emerged as saintly and kind. The woman was interested in occultism and practiced meditation. After his death—and against friendly counsel—she began to try to get in touch with him psychically, hoping that his spirit would serve as her guide. She brought all his belongings from the nursing home where he died and kept them in her bedroom; using his photograph as the focus for her meditations, she constructed an altar around it. Fortune relates what resulted:

> It soon became noticeable that she, who had previously had a very lovable and gentle disposition, was gradually changing, so that not only in temperament, but in facial expression, she was growing like her late husband. Next a curious thing ensued. Her husband had died of an inflammatory spinal lesion which caused

no pain at the site of the trouble, but intense pain in the nerves that issued from the spine at that point, so that the pain was referred to a particular distribution in the hands and arms, more upon one side than the other. The lady developed a severe neuritis that exactly corresponded in its distribution to her late husband's symptoms.

This shows, according to Fortune, that the woman was successful in drawing her discarnate husband back to herself. He was now carrying on his post-mortem existence in his wife's body.

CARRIE

An even more recent example of possession by the demonic discarnate is presented in *Mind in Many Pieces* (1980) by Dr. Ralph Allison, a California psychiatrist whose experience with certain patients has led him to accept the reality of possession as a working hypothesis for therapy.

Carrie was a multiple personality patient with whom Allison had done a great deal of work. Late in 1972, when the girl was being treated for depression and drug and alcohol abuse, a nurse friend of hers told Allison of a curious incident. During a mind-dynamics course which investigated ESP and which the nurse attended, the instructor was demonstrating his ability to enter the mind of another to discover what troubled that person. The woman gave him Carrie's full name and physical description to see what he could do for her but when he concentrated on Carrie, he became agitated, saying he could not get into her mind, but had witnessed some kind of evil force around her. He said he sensed the force as a human being who had died and was now using Carrie's body and he came up with the name "Bonnie Pierce" or "Price," and the information that in 1968, when only in her twenties, she had died of a drug overdose in New York. She was now continuing her addiction to drugs through Carrie, herself a drug user and so a good victim for her invasion.

Allison listened to the story, but was skeptical about its validity. Carrie was at this time in a very serious state. She was not only oppressed by a long-standing fear of choking to death but also convinced that she would die on the next New Year's Eve. Her drug abuse was becoming worse and she was having lapses of memory at the end of which she would find herself in embarrassing or dangerous circumstances. Allison tried everything he could think of to help her but with no noticeable results. In desperation, he began to think about the spirit-possession story and after much consideration, decided to treat the girl as though she really were possessed. He would try an exorcism.

In the presence of another doctor, Allison first hypnotized Carrie. He talked to her for a while and then asked if a "Bonnie" was present, giving the impression that this Bonnie might be just another of Carrie's multiple personalities. She was so familiar with the discovery of new personalities in herself that she treated the question matter-of-factly, replying that there was no Bonnie present. Allison's colleague then suggested he put Carrie into a deeper state of hypnosis. Now when he asked Carrie if someone named Bonnie was influencing her life, she became agitated, replied that indeed she was and said that she wanted to be rid of her. Allison then suspended a hypnotist's crystal ball over Carrie's head and in a commanding tone of voice, ordered the spirit of Bonnie to enter it. He repeatedly commanded Bonnie to leave Carrie in peace and go to wherever it is that spirits go. He stipulated that when the crystal ball he was holding stopped swinging, it would be a sign that Bonnie was gone. He noted with surprise that the crystal was moving energetically in a circle, even though as far as he could tell his hand was steady. He also gave Carrie the hypnotic suggestion that she would raise her right index finger when she sensed that Bonnie had left.

Suddenly the rotations of the crystal ball slowed and at the same time Carrie lifted the signal finger, indicating that Bonnie had departed. Then Allison told the exhausted girl she could rest and added the suggestion that when she came out of the hypnotic state she would be a new person.

The two and a half minute exorcism brought about a dramatic change in Carrie. Ten minutes after it was over, she began describing the changes of which she was aware. She said she had always felt there was something present with her, some kind of spirit or shadow. She had hated to close her eyes, because then she would become aware of it. She described it as a haunting evil feeling that she was going to die. But now, Carrie said, that vision or feeling was gone and she felt a hope she had not felt before.

The results were lasting. Carrie's fear of death by choking never returned. And she no longer worried about New Year's Eve.

THE CONFUSED OR BENIGN DISCARNATE

Possession by the discarnate is not always perpetrated to accomplish some selfish or evil purpose. Sometimes the possessor is simply confused and has become entangled with his victim accidently.

A TORMENTED MUSICIAN

In his book *The Gateway of Understanding* (1934), Chicago physician Dr. Carl Wickland, describes the case of a young musician who got involved with an occult group, sitting in "dark psychic circles," hoping to develop his psychic abilities. He became vulnerable to spirit interference and was tormented by spirit voices. He also complained of great distress in his stomach and refused to eat, having to be force-fed. He finally displayed such severe emotional disturbance that he had to be placed in a mental institution. His brother eventually brought him to Dr. Wickland because he believed spirit possession was involved. Indeed, over a period of three weeks, nine spirits were removed by means of Wickland's static electricity treatment which involved driving the spirits into his wife, Anna, a spiritualist medium. The young man improved and was soon able to return home and carry on with his life. The Wicklands were informed five years later that he remained completely well.

One of the spirits removed was of the "confused" type, a spirit called "Reuben" who took control of Mrs. Wickland during a session in which the young man's brother was present. The latter immediately recognized the name, speech and mannerisms of a butler whom the patient's family had employed for thirty-five years. He had died of stomach cancer after a long illness.

When he first began to speak, the spirit complained of a pain in the stomach and said he was so sick he could not eat anything. Upon recognizing the patient's brother, he begged for his help:

Spirit: . . . You will not leave me, will you?
Brother: No, indeed. We are all going to help you.
Doctor: Do you know that you have lost your physical body?
Spirit: You mean I died?
Doctor: You left the physical . . .
Spirit: Where is your brother? Did you say he was sick?
Brother: He is going to be better now.

109

Doctor:	Evidently you have been attached to him so closely that he complained of suffering just as you did. . . . Now that you are away from him he will gradually improve. . . . You are no longer sick. Take your mind off that condition. You must progress now.
Spirit:	Am I going to heaven?
Doctor:	You will go to the spirit world, where you will find your kindred.

At this point Reuben began to speak of things that occurred when the brothers were young. The patient confirmed that they had happened. When the spirit realized his pain was gone, Dr. Wickland was able to bring the session to a quick conclusion:

Doctor:	You have been interfering with this gentleman's brother. He had been studying the occult and became sensitive. You contacted him without realizing it and caused disturbance.
Spirit:	Did I do that? Please forgive me.
Brother:	Don't worry about that now.
Spirit:	God bless you.
Doctor:	Intelligent spirits will help you to learn about your new life.
Spirit:	They want me to go with them. Goodbye.

An Intimate Bond

In *Healing the Family Tree* (1982), Dr. Kenneth McAll, a British psychiatrist whose work will be discussed in the following chapter, describes a case in which the possessing discarnate was neither demonic nor confused. Rather, the possession was established with full consent of both possessor and host, and so could be termed "benign," even though it caused considerable disturbance in the possessed.

A young woman of twenty-three who had been medically diagnosed as schizophrenic was brought to McAll for treatment. She had received training as a schoolteacher, but a recurring disturbance led to her being certified many times. Therapeutic drugs, shock treatments, and the efforts of sixteen psychiatrists had been unable to cure her.

In her first interview, the woman, Georgina, confided to McAll that her trouble centered around "blackouts" which came without warning and lasted for three to fourteen days. These periods were characterized by bizarre behavior and subsequent amnesia. As an illustration she spoke of how she once blacked out on her way to the bank with school money; the next thing she remembered was standing in the street loaded down with articles she could not recall buying.

At the end of the interview Georgina suddenly blurted out a difficult confession. She told McAll that she had for years been involved in a lesbian relationship with a nurse who was now deceased. Since her death Georgina would spend days on end lying abed, oblivious to everything around her, daydreaming herself into contact with her dead friend. In that state Georgina would hold long conversations with the nurse, submersed in an intimate communion that was tantamount to possession.

McAll treated the condition by using the services of a priest to exorcise the possessing spirit. Much relieved, Georgina afterwards described the sensation of having a hole in her head that now felt clean. As a result of this treatment, the blackouts ceased and, according to McAll, she is today happily married.

PSYCHIC CREATIONS

Western occult tradition holds that all thought has effects which go beyond the mind of the thinker. Thus, if "thoughts are things" and if an individual or group focuses with force upon some thought, an objective psychic creation will be produced.

If the energy applied to the thought is powerful but confused, a "thought-atmosphere" with a particular emotional tone will result.

If the energized thought is well-defined, it will become a "thought-form," which will both exist as an entity and have a power and endurance proportionate to the energy put into it.

Occultists believe that both creations affect emotionally and mentally those to whom they are directed or who enter the environment where they exist. Whether this influence is positive or negative depends on the quality of the original thought. Thought-atmospheres and thought-forms are usually produced accidentally but occult tradition teaches that psychic creations can be deliberate.

There are those practiced in the art of magic who set out to create entities by the power of thought. Whether working alone or in groups, their procedure involves the concentration of imagination and will. An experienced occult worker can apparently charge these thought-entities with so much energy that they take on an independent life, operating as quasi-intelligent beings in their own

111

right, moving in and taking over any individual who is open to such invasion. There are thought to be evil practitioners of the magic art who create such entities for the express purpose of possessing some victim and bringing him harm.

THOUGHT-ATMOSPHERES AND THOUGHT-FORMS

A colleague of mine with eighteen years' experience as a psychotherapist once said to me that his work had brought him to a peculiar realization.

In his office, the client usually sat in a particular comfortable chair. Often, he would see a number of clients consecutively, with only a few minutes break between sessions, and over the years, he had noticed that certain people had a remarkable unconscious sensitivity to the mental-emotional climate of the person who had preceded them in the chair. If the previous client had been particularly grieved about something, the sensitive would feel an unaccountable sadness when he or she sat down; if the recent occupant of the chair had been experiencing rage or terror, the sensitive would be overcome by the same emotions. Though such sensitivity is not common, those who have it are responding to a thought-atmosphere created in a particular physical space—and which endures at that spot for some minutes before dissipating. In this case, once the psychotherapist realized the problem, he shifted the furniture in his office as necessary.

In *Psychic Self-Defense*, Dion Fortune deals with the type of creation that can be experienced as a haunting. A friend of Fortune's had moved into a suite of modern apartments in which she could never feel comfortable. At dusk one evening she walked into her drawing room and saw a man standing with his back to her, apparently staring out the window. Turning on the light, she found no one there. Her maid also thought she had seen a man walk down the hall towards that same room on occasion. Sometimes the door of the room would open of its own accord.

The woman grew steadily more unhappy in her new home until one day, standing at that same window, she felt a powerful urge to throw herself out. She now was certain there was some external factor involved and so looked into the history of the place:

. . . It was the site of an old madhouse of sinister reputation. The form that she and her maid had seen was probably that of some unfortunate patient of suicidal tendencies who had succeeded in giving effect to his impulses on a spot corresponding to the situation of her room. The terrific emotional forces generated by his brooding and last desperate act were photographed on the atmospheres, as it were, and suggested to her mind thoughts of self-destruction just as the ill-temper or depression of a companion will induce a similar mood in ourselves without any word spoken.

In this case the thought-atmosphere had apparently lasted decades rather than minutes. Like the previous example, it had not been deliberately created.

OCCULT CREATIONS

Those experts at creating psychic entities who use their knowledge to gain power for themselves and destroy their enemies are called occultists of the dark path; those who use such knowledge for good are called occultists of the light path. The psychic entities—or artificial elementals, as they are sometimes called—thus formed are more powerful, more intelligent and longer lasting than those formed spontaneously. In *The Astral Plane* (1973), C.W. Leadbeater, a theosophist author, says of these entities:

Occultists of both the white and dark schools frequently use artificial elementals in their work, and few tasks are beyond the powers of such creatures when scientifically prepared and directed with knowledge and skill; for one who knows how to do so can maintain a connection with his elemental and guide it, no matter at what distance it may be working, so that it will practically act as though endowed with the full intelligence of its master.

Chapter 7
The Cures

Over the centuries there have been two basic approaches to terminating the state of possession: *commanding* the possessing spirit to leave and *persuading* it to leave. The first approach is the best known and is called exorcism, as we have already seen. The second has taken a great variety of forms in many cultures and has never been given one generic name.

Like command, persuasion presupposes that one is dealing with an intelligent spirit, a person of some sort. But when the unwanted possessing entity is a psychic creation, the approach must be very different and will involve the *application of psychic force.*

EXORCISM

In the Christian tradition the power called upon when commanding a spirit to leave is that of God and especially Jesus. The Catholic tradition also asks for the aid of the angels of God (especially Michael the archangel, ancient foe of the devil), Mary, the mother of Jesus, and the saints.

Because he believes God's power is supreme, the exorcist is confident of final victory though the evil spirit may claim many casualities along the way. Exorcism can hold great peril for victim, exorcist and aids. There have even been instances of exorcisms that ended with the death of victim or exorcist. Nor is it unusual for the exorcist to be subject to powerful physical and spiritual attack—or even to end up possessed himself, particularly if he forgets that he is simply the agent of divine power and attempts to engage the possessing spirit on a personal basis.

The hallmark of exorcism is violence. Force is used to counter force. Sometimes this spiritual violence expresses itself in tremendous physical havoc. Furniture and other objects may be demolished. The victim may be horribly tortured during the process;

he may suffer cuts and bruises, swell to enormous size, or vomit huge quantities of foul-smelling substances. He may become stiff as a board, have his tongue increase in size and protrude, or be reduced to a near-death state. Paranormal phenomena are not uncommon, as we saw in the Karen Kingston case, for example.

The exorcist takes it for granted that since the possessing spirit is basically evil and unconvertible, the only way to resolve a state of unwilling possession by evil spirits is to call upon some higher power to unmercifully throw the invaders out.

PERSUASION

Not all of those who deal with victims of unwilling possession believe that exorcism is the answer. Many workers hold that some— if not all—cases of possession involve spirits of discarnate human beings who can be reasoned with. They see their main task as persuading the possessing spirit to come to terms with his condition, depart from his unwilling host and move on to the phase of existence which is proper to his discarnate state.

THE USE OF PERSUASION

One of the most important practitioners of this art was Dr. Carl Wickland who was mentioned in the last chapter. Though Wickland was concerned to relieve the sufferings of possession victims, he was equally concerned about the earthbound spirit who had intruded. Being a Spiritualist, he believed that often the discarnate spirit had accidentally blundered into the "magnetic aura" of the victim and become trapped there. His approach fit the Spiritualist tradition of "rescue work," in which wandering earthbound souls were contacted, enlightened and sent on to the next world.

In most cases, it seems, his persuasive powers carried the day. But when the possessor would not respond to Wickland's arguments, he had to send it off to a "dungeon" prepared by helper spirits where it would be held until it gave up its "selfishness." In this way the spirit could be prevented from re-entering the victim.

One instance of Wickland's work has already been cited (see Chapter 6); however, one more example taken from the *Gateway of Understanding* may be of interest. In this case a Mr. P.H. had come to the Wicklands with a palsy in his hands that was of several years duration. Two spirits were discovered to be possessing him: the second caused the shaking, and with its removal the problem was cleared up. The first provides a good example of release through enlightenment, the spirit having first been induced to take over Mrs. Wickland, and so speak through her:

Doctor: Good evening. Who are you?

Spirit: I don't know who I am right now. Just leave me alone; it's bad enough to shake without talking.

Doctor: Why are you shaking?

Spirit: I don't know. I suppose because that man (referring to patient) does. . . . [He] bothers me, and I don't like him at all.

Doctor: Any reason why?

Spirit: Because he won't let me work.

Doctor: Are you an active person?

Spirit: I am active if only I can get to do what I want. I want to do something, if the work is not too hard.

Doctor: What work did you do?

Spirit: Contracting for buildings and greenhouses for Howard Smith, German's and Paul Howard. (Nurseries in Los Angeles)

Doctor: Did you know P.H.? (patient)

Spirit: Yes, he worked for me; I was the boss. But I haven't worked for some time now.

Doctor: You have lost your physical body and do not understand it. You drifted about and evidently got into this man's aura. Now you must leave him. He is sensitive to spirit influences and you are one of the spirits that bothered him. You have been an earthbound spirit without understanding that fact.

Spirit: Spirit! I don't care for such things.

Doctor: When you had your own physical body, did you ever think where you would go when you died?

Spirit: Wherever they all go. Where am I now?

Doctor: You are controlling the body of a woman; she is a psychic sensitive and allows spirits to use her organism so they may be helped. We are following research work to learn what becomes of the dead. Can you remember whether anything unusual happened to you?

Spirit: A couple of winters ago I was caught in a severe storm. I got wet through and took cold. I was sick and then I went to sleep [died]. When I woke up I felt all right but many queer things happened. I went to work but nobody took any notice of me. I would tell them to do things but they didn't care what I said. I got so mad I wanted to strike them.

116

Doctor:	Even had you struck them they would not have noticed you.
Spirit:	I sat looking at things for a while and all at once I felt very strange. I seemed to have gotten closed up with some man [entered patient's aura] and I shook as if I had a stroke. I heard somebody say I was paralyzed. I wasn't, but I couldn't stop shaking [patient's condition]. It made me so angry.
Doctor:	Now you have been taken away from that man and we can explain matters to you. Do you realize where you are?
Spirit:	Not exactly.
Doctor:	You are in Los Angeles.
Spirit:	That is where I live.
Doctor:	What is your name?
Spirit:	Wagner.
Doctor:	Now you must go with spirit helpers who will teach you how to progress and, when you have learned how, you can help the man whom you have been troubling.

The spirit was then taken away. When Mr. P.H. was asked whether he had known anyone named Wagner, he said, "Why, yes, I used to work for him and after he died I bought his business." These circumstances were entirely unknown to us.

There are two contemporary workers who deal with possession in a very similar fashion: Dr. Martin Israel and Canon John Pearce-Higgins, both clergymen of the Church of England. Canon Pearce-Higgins early became convinced that many cases of possession were neither symptoms of emotional derangement nor signs of the devil's presence. He believed with Wickland that they were mani-ifestations of "earthbound" spirits. He began working with victims of possession with the aid of a well-known medium, Ena Twigg.

Mrs. Twigg and other mediums who later assisted the canon would allow themselves to be taken over by the possessing dis-carnate, giving the clergyman an opportunity to speak with the spirits. Eventually he developed a religious service to precede these confrontations, finding the combination of liturgy and conversation to be a particularly effective way of clearing up difficult cases.

Canon Pearce-Higgins dislikes being called an exorcist because the Christian concept of exorcism implies cursing or condemning the possessing entity to everlasting damnation. That approach is unacceptable, he says, when the invading spirit is a discarnate human being. Pearce-Higgins refuses to judge or condemn anyone, believing that even the most refractory may some day repent. When he deals with a possessing entity, his view is that it needs as much help as the victim.

Dr. Israel, who is both a clergyman and senior lecturer in pathology at the University of London, holds much the same view. Although he speaks of himself as an exorcist, his practice is not to condemn the possessor. Dr. Israel's view on this is quoted in *The Devil's Dominion* by Anthony Masters, a British journalist and author:

> Only when the spirit is able to lovingly forgive—to come together in spiritual harmony with its victim—then can an exorcism be deemed complete and successful. This can often be achieved in the cases of possession by human spirits.

In the same work Dr. Israel's views on the origin of spirit possession are given:

> Possession is very much on a sliding scale. Generally speaking a person is possessed by a relative or friend whose discarded personality is left behind after death. The reason for this is that the dead person is still demanding something from the living. Generally speaking they died feeling angry, or sorry, about the living person they eventually possess.

This passage is rather remarkable in the literature of possession. Up to this point, there have been only a handful of workers who have recognized the importance of the phenomenon of possession by family members.

WHEN PERSUASION CANNOT BE USED

There are times when trying to deal directly with the possessing discarnate would be imprudent, particularly if no experienced worker is available to help.

In an article entitled "Dangers of Automatism," Canon Pearce-Higgins describes how easily unsuspecting persons can become victims of possession by unscrupulous spirits:

> If you use a glass or ouija board or planchette or automatic

writing, what are you doing? You sit down and invite some external forces to make use of you. You do not know who is going to come. Your own motives also have much bearing on this. If you are going to do it for kicks, or out of idle curiosity, you will get jokers and pretenders answering your call, because there seems in the spirit world to be a law that "Like attracts like." Even if your motives are really serious, it is not necessarily a protection because it is so much easier for earthbound spirits to jump into control, than it is for those who have already made some progress and who apparently find it difficult to "gear themselves down"—to get down to our level of consciousness which they have now left behind.

So that is why these apparently simple methods of attempting contact with the dead are extremely dangerous. All the experienced mediums I know say the same—don't do it—and they know, because they so often have people brought to them who are obsessed or possessed by some mischievous or damaging spirit who has got control of them and won't let go.

In an article entitled "How to Guard Against 'Possession' " (1970), Paul Beard, President of the College for Psychic Studies in London, talks about what to do if invaded by one of these harmful spirits. It is a prescription for self-cure and since it does not involve any direct dealing with the possessing entity, it can be tried without fear of becoming even more deeply mired.

Here, the essential element is "starving out" the entity, doing everything possible to deny the possessor access to oneself. This means first of all to completely cease the activity through which the entity gained access in the first place. While the entity may object, it must be ignored. Secondly, if it is sufficiently established in the victim to be able to "talk" to him inside his head, such communication must be strongly resisted. Beard writes:

> Every attempt to argue with the obsessor [possessor] must be avoided. As long as the obsessor can talk to or think with the victim, it will result in his strengthening his hold. He must at every attempt be cut dead.

Beard recommends distraction as a powerful weapon:

> The best remedy . . . is a complete focus of attention upon other things. Reading, music, T.V., the cinema can all be helpful, as can visits to friends, sharing in others' family life, . . . Once even

119

a few minutes of complete attention on something else is secured, the victim can feel a good stride forward has been made. The aim will then be to secure more of these complete acts of attention and gradually to lengthen them, and thus loosen the hold.

Also recommended is a technique of visualization of white light:

When in particular trouble the victim can mentally visualize being completely encircled in a cocoon of light, or can mentally draw around him or her what can be pictured as wings of protection, made of brilliant white light. Help may usefully be sought from a prayer group.

The experience of Pat, a young woman of my acquaintance, will well illustrate a successful self-cure of a state of possession. A girlfriend, Sam, had invited her to spend a weekend at her grandparents' farm and although Pat was looking forward to the trip, she had vague uneasy feelings for which she could find no justification. She made the trip with Sam and her parents. On arrival, Pat was immediately intrigued by the 150-year-old farmhouse and she set out to explore it. In an attic room, she felt overwhelmed by feelings of uneasiness and fear. Her hosts, who were dabblers in the occult, spoke vaguely of "influences" in the house.

The next morning, Sam's mother, Kate, began speaking about reincarnation, claiming the ability to see who people had been in past lives. Pat, she mentioned casually, had once been Elizabeth Barrett Browning. This intrigued Pat, who had heard of the poetess, but knew nothing of her life or work.

Later in the day Sam suggested that Pat try automatic writing. Reluctant at first, she then agreed and took pen in hand. She allowed her arm to relax upon some writing paper and immediately found herself slipping into a trance state, as she describes in *Self Possessed*, her account of her experience:

Before I knew it I fell into nothing short of a drugged state. I could still see Sam and the room. I could hear external noises—Kate in the kitchen, the birds outside the window—but I could not focus my attention on anything else but a kind of visceral fear I was experiencing, my increasing coldness and a disturbing numbness that was proceeding up my right hand and arm . . . I wanted to stop myself, but I couldn't. Under Sam's silent but penetrating gaze, I felt powerless to change position or cry out.

> The more highly electrified the room became the more drained I began to feel. My head felt as though it was full of cotton. My body had become a dead weight. Worse than that, it seemed like a stranger to me.

In her altered state of consciousness, Pat "saw" the figure of a woman suddenly appear behind her. Although Pat was staring ahead of her, she seemed to view the woman frontally. The apparition was petite, dressed in a mauve gown which reached her ankles. Pat could not make out the woman's face clearly.

> The doll like entity came closer and closer until I could smell its perfume, and feel it literally beginning to press into the curve of my back. My motor functions began to fail. My head dropped onto my chest, though I did not pass completely out. Gradually I felt the almost imperceptible usurping of my body's energy by this strong and only too tangible force until I knew it, or she, was becoming one with me, invading my body.

At this point Pat's numb right hand began to move the pen across the sheet of paper before her. Four words appeared on the page: "Elizabeth Barrett Browning here." This sentence was written slowly, but now the words began coming swiftly:

> "We are very nervous to be here with you, Patricia. . . . I am sorry my handwriting is so illegible, but as you must understand, I am new to this and am unaccustomed to the instrument you hold in your hand. I am best with the quill. Robert and I must get used to our new surroundings. I feel like a small child experiencing feelings for the first time . . ."

Pat's hand continued to spell out sentences from "Elizabeth" with movements completely outside her conscious control. After a time the energy in her hand seemed to diminish and the writing came to an abrupt end. Pat looked up, stunned and dazed; her hosts were delighted. She remained in a partially dissociated state for the rest of the evening.

A second automatic-writing session was held that evening, and a third the next day. On these occasions Pat experienced the same sensation of being possessed by an outside force at the beginning of the session. Writing from Elizabeth continued to flow as before. During the second session Pat was taken over by a number of

121

other entities who wrote messages of a coarse nature. She had been a somewhat reluctant cooperator in the Browning writings, but these unruly intruders greatly disturbed her. The third session contained a communication that caused even more serious doubts about the whole affair. She had asked Elizabeth a question and waited for an answer to come through the pen. The question was: "Where do you live now?"

> There was a long pause before my hand began to move again. "Everywhere. . . . Nowhere. We . . . are . . . you . . . and . . . you . . . are . . . us. We have found . . . our home . . . through your eyes."
>
> "My eyes," I thought, somewhat startled. Why couldn't they use their own manner of perception? Suddenly "Elizabeth," my friend, seemed more than a little reticent about answering any further questions about her and "Robert's" whereabouts. In retrospect, I suppose, this is when the lightbulb finally began to flicker in my head. How did I know for sure this was Elizabeth Barrett Browning and her husband Robert?

Before Pat's doubts could go too far, however, the communicators introduced a diversion. Now Pat's deceased brother, Tom, began to communicate through the automatic writing. The handwriting seemed to Pat to be his and the message was one of love and comfort. Pat felt very moved and immediately told Sam about it. This led to a rude awakening:

> I looked at Sam, and wiped my eyes with my shirt sleeve. "Tom came through, Sam, isn't it great?"
>
> Her next words crushed me. "Oh, that wasn't Tom," she snapped. "They'll pretend to be anyone."

As Pat was preparing to leave that afternoon, she had a conversation that put her in a state of real alarm about what had been happening. Kate opened up the subject:

> "Something left this house," she said with a timorous voice. "Something . . . or . . . someone . . . who was attracted to Pat's aura."
>
> I shuddered.
>
> "Of course, Pat did it." Kate exclaimed, in the background. "She let the force work through her, right out of the house."

"You see," she smiled putting her arm around me. "We told you, you were a medium, that you had the gift . . ."

What was she telling me? Could this invading entity have no true identity of its own. Could it be that it was not Elizabeth but some dormant energy that had been locked up in the house's attic all these years?

"The older the house," Kate continued breezily, "the more the spooks . . ."

Sam began feeling uneasy and embarrassed about the direction the conversation was taking. She then admitted to Pat that perhaps more forces had been working through her than they had realized, negative forces of some kind. Now Pat felt close to panic:

"How do I get rid of them? How am I ever going to get rid of them?"

"Pat, if you just ignore them, they'll decrease in energy and leave you alone. Don't worry," Kate tried to placate me. "The one good thing is, it's out of this house. Grandma and Grandpa have been tormented by this thing or things long enough."

I couldn't believe her callousness. "You never told me they'd had problems," I blurted out angrily. . . ."

By the time Pat returned home she knew she was in serious trouble, and a close friend who was waiting for her became greatly alarmed: she seemed almost out of touch with reality. He tried in vain to bring her around but by now she was hearing the pretended "Elizabeth's" voice inside her head:

"Patricia we need you. If you refuse to speak to us we shall live in your room, in your walls! Speak to us. You are us, and we are you. . . . No matter how hard you try to block us out, we will always be part of you."

This was the beginning of a struggle between Pat and the un-known entities within her. She knew instinctively that she must not give in to the request to do automatic writing, for the entities would consolidate their hold upon her that way. Yet soon after her return home, she was trying to write down an address being given by telephone when her hand began writing of its own accord, spelling out a message from the entities.

By the next evening, Pat had hit upon the strategy that would eventually work. Although she knew nothing of the specialist writings in these matters, she took up the approach recommended by Beard:

> The only thing I could do was to shift my thoughts completely off the voices and on to something else. . . .
>
> I got up, walked over to my bookcase and picked out the trashiest novel on the shelf. At first it was painfully difficult to maintain my concentration on a page without experiencing the sensation that someone very menacing was pressing its face against mine. I tossed so violently in my bed that the sheets were repeatedly pulled right out from under the mattress. At least re-making the bed provided a diversion.

With unremitting application of the "starvation" technique Pat was beginning to regain the mastery of herself. After a few days her ability to concentrate began to return. By the fifth day she was able to do some schoolwork that had been awaiting her attention. As she did so, the influence of the entities diminished:

> If I didn't comprehend something, or if I felt I had missed a line because my mind was being pulled in another direction by the unseen voices, I would read the line again, over and over, until the voices reduced in volume, and I could fully involve myself in the words, their sounds and form.

Through sheer determination Pat succeeded in keeping up her regime of distraction. By doing so, she was rewarded with complete success:

> As I began to disentangle myself from the entity's influence, I finally found myself able to see it, watch it visually recede. First the form of the woman in the mauve dress gradually melted away into a pulsating mauve mass, then seemed to merely become a low grade vibration or energy field . . . until it receded, almost like visual sound waves, not only out of my bedroom, but out of my house.
>
> The process was physically and emotionally taxing and the experience challenged my way of looking at the world the way nothing before had.

In the occult tradition, thought-entities which have achieved quasi-independent existence may be good—angelic or godlike creatures—or they may be evil—demonic creatures—depending upon the quality of the thought that went into their making. According to the occultist, such demonic thought-entities roam a dimension just outside the scope of our ordinary awareness. Those who have been born with or have developed a special sensitivity can see these creatures.

Because such evil thought-entities will dwindle to nothingness without a renewal of energy, they seek to dwell in substantially existing creatures, such as human beings, so as to partake of theirs.

Occultists are quick to point out, as we have seen, that "prevention" is the best remedy for the problem. And an important aspect of this is the development of moral strength of character. Possession only comes about when an entity can find some weak spot in the victim's aura and one of the principal ways a person's protective aura may be weakened is through the generation of evil or destructive thoughts from within. The evil thought-entity in that way finds a welcoming vibration without which it would have no means of access.

When demonic thought-entities do succeed in possessing someone, the occultist must use an accumulation of positive psychic force to do one of three things: (1) bind the entity and isolate it from its source of energy so that it will fade away; (2) dissolve it with a powerful concentration of positive energy; or (3) send it back to the mind that generated it. The occultist may invoke divine authorities in the process of carrying out this form of exorcism. In so doing he claims to tap powerful sources of energy which have been built up for untold ages, enormously increasing the force he can bring to bear upon the demonic entity. How they manifest in that person will, according to the occult understanding of these things, depend on the philosophic or religious views of the victim. In *How to Protect Yourself Against Black Magic and Witchcraft* (1978) Leslie Shepard describes the occult point of view:

> Possessing entities may assume such symbolic names as Lust, Pride, Lies or Doubt, as well as traditional names like Satan, Lucifer, or Belial. Even more resounding names have often been used in black-magic conjurations, and many demonic entities often pass under the traditional names of angels. In fact, names of demons are as arbitrary and numerous as human names, and since the ancient Talmudic rabbis assumed there were nearly seven and a half million devils, the possibilities are enormous. In general possessing entities draw their names from the mental

background and associations of the victim, in much the same way as benevolent entities at Spiritualist seances. Even though such names and personalities are artificial, they provide a means of communication with the entity, making its control possible in exorcism.

It is clear that there is a great difference between the occult understanding of exorcism in this context and that of the traditional Western religious traditions. As mentioned in the section on exorcism above, those traditions see the rite as dealing with substantially existing personal spirits—whether nonhuman or human. These spirits are considered to be indestructible and immortal. The rite of exorcism uses the authority of God to drive them out of the victim and back into some version of hell where they will be imprisoned for eternity.

A good example of the occult method of dealing with a possessing thought-form was related to me by Tamarra, a high priestess of the Wiccan religion, an ancient pagan faith that has its roots in the mists preceding recorded human history and is still practiced today. The case involved a woman in her forties, originally from a Caribbean island and now the resident of a large North American city where she worked as a computer operator. Although the practice of psychic attack was not uncommon in her country, she had never been directly involved with it and frankly did not believe it. Yet she started to experience symptoms which, according to Tamarra, were typical of severe thought-form attack in her native culture.

The woman felt herself being clawed by a creature which seemed, from tactile sensations on her skin and hissing sounds she could hear, to be a lizard. But since she could not see it, she eventually came to believe that it must be a psychic manifestation. It nevertheless left long, thin scratches on her neck and lower back. As the attack continued, the scratches also appeared on her abdominal area and inner thighs.

This, according to Tamarra, was a typical pattern of progression for attacks by such thought-forms: first external, then moving inside the body through the breathing apparatus or, as in this case, the sex organs. Once ensconced in the abdominal cavity the thought-forms entwine themselves with certain organs, causing cramps and nausea.

According to Tamarra, the lizard shape for the attacking thought-form is usual for the particular culture but it was not usual to see such physical manifestations as the scratch-marks.

When the symptoms first appeared, the woman suspected the cause might by psychological and so consulted a psychiatrist, who prescribed tranquilizers. They were of no avail, however, and the symptoms grew worse. She then sought help from Tamarra who knew that hysterical conditions can cause eruptions on the body and so advised her to seek further medical diagnosis. Tamarra's policy was to exhaust orthodox methods first but when nothing further could be discovered medically, she agreed to try helping the woman with her own occult arts.

Apart from the symptoms of attack, the woman seemed to be completely normal. She was well educated and down-to-earth—someone in close touch with the realities of practical life. She felt unusually upset only with the onset of an attack and with their increasing severity, she was becoming quite unnerved.

After trying low-key methods of dealing with the lizard thought-form, Tamarra decided to use the full power of occult ritual exorcism. This meant a four-hour session in the temple she used for ceremonial magical practices. Tamarra says that during the ritual she drew the lizard entities out of the woman and into herself. Using the power of the ancient rite, she was then able to dissolve them completely. After the session the woman felt exhausted but, for the first time in years, completely free of all symptoms.

So she remained for two and a half weeks. Then she began to experience a return of the trouble and called Tamarra. The woman had been told to do certain things to ensure that she remain free of the condition but she was not properly following them up, and thus placing herself in jeopardy of a complete recurrence. However, she did not return to visit Tamarra so she never learned the outcome of the matter, though she had a suspicion about it.

Tamarra knew that when a thought-form has possessed a person for a long time and is removed, the victim still retains a vivid memory of it—much like an amputee and a missing limb. Unless certain measures are taken to deal with the victim's imagination, he or she may inadvertently recreate the thought-form from the vivid memory and again become its host. Because these creatures are the products of the mind, the victim is just as capable of creating them as the attacker. Tamarra further points out that the original possessing thought-form, although produced by an outside agency, may be greatly increased in power when the victim becomes aware of it, so feeding it energy.

Other occult practitioners who deal with possession by destructive thought-forms agree with this assessment of the danger, emphasizing that the job is not finished when the entity is removed. Not only may the victim recreate it, but the original thought-form may itself return if it was only driven off and not destroyed. For that reason, it is recommended that the victim take certain precautions to protect himself or herself from future invasions. These are virtually the same as the "prevention" methods described earlier (see page 118).

Another procedure often recommended as a preventative measure is to call upon positive thought-entities for support and protection. The occultist holds that just as evil thought-entities exist and affect individuals, so also do good thought-entities which can be invoked to reinforce against evil.

Chapter 8

A Note on the Second Self and Possession

In Part One (Chapter 2) we explored the growth of knowledge about the second self after the discovery of artificial somnambulism. As understanding of the complexity of the second self developed, it was hoped that it would help explain the puzzling phenomenon of possession. Some investigators saw in the creative power of the subconscious the total explanation of possession; others believed that many cases did not yield to that approach.

SUBCONSCIOUS PRODUCTIONS

ACHILLE

The case of Achille furnishes a classical example of the analysis and cure of diabolical possession following the principles of the psychology of the subconscious. It was undertaken in the year 1890 by Professor Pierre Janet, the renowned psychologist whose work was referred to in Part One of this book. Achille had no obvious psychological problems but one day, soon after returning home from a business journey, he became somber and taciturn—to the point of being unable to speak at all. He took to his bed and lay there mumbling incomprehensibly. Achille's wife and children believed he was about to die, and sat with him waiting for the end. He now lay motionless in a stupor.

But two days later Achille suddenly sat up in bed with his eyes open wide and burst into a demonical laugh that shook his whole body and twisted his mouth grotesquely. He laughed convulsively for more than two hours, then leapt from bed and called for champagne, saying that it was the end of the world. Then he cried out, "They are burning me—they are cutting me to pieces!"

129

This was followed by an agitated sleep. When he awoke, his limbs became contorted, he said he was possessed by the devil and began to utter blasphemies. His distraught family sought professional help and Achille was eventually taken to the famous Salpetriere Hospital where pioneer work was being carried out on hysteria and hypnosis. There he was placed in the care of Janet who immediately recognized the classical signs of diabolical possession. Achille asserted that his curses against religion were attributable to the devil, who was in control of his tongue. He remained in an extremely agitated state.

Janet had no success in trying to hypnotize Achille but finally decided to try inducing automatic writing. It worked. Soon Janet was asking the "devil" questions and receiving answers through writing while the possessed, ignorant of the whole process, raved on.

Eventually Janet tricked the devil into putting Achille into a hypnotic sleep. Now he had the upper hand, with Achille able to tell him the story of what had been happening.

On the business trip preceding his possession, Achille had been unfaithful to his wife. He was so distressed about this and so afraid he might accidentally reveal the deed to his wife that he fell into a gloomy silence. His guilt led to morbid fantasies, and he felt that the devil himself had entered his body.

Janet now believed he had the whole picture. The devil was not involved. Achille had been driven to create his own demon. Because he could not forgive himself for his crime, Achille had become hopelessly possessed by his inner avenger.

Janet was not satisfied with simply analyzing Achille's affliction but was determined to do something about it. Final resolution was reached when he induced the hallucinatory figure of Achille's wife before his mind's eye. The man confessed his crime and obtained forgiveness from the spectre. With that the possessed state was terminated and never recurred.

Mr . John McB

A good example of a psychoanalytic explanation of the state of possession is given in an article entitled "A Case Illustrating So-Called Demon Possession" which appeared in the *Journal of Abnormal Psychology* in 1911. The article was written by Dr. Edward Mayer, Clinical Professor of Neurology at the University of Pittsburg. It is the story of a young man who came to Mayer complaining of a voice he heard talking continually inside his head. The man, whom Mayer calls McB, wrote a detailed description of his experience of the voice:

> He says he is the devil from hell and he is going to take me to hell as soon as he gets ready. He makes me speak words as if he has my tongue in his control when he is talking to me; but if I talk to any person, I have control. . . . He talks to me all day and night, waking me at night to tell me what he made me dream. He makes my head hurt in the back and it feels hot, and he says it will be worse later on with me. "John," he says, "you never will have another minute's peace as long as you live, and when you die it will be worse. . . . Let's write a book, John, about hell. I have asked you often and if you don't I will carry you to hell."

Mayer found it very difficult to get any information from the man about his personal life. When McB revealed that he was married and now separated from his wife and children, Mayer thought that would be a useful line of inquiry to follow. However, McB would volunteer nothing else.

Mayer eventually succeeded in getting McB into a passive state to learn more about his marriage situation. McB said his wife was childish and jealous of his work, and used to unpredictably leave with the children and go to her mother. He feared her too, believing she set spies to watch him and that she attempted to hypnotize him when he was asleep. At this point McB also admitted that he had taken to drinking as an escape.

When Mayer visited McB's wife, he found a woman quite different from the one described. She was quiet and concerned about her husband. She said that her frequent desertions were because McB would beat her.

Mayer now realized he was working with a badly disintegrated personality. McB presented to the world the picture of a refined, quiet, agreeable man. No sign of his disturbance showed through in his public life. Yet he was subject not only to a severe drinking problem, but also to fits of violence and unreason. Further questioning revealed that McB knew nothing about his irrational episodes. This indicated to Mayer a type of double personality where the repressed second personality had eventually surfaced in McB's consciousness as a demon.

Mayer used a psychoanalytic approach to McB's therapy. He helped him see the nature of his intense emotional state and how its repression had led to audible hallucinations. As is often the case with individuals subject to dissociations, McB was a good subject for therapeutic suggestions. His last communication on the matter was:

> The talking I heard is just about gone: I have become able to be indifferent and not pay attention to it. I may get two words mixed up, half the sound of each or the wrong word first and then it will say, "I made you do it." This is about all I have to contend with at present. I feel sure that I will be like I was years ago again.

Mayer was not certain how deep his cure of this case of seeming demon possession went. He believed McB had a basic temperamental flaw which no therapy could alter. He was convinced, however, that his analysis of the problem had been accurate.

A COMBINED EXPLANATION

Although workers like Janet and Mayer reduced cases of possession to subjective productions of the subconscious, there were and are those who believe it to be more complex. They hold that while many cases of seeming possession are neurotically or psychotically manufactured by the victim himself, others are what they claim to be—invasions by external entities.

HYSLOP'S WORK

One such was James Hyslop (1854–1920), Professor of Logic and Ethics at Columbia University until 1902. He took up in earnest the problem of whether spirit possession might sometimes be involved in cases where a number of personalities manifest through an individual. Writing in 1906 in his book *Borderland of Psychical Research*, Hyslop pointed out that there was a great need for a criterion for distinguishing between the subconscious mental action of a multiple subject and the intervention of external agencies.

He would later develop a test that he considered actually filled that need in regard to cases of possible possession by spirits of the departed. Hyslop had been struck by the "Miss Beauchamp" case of multiple personality (described in Chapter 3) which Morton

Prince had recently brought to public attention. Suppose, Hyslop thought, an investigator were to bring an individual who exhibited a secondary personality to a medium who had absolutely no knowledge of the case, and the medium should produce detailed information about a spirit possessing that individual. If these details corresponded to the secondary personality exhibited, the investigator would have strong evidence for a true case of spirit possession.

Hyslop soon found a chance to test his hypothesis. In 1909 Walter Franklin Prince (1863–1934), an Episcopal clergyman from Pittsburg (and no relation to Morton Prince), had made the acquaintance of a young woman who in 1911 began to show signs that a secondary personality was present. In psychological literature this patient came to be known as "Doris Fischer."

Doris, in fact, had a number of secondary personalities. Hyslop and Prince managed to trace the psychological origins of three of the four secondary personalities present. "Margaret," who could be very cruel, was formed at age three, when Doris's drunken father threw her down on the floor so violently that her head was injured. "Sick Doris" emerged at age seventeen, when her dearly loved mother died. "Sleeping Real Doris," the somnambulistic state of the normal self, seemed to have been formed when Doris suffered an injury to her head and back at age eighteen. The two investigators could not, however, find an adequate explanation for "Sleeping Margaret." She spoke as the girl slept at night, showed great astuteness and even helped to formulate Doris's therapy.

To test the Doris Fischer case in terms of his theory, Hyslop brought the girl to a medium named Mrs. Chenoweth. The result was a series of dozens of sessions in which the medium produced information of remarkable relevance to the condition of the girl, though she neither saw her nor had access to any information about her. Hyslop wrote up his findings in a report of more than 850 pages which appeared in the 1917 *Proceedings* of the American Society for Psychical Research.

His conclusion was that there was strong evidence for spirit possession (or "obsession" as he called it), but not in the form he had anticipated. "Margaret" was apparently a discarnate human spirit who was intervening in Doris's life, whereas "Sleeping Margaret" was Doris herself in a partly dissociated state. There were, in Hyslop's view, some indications that "Sick Doris," too, was a discarnate spirit intruding into Doris's life, but this aspect of the case was never fully clarified.

Hyslop continued to investigate cases of multiple personality in this way. He came to believe that many of these cases and mental illnesses of other kinds involved some sort of influence from discarnate spirits. As he said in *Contact with the Other World*:

> All that I desire to do in this discussion is to suggest the wide application of the hypothesis of spirit intrusion in the treatment of cases regarded as incurably insane. . . . We have proved enough to suggest the possibilities; and any physician who recognizes them and the facts will open his mind to revolutionary possibilities in the diagnosis and cure of cases usually regarded as hopelessly insane. Doris Fischer was so regarded by the physicians who saw her. Dr. Walter Prince, however, cured her by care and suggestion. . . .

Hyslop wrote these words in 1919, about a year before his death. He had for some time been involving a colleague, Dr. Titus Bull, in his researches. Dr. Bull carried on and in 1927 established the James H. Hyslop Foundation which had as its purpose further experimentation to discover the spiritistic component of mental illness.

LHERMITTE'S WORK

The work of the French Catholic psychiatrist Jean Lhermitte provides a good illustration of the combined explanation as applied to possession by the devil. Lhermitte, a neurologist and member of the French Académie Nationale de Médecine, is considered an outstanding authority on the subject. His book *True and False Possession*, written in 1956, is his most detailed exposition of possession.

Lhermitte believes that there is such a thing as true diabolical possession in which a demon takes control of the victim's body and speaks through his mouth. The condition may arise when an already existing mental disturbance makes access to possession easier.

Lhermitte cautions that one cannot rely so much on external appearances when diagnosing such cases, as on a sensing of the victim's inner state. Here a sort of discernment of spirits plays an important role. Next to that, the most reliable approach is observing the victim's response to psychiatric therapy. Any individual who shows the signs of possession and does not respond to orthodox treatment—particularly if one cannot trace the gradual development of the state through ordinary psychological means—may need the aid of the exorcist.

Lhermitte says that there are two types of pseudo-possession (or demonopathy as he calls it): paroxysmal and lucid. The first is experienced as an attack and tends to cloud the consciousness of the victim, producing amnesia for what takes place then. Sometimes this will be an epileptic attack, with convulsions and ensuing unconsciousness; at other times both the physical and moral personality are transformed, with bodily convulsions accompanied by grotesque and obscene words and gestures. Lhermitte links this type of attack to the hysterical neurosis.

False possession of the lucid type is very different and much more difficult to treat. Here instead of the victim and "demon" alternating control of the victim's consciousness, both seem to be present simultaneously, coexisting as two personalities who hate and fight each other bitterly. The "normal" personality experiences words forming themselves without his consent, and perverse scenes may be insinuated into his imagination. Sometimes there are even overt dialogues between the normal consciousness and the "demon."

Lhermitte sees lucid false possession as an instance of conscious dual personality where the victim has created this artificial personality but does not recognize it as his own. Those feelings and tendencies which he has not been able to accept coalesce in this artifact and rise to the surface to torment him.

Lhermitte believes that cases of apparent possession are not as uncommon as may be thought. He holds, however, that the phenomenon must be approached with great caution and a thorough examination made of the psychological aspects in any case encountered.

McAll's Work

The British psychiatrist R. K. McAll began his work with possession as the result of an experience he had as a surgeon working in China during the Sino-Japanese War (1937–1939).

McAll witnessed the instantaneous cure of a madman by a simple exorcism that a woman performed in the name of Jesus Christ. He wanted to know more about the nature of such afflictions and the means of cure. McAll eventually returned to England and in 1956 he decided to go back to university and specialize in psychiatry, devoting himself to the study of serious mental disturbances, and often living in close quarters with those considered to be insane.

In the course of his practice many were sent to Dr. McAll who would not respond to the usual methods of psychiatric treatment. Some of these would speak of being aware of "spirits" or "voices" from another world. McAll took these assertions seriously and eventually concluded that the voices were real and that much could be learned if attention were paid to what they were saying and how the victim was experiencing them.

In 1971, writing in the *International Journal of Social Psychiatry*, Dr. McAll suggests that "demonosis" or the "possession syndrome," as it had come to be called in psychiatric literature, had to be accepted as a reality "even in a sophisticated British culture."

In a recently published book, *Healing the Family Tree*, Dr. McAll develops in much greater detail his view of the nature of possession and its treatment. Again, he acknowledges the importance of recognizing emotionally based symptoms which are simply the production of the victim's subconscious mind, and recommends that the usual psychiatric methods be tried first. But McAll says that when conventional treatment fails, the doctor is justified in looking further afield for explanations. However, sometimes the disturbance is not a simple one, particularly in cases of demonic possession, where there is frequently a mixture of mental illness and occult control.

McAll acknowledges two basic types of possession: possession by human spirits and demonic possession, which often results from dabbling in the occult. Where the possessing spirit is human, it may be living or dead, known or unknown to the victim. McAll makes an original contribution to the literature of possession in his exposition of how possession by the living may easily pass over to possession by the dead.

He points out that the relationship between mother and child may be so possessive that it actually becomes possession in the true sense of the word and goes on to describe the case of a woman who came to him, disturbed, and talked wildly about her son. When McAll was unable to get her off the topic, and so suggested that there was something wrong in their relationship, his patient became furious and left.

Some time later she returned in a calm state and told the doctor a remarkable story. During her first visit, she had not revealed that her son was confined to a mental institution, diagnosed as schizophrenic. On her way home that day, she had gone into a church and sat down. She heard a voice tell her that she never cut her son's umbilical cord. As there was no one else in the church, she believed that God must have spoken to her. There and then, she decided that she had to free her son and experienced a sensation of actually taking a pair of scissors and cutting the cord. She was immediately transformed. Soon afterwards, she received a letter from her son in which he told her that on the same afternoon, he had suddenly experienced a surge of release. He felt he was himself again and wanted to begin to make visits. He was later discharged, completely cured.

McAll sees in this case an instance of the mother's possessiveness becoming possession. He believes that family induced possession is not unusual; it may just as easily be exercised by the dead as by the living. The bonds of family relationship are very powerful. Departed members of one generation may easily establish a possessive control over living members of the next; such possession can even skip a generation and fall upon a grandchild. McAll will often have patients draw up a family tree and try to determine whether any members were subject to behavioral disturbances.

Once McAll has helped the victim to establish the identity of the possessor, treatment can be undertaken. Where the possessor is living, McAll tries to get that person to let the victim go. Where a departed spirit is involved, McAll uses prayer and the Eucharistic rite to help the restless soul find peace and depart.

The length of time involved in freeing the possessed from the possessor varies greatly. Sometimes a simple prayer has immediate results. Sometimes repetitions are needed. Nor is the treatment always finished with the departure of the possessor. McAll compares release from spirit control to release from control from alcohol. The state of possession has produced a kind of spiritual illness that must be healed. A state of dependency upon the possessed state is often produced, with a resulting weakness of willpower. Like the reformed alcoholic, the formerly possessed needs the extended help of knowledgeable, sympathetic persons.

When McAll takes up the subject of *demonic* possession, he emphasizes even more sharply the psychological aspect of diagnosis and treatment, insisting that a medical examination precede any attempt at treatment, so that any neurotic or psychotic sources for suspected demonic possession can be uncovered. In his view there are three possible causes of its symptoms: (1) mental illness; (2) a combination of mental illness and demonic control; or (3) demonic control alone.

In his treatment of cases of apparent demonic possession McAll has helped individuals in all three categories but now concentrates on those in the last two. It is interesting to note that he has found such cases usually have a history of experimentation with the occult. McAll also affirms that demonic influence can be passed down through the generations of a family. As with treatment of possession by the discarnate, his method consists of prayer and the Eucharistic rite. But with demonic possession, he emphasizes that the individual must put all occult practices behind him.

Part Three
A Therapist's Casebook

Chapter 9

Possession and the Emotional Life

The preceding part of this book gives an idea of the many kinds of possession experiences and the various approaches that have been used to remedy the condition. There are two basic tacks that have been used in treatment, as we have seen. The first is concerned only for the welfare of the victim. The second is concerned for both victim and possessor. But both approaches seek a speedy remedy that is as uncomplicated as possible.

I have discovered in my practice as a therapist, however, that there are some cases where speedy resolution is neither possible nor desirable. Sometimes possessor and victim need to reach a deeper understanding *together*, so that each appreciates the cause and meaning of their situation from the other's point of view.

THERADRAMA

I have been working as a therapist for over fifteen years. I was trained in the therapeutic art termed "theradrama" by its originator, Lea Hindley-Smith. Hindley-Smith was trained in psychoanalysis in London, England, and during the Second World War began a therapeutic practice there. After the war she moved to Toronto and in the 1950s continued developing some new approaches to therapy that she had begun in England. She went on to write a number of books on the art she termed "theradrama."

Theradrama is concerned with bringing to consciousness the hidden patterns that influence the life of an individual—patterns that derive from basic family structures handed down from generation to generation. These structures are considered to be living realities, constantly exerting their influence, even after the individual has left the bosom of his original family. They maintain their power in all of his relationships and are reconstituted in full force when he establishes a new family of his own.

140

The influence of these family structures is for the most part unconscious. For that reason, both therapist and client must carry out a penetrating exploration to discover the nature of the latter's particular family structure and how it has influenced his life. This also means, where possible, going back in time to gain a sense of the ancient family character that shows itself in each new generation.

Theradrama is so named because the individual repeatedly "dramatizes" his unconscious family patterns in his daily life. These blind dramatizations can be the source of unhappiness in relationships and frustration in creative development, but once they are brought to consciousness, the individual may be freed of their control and able to alter his life patterns.

The process of bringing these patterns to consciousness always carries with it painful emotional realizations that may be strongly resisted. Successful resolution requires the determination to persevere through these demanding phases of the process and the willingness to resist the tendency to reintroduce the old dramatizations in order to diminish the pain.

The next stage of theradrama is to help a person discover a *sense* in his life, a *direction* inherent in its events. Though this meaning is inherent in a person's life, he may have little or no conscious awareness of it. He may view his life as segments, occurring consecutively, but with no continuity. The theradramatic process works toward attaining a perception of its *unity*.

A person in the grips of disturbance is likely to be aware only of the present. The past has no significance, except perhaps as a source of woe. The future seems dark or blank. He is overwhelmed by the emotions of the moment and cannot find perspective. Without perspective he cannot feel hope. The events of life strike him as meaningless experiences, coming into existence and passing out again by the merest chance.

Theradrama seeks to establish the perspective of meaning and so generate hope. If the individual can see meaning in his life—even in his sufferings and mistakes—he will feel hope. If he can sense that his life constitutes an unfinished production which his unconscious greater self is working away at, he will be encouraged by that awareness. This perspective throws light on his experiences as they occur and provides guidance at points of decision.

Theradrama is not linked to any particular therapeutic technique or psychological system. I have made use of psychodrama bio-

141

energetics, abreactive therapy, group therapy, house-group therapy, work therapy and other techniques. I have been influenced by Wilhelm Reich, Carl Jung, Pierre Janet and others, but for me the strongest systematic influence has come from Freud. His analysis of the personal unconscious and the sexual dimension in family structures has been crucial to my therapeutic work.

In the last analysis, however, both system and technique must be subjugated to the needs of the particular client. How one sees the client is a matter of inspiration. And this brings me to mention how I became aware of the phenomenon of possession in my therapeutic work.

THE ELUSIVE ELEMENT

I have found when working with certain clients that some of their experiences do not fall neatly into the categories devised by the great masters of psychology. There will be an elusive element that does not yield to the more conventional therapeutic approaches. It may be some pervasive feeling—guilt, for example—that cannot be explained no matter how one searches the client's remote and recent past. It may be a sense of being tormented on the inside by a harsh persecutor whose identity cannot be satisfactorily established. It may be the conviction that some influence which is "not oneself" enters into the responses and decisions of daily life— an influence whose alien quality remains no matter how much analysis is done.

Now the therapist may rightly question in such cases whether his analysis has gone far enough. It may be that he simply has not applied the process deeply enough to touch upon the elusive element. It may, in other words, be a matter of therapeutic failure due to a lack of skill on the part of the therapist. This explanation must be considered first, for failure of therapy inevitably comes into the experience of every psychotherapist. Sometimes it is a failure of imagination. If the therapist cannot allow his imagination to move beyond the framework of his training, he will be unable to really take in what the client is trying to tell him.

I found that I was doing this some years ago. While I was not tied to the system of one particular psychological master, I *was* caught within the structure of the system I had distilled from many. When I finally did question my own closed framework, I discovered this remarkable fact: some of my clients were actually telling me that they felt possessed by entities alien to themselves. They experienced these entities as personal presences dwelling within them and subtly communicating with them.

I found that if I really took these clients' descriptions of their experiences seriously, that element in their therapy which had so long remained elusive could be firmly grasped and dealt with.

This was difficult for me to do at first because I did not feel comfortable with the concept of possession. I was not convinced that the human "spirit" could operate outside its own body, much less that it could actually take control of the body of another.

However, the solution I arrived at was to go ahead and treat these cases *as if* they were exactly what they appeared to be: the possession of one individual by another. It seemed to me that whether or not I believed in the reality of spirit possession, I might be able to help these clients by accepting their description literally. After all, I reasoned, I did not have sufficient evidence *against* its reality to stand in judgment about another's experience.

So that became my therapeutic approach to such cases and in treating them as *bona fide* instances of possession, I had to take the *possessor* into account—a third person who also has to be treated therapeutically.

From the time I first adopted this *as if* approach, I began a thorough investigation of the phenomenon, as detailed in Part Two of this book. This led to my acquiring a considerable library related to all aspects of the paranormal. In particular I made a study of the history of psychical research, the scientific study of paranormal phenomena, and discovered that even before the turn of the century, there was a body of well-documented and carefully evaluated data on these matters—a body of data almost unknown today— much of it produced by the Society for Psychical Research, founded at Cambridge, England, in 1882. It revealed to me that not only was there insufficient evidence *against* the reality of the phenomenon to rule it out, there was actually impressive evidence in its *favor*.

As time went on, I came across references to other therapeutic workers who were taking the possession experience seriously, some of whom have been mentioned earlier in this book. But here I must mention one man whose approach is remarkably similar to mine: Wilson Van Dusen, a well-known American psychologist.

In his writings, Van Dusen tells how he works with the "hallucinations" of his clients. By "hallucination" he means a clear sensory

143

perception of things that the client experiences but others do not. Van Dusen tells us that often his clients' hallucinations took the form of inner voices to which he could actually speak. In an article in *New Philosophy* entitled "The Presence of Spirits in Madness" (1967), Van Dusen writes:

> It took some care to make the patients comfortable enough to reveal their experiences honestly. A further complication was that the voices were sometimes frightened of me and themselves needed reassurance. I struck up a relationship with both the patient and persons he saw and heard. I would question these other persons directly, and instructed the patient to give a word-for-word account of what the voices answered or what was seen. In this way I could hold long dialogues with a patient's hallucinations and record both my questions and their answers. My method is that of phenomenology. My only purpose was to come to as accurate a description as possible of the patient's experiences. The reader may notice I treat the hallucinations as realities because that is what they are to the patient.

Van Dusen then goes on to mention that his patients were usually perfectly ordinary people who found their experience as baffling as he did. I have also found this to be true.

It was gratifying to discover that an approach I had felt compelled to take was being used by others, and for me it confirmed the importance of intuition in therapeutic work.

Another interesting aspect of the work is that not even the client need believe in the objective reality of possession for this approach to work. A number of my clients who, from beginning to end of the possession therapy, disbelieved in—or at least had serious doubts about—the reality of their inner presences were nonetheless relieved of their condition.

Over the last seven years I have worked with approximately fifty cases of apparent possession with symptoms ranging from slight distress to serious disturbance. Results have varied from minimal change to radical improvement of the client's life, and the types of possession cases have also varied as will be seen.

POSSESSION CASES IN CONTEXT

There are a number of categories of possession, as described in the second part of this book, which I have never encountered and I think this is simply because so much of my work as a therapist has had to do with understanding the individual's experience within his original family context. The bulk of possession cases that I have treated are thus family related, involving a person or persons who are related to the host by blood. I have divided the cases I have worked with into five categories:

Possession by the deceased. This is the most common type of possession I have dealt with. The possessing entity is the discarnate spirit of some blood relative of the victim or host, most often in the direct ancestral line, and commonly a parent or grandparent.

Possession by the living. I have encountered some such cases, always involving family members. In my experience, possession by the living does not mean possession by the "whole" personality of the possessor, but rather by some "fragment."

Possession by group-minds. A group-mind as mentioned briefly in Chapter 11, is a psychic entity formed when a number of individuals come together and concentrate on a particular idea or task. It has a mental/emotional life of its own and exerts a very strong influence on its members. The family is an example of a naturally formed group-mind and if its influence over a member is so strong that it controls the individual's basic emotional life, the situation can rightly be called possession. I have seen instances of this.

Possession puzzles. Some cases that I have treated do not fit into any particular class and so I have grouped them together under this heading.

The cases that follow were chosen to illustrate as fully as possible the various aspects of my work with possession. Rather than give a detailed account of the thinking behind the treatment procedure in each case, I have included a chapter at the end of this section on the general nature of the therapy involved.

In reporting these cases, I will talk about the personalities that speak through the clients *as though* they are separately existing individual beings. I want to give as accurately as possible a sense of how the "possessing entities" come across, while still remaining undecided about the essential nature of these experiences and the objective status of these entities. By speaking about the intruding beings as real persons I do not intend to try to convince the reader of their objective existence. I want only to bring home the striking nature of the possession experience as undergone by my clients.

The reader must also understand that the material presented in these cases was obtained as part of a process of therapy; my sole concern in working with these clients was to alleviate their problems. This has significant implications in terms of the present book.

In my work as a therapist I have never attempted to elicit from the client information that might *prove* the objective existence of the possessing entity. I have never, for instance, sought to obtain specific data that could, through verification, be shown to be known only to the supposed possessor and not available to the client through any normal means. Though I believe this kind of parapsychological investigation is important and should be done, I have not been able to bring myself to experiment with my clients in this fashion. I have either accepted whatever information came forward spontaneously or asked about matters directly relevant to the therapeutic process. For that reason, no hard evidence for the paranormal appears in the cases summarized here.

A final note. In one chapter of this section certain reincarnation-type experiences are included—not because I consider them as examples of possession, but because they also constitute important instances of multiplicity-type phenomena.

Chapter 10

Possession by Family Members

SECTION A: DISCARNATE FAMILY MEMBERS

The three cases described here are of the type I have most frequently encountered in my work, where the possessing spirits were deceased blood relatives. In each case they were very conscious of that special connection which the ties of kinship produce.

THE HELPFUL GRANDMOTHER

Some years ago a colleague of mine, Jenny, directed to my care a young woman named Sarah Worthington, who had recently become excessively agitated and despondent. Jenny had been her therapist for some years and Sarah had learned to trust her deeply. There had been good progress until recently, when Sarah had fallen into a dangerous depression accompanied by strong suicidal impulses. Jenny became convinced that there was some element within Sarah that would not yield to any of the usual therapeutic approaches and so asked for my assistance.

The three of us met in my office. I had known Sarah from a time when she was in one of my therapeutic groups. We talked for a while about how she was feeling. When I asked her if she would try an experiment to see if we could get to the source of her distress, she readily agreed.

I then asked Sarah a question that I had found useful in detecting unusual influences: "Have you ever been aware of anything like an interior conversation—as though you were speaking to someone in your mind and that person was replying?"

"Yes," Sarah answered. "Something like that seems to be going on much of the time."

"Can you tell us about it?"

"I can't say much about it. I just know it does happen like that."

"Well, let's try to see what is going on."

I asked Sarah to recline in a comfortable position and close her eyes. With some guidance she soon entered into a deeply relaxed state.

I continued: "Now try to focus on one of those interior conversations. You will find words coming into your mind that are part of it. I want you to take the part of the person you are conversing with. Speak for that person, whoever it is. Bring that inner voice right out. You can do it very well. You have nothing to fear. Go ahead."

Sarah's body tensed and the words that came out startled us.

"I'm hot! I'm hot! Oh, the heat!"

While these first words were startling enough in content, they were more so for the change in quality, volume and pitch in Sarah's voice. As she continued, it was clear that this was the voice of a woman accustomed to exercising authority. The tones were deeper and fuller than her own. Her usual tentative manner was gone. The voice seemed for all practical purposes to be that of another person.

Not being sure, however, if we were talking to Sarah, to a split-off part of her personality or to something else, I continued the questioning.

"What is happening? Can you say more?"

But by now she had sunk back quietly on the couch. The agitation had disappeared. She did not answer my question.

"Can you say more? What is upsetting you?"

The same powerful voice continued in the abbreviated phrasing that would prove characteristic: "Unhappy."

"Why are you unhappy?"

"Don't know."

"Is there something you want to say or do?"

"Help Sarah."

This was the first direct indication that it was not the usual Sarah who was speaking.

"You want to help Sarah? Well, tell me, what is your name?"

"Sarah Jackson."

"Who are you?"

"Grandmother."

"Sarah Worthington's grandmother?"

"Yes."

"Her mother's mother?"

"Yes."

"How are you going to help Sarah Worthington?"

"Don't know."

"Well, Sarah Worthington is feeling very desperate about her life right now. Perhaps you can help her. That is why Jenny and I are here also—to help her. Would you like to work with us and see what can be done for Sarah Worthington?"

"Yes."

By now we had come to the end of our allotted time and Sarah was showing signs of exhaustion.

"We are running out of time for today. Would you like to get together with us again soon?"

"Yes."

"Okay. But for now I want you to step back so that Sarah Worthington can return. You are moving back, back, back. Sarah Worthington! You are coming forward. Coming forward very strongly now. You are here now, Sarah Worthington. You are here, fully present. Open your eyes."

Sarah opened her eyes and looked around. I told her it had been a good session and we would continue the work at our next scheduled time. She clearly had no memory of what had just taken place and could not account for the time that had elapsed. She did not know we had been speaking with a "Sarah Jackson," and we did not mention it.

The next time we got together Sarah relaxed again on the couch and immediately Sarah Jackson came forward.

"Hot! So hot! Jason! Where's Jason? I can't find him."

"Sarah Jackson, what is the heat? What is happening?"

"Fire. The fire is hot."

"What is burning?"

"Houses. All on fire. Where is Jason?"

"Who is Jason?"

"Jason. My son. Heard there was a fire. Came home to find Jason. All the houses burning. Oh, Jason!"

As we continued, the picture took shape. The year was about 1910. The Jacksons lived in downtown Toronto and Sarah Jackson had been away from their house from early morning on this particular day. Her husband had earlier departed for work, leaving Jason, their son, who was seven, alone. When news of a neighborhood fire, which was spreading quickly, reached Sarah Jackson, she rushed home. The heat was intense, as the fire was very close.

She could not find Jason. Panicking, she ran through the burning streets calling his name. He had been taken by neighbors to a safe place but Sarah Jackson spent a very desperate hour fearing the worst and for some reason, this traumatic experience was in the forefront of her consciousness when she first came through.

Sarah Worthington had been named after her grandmother Sarah, who had died some fifteen years before. The piano she played daily was a bequest from her. As we talked with Sarah Jackson she spoke of the piano and her love of music, indicating that shortly after her death, she had somehow entered Sarah Worthington as she played her piano and had been a living presence within her from that time. She was there with the intention of helping her granddaughter, but her presence amounted to a kind of possession that was confusing and frightening the young woman.

The sessions went on for two months, two or three times a week. Sarah Jackson had to unburden herself of her own pre-occupations before she could be of much real help to her granddaughter. She was plagued by disturbing memories of her own life and by feelings of regret and guilt about her daughter, Elizabeth—Sarah Worthington's mother—whom she had treated with coldness and indifference. Sarah Jackson had loved her son, Jason, but sent Elizabeth away to live with relatives for a long time when she was very young. Elizabeth took this as a rejection and never recovered from that trauma. There had also been sexual interference from Jason, encouraged by Elizabeth's father, and though Sarah Jackson was subliminally aware of what was going on, she had ignored it.

This combination of unfortunate events deeply scarred Elizabeth and manifested also in a rare psychosomatic disease, which developed in adulthood and remained with her for life, and in her mistreatment of her own daughter, Sarah.

Elizabeth also had a son whom she favored in the way her hated brother had been. But she treated Sarah as a nuisance, and taught her that women are nothing and men everything. She would constantly humiliate Sarah while praising her son. As for her father, he had hoped for a son when Sarah—their first child—was born, and from then on, treated her like a boy. She was dressed in boys' clothing and encouraged in typically boyish interests so that it was hardly surprising that Sarah could not appreciate herself or her femininity.

Sarah Jackson had been aware of all this and at the time she died, seems to have felt particularly guilty about how she had indirectly contributed to her namesake's unhappiness. But any relief she hoped to bring to her granddaughter by her interior presence had failed. She had instead added confusion to desperation.

However, the moment Sarah Jackson could make herself known directly, having cleared away much of her own confusion, she was of real service. She not only offered valuable perspective on what Sarah Worthington had been going through, but also helped establish communication between the girl and her mother. She offered her reassurance and support in Sarah's struggle with everyday problems.

These sessions produced a great sense of relief in our client. After the first two weeks she began to realize what was transpiring during the sessions and as they continued, to retain more and more of the content. She was at first astonished that her grandmother was speaking through her but as she grew to accept this, she gained a much broader view of the forces that had been at work in her life. She saw her parents more realistically and felt heartened by her grandmother's concern.

At the end of two months, the basic work had been done. Sarah's suicidal impulses were gone and she began to turn her attention to her career and the important friendships she had been neglecting.

Though Sarah Jackson ceased to be with her as a possessing presence, she still thinks of her grandmother as a kind of beneficient presence in her life.

The Confused Father

Susan was a very successful young woman in her professional life. Considered an extremely capable counselor and social worker, she inspired confidence in both colleagues and clients. However, in her early twenties she had entered into a marriage that soon ended in divorce and this was followed by other unfortunate relationships.

Shortly before the work described here began, Susan had broken up with a young man. Although he had his problems, Susan had pushed the situation to a point where it could not be repaired, becoming cold and closed, declining to work things through. Susan had made the situation irredeemable and recognized the fact. There was a strong feeling of vengeance and she knew it was time to do something about it.

Over the four months since the relationship ended, Susan had become convinced that this vengefulness originated in her feelings toward her father. But that was not all. She also felt that her father, now dead for many years, was actually "with" her in some very concrete way, and that his presence was helping to keep her vindictive feelings alive. She believed, in fact, that she was possessed by him.

Susan, her own therapist and I met for the first session in his office. Susan was nervous. She had to be allowed to relax and sink below the agitation she was experiencing and so I asked her to put aside any expectations of what "should" happen and let things develop on their own.

Susan became very relaxed. In answer to a question about what she was experiencing, she said, "He is here. My father."

When I asked if he felt close, Susan replied that he did and that she wanted him to communicate with her. I said she would find that he could speak through her, if she wanted that.

Susan relaxed further, and I noted that subtle shift in facial expression that I have observed so often in these cases. Now her words were in a lower pitched voice, delivered very slowly.

"What do you want?" the voice said.

"To talk to you," I replied.

"Leave me alone, I don't want to talk." The delivery was sluggish, as though thoughts were being gathered with great difficulty.

"Why don't you want to talk?"

"I am tired. I need to rest."

"Who are you?"

"John."

"John who?"

"John Driscoll."

"Susan's father?" I asked.

"Yes. I am tired. Why are you bothering me?"

"We have been asked to. Do you know where you are?"

There was a long pause, then, "I don't know."

"Do you know who I am?"

"No. I am too tired. Let me rest."

"Now look, John. I know you want us to leave you alone. I know you feel too tired to be bothered, but we have a problem here. You don't know where you are or who we are. Wouldn't you say that is peculiar?"

"Yes. It seems so."

"Why do you suppose things are so unclear to you?"

"It's the fog. There is a fog all around. I can't see anything clearly."

It was like talking to a man who was asleep and speaking from a dream. He did not wonder about things that were strange but accepted everything as given, just as in a dream even the most bizarre circumstances go unquestioned. There was no spontaneity and his mind was sluggish, nearly to the point of paralysis.

I knew that Susan's father had died from injuries sustained in an auto accident. In a strange premonition Susan had seen her father's car surrounded in a black haze a week before his death.

Those who write about human survival of death believe that the way one dies affects one's state immediately afterward. Where there is gradual progression toward death, as in disease or aging, the individual has a clearer consciousness of his condition. But with a sudden death, there is often great confusion. The person does not realize he is dead; rather, he experiences a period of fogginess which gradually clears as his true state dawns upon him.

If one accepted the possibility that John was still around after his death, he was a classic example of this latter state of consciousness. The passage of years had not helped him clarify things and I speculated as to whether this might be because he had remained attached to his daughter, insulated from other influences.

It seemed important that John get a clearer picture of where he was. I asked, "Do you know where your daughter Susan is?"

"At home, I suppose."

"No, she is here."

"Oh." He seemed completely indifferent to the exchange.

"Now, John, would you like to find out what is going on?"

"I guess so."

"Well, we can help you do that, if you will allow it. Would you like that?"

"I guess so."

"All right. We are going to end this session now, but we'll be getting together again to try to see more about this. Are you agreeable?"

"Yes."

After asking John to "move back," I called Susan "forward." She remembered everything that had taken place in the session, felt relieved that the process had started and was amazed at the state her father was in.

The next few times we got together were spent trying to get

John to at least question where he was and what condition he was in, but his confusion was so great that we could not make much headway. When we told him that he was with Susan—that he was in fact in her—he could not believe it.

I next asked John to become aware of his body and he was astounded to find that it was female. When we told him it was his daughter's he accepted this, though with surprise. This realization seemed to shock him into greater alertness so that he even began to question things for himself. This was the breakthrough we needed. Now we could do some real work.

In this case the real work had to do with John's recalling to his consciousness certain unfortunate things he had done, looking squarely at their consequences and experiencing the guilt he had so long avoided.

Susan had known before we began this work that her father had interfered with her sexually when she was very young. Therapeutic work two years earlier had uncovered memories of her father putting his penis in her mouth when she was a baby. This had happened periodically until she was three years old. In that earlier work Susan had not only recalled the incidents, but re-experienced them emotionally, realizing why up to that point in her life, sex had always involved fellatio. After the work with these early memories, Susan lost all interest in oral sex—a fairly good indication that the work we had done was on target.

But we were to discover that there was more to the story. As the fog lifted and John's thinking became more focused, he began to face other disturbing memories.

He was shocked when he remembered the early fellatio incidents, and realized he was accountable for the ways this had affected his daughter's life. But John's next set of disturbing memories surprised us all, for he recalled that when Susan was just in grade school he would go into her bedroom at night after she had fallen asleep and fondle her genitals. Susan did not appear to awaken and he would leave after a few minutes. He apparently did this frequently over the years until Susan was sixteen. He had suddenly perceived her as a fully developed woman, become frightened about what he was doing and stopped.

At the end of this session with John we spent some time talking with Susan about it. In her adult life she had no conscious memories of these incidents which meant that if she was aware of her father's actions when they occurred—which seems likely—she had immediately repressed that awareness. Also, throughout the whole period of these events, Susan's mother seems to have been oblivious to what was taking place.

Susan told us that all through her adult life, she had difficulty getting to sleep. She had always felt as though someone was watching her as she was falling asleep. Now, after this session with John, this particular problem disappeared, never to return.

As the work with John progressed, it became clearer to Susan that she must come to terms with her own role in the neurotic tie between herself and her father. From the time of her adolescence she had felt an irritation with him, bordering on contempt. While not consciously aware of the sexual incidents at night, she sensed her father's attraction to her as she matured and sometimes took the opportunity to behave in a provocative way. She enjoyed seeing him squirm uncomfortably as she tried out her new-found sexual power and without fully realizing why, was driven to make him suffer for his sexual feelings towards her.

Susan's contempt for her father spread to her relationships with young men as they began to enter her life as a teenager and an adult. She would feel very interested in her boyfriends and responsive to them at first but before long, grow unaccountably impatient and angry with them. This became a pattern with disastrous results for her love life as the unresolved sexual tie between Susan and her father was played out time and time again.

At this point in the work Susan had to come to terms with her desires for vengeance against her father for only then would she be able to let him go. And only if she could accept him as a human being, flawed as he was, would her love relationships have a chance.

As her father confessed his actions, Susan began to mellow toward him. He had been a tortured man long before he mistreated her, himself a victim of sexual mistreatment early in life. Susan appreciated his courage in speaking so candidly and soon felt compassion for him. It was a short step to complete forgiveness and acceptance.

Once John had reached sufficient clarity of mind to realize where he was, we periodically spent time reconstructing the events around his death and developing a clear picture of his present state of existence. He recalled the drive that ended in the fatal crash, and began to realize that when he died he had been afraid to go on and had been drawn to Susan as a place of refuge. She was vulnerable to this invasion because of his previous sexual interference. Once

155

he had taken possession of her, he had remained in a kind of foggy sleep, his thoughts and feelings subliminally impinging on Susan's, causing her much confusion.

Now that he recognized clearly that he had died, he became curious about the next phase of existence. We periodically asked him to become aware of that next phase through a process of mental visualization. We suggested he consider that up to now he had been looking "down" at Susan and the events of this world, completely preoccupied with earthly concerns. He would now find that he could look "up" and if he did, he would see new things.

John followed our suggestions and soon began to see a "light." Eventually he recognized human presences in that "light": his aunt and his mother, both long deceased. John realized that he would have to leave Susan, now that they had reached the point of resolution, yet he said he was still afraid to go on, even though he wanted to. Then one day, after about six weeks of sessions, we called upon John and he was not there. He had taken that final step on his own, and Susan was free of the possession.

Susan experienced a palpable change in her state of being after the work. She had always felt as though there was a shroud over her, as though she lived behind a veil, slightly separated from people. That feeling disappeared completely with John's departure.

Her attitude toward men also altered radically and a few months after the completion of this work Susan fell in love with a bright and successful young man. Her feelings for him were free of the ambivalences of her previous love relationships. They were soon married, and their life together since has been a witness to the permanence of the changes within Susan.

One further interesting point about this case is that shortly after her father's death, Susan developed a severe phobia for birds. She could not understand this since she had a pet budgie for years and loved to let it fly around her room and land on her shoulder. But she had suddenly become terrified of any bird that flew near her. After the completion of our work with John, Susan lost that phobia. She believed that to her unconscious any bird represented her father's spirit which had entered her at the time of his death. But now the possession was over and she no longer responded to birds symbolically.

THE SECRET SISTER

One day my colleague Elizabeth Harding came in to consult me about a client named Jean. This young woman had apparently always spoken quite freely with Elizabeth about her life and family background, describing a brooding, angry father, a remote mother, and a retarded sister, now deceased. Then one day Jean had brought in an early family photograph and when Elizabeth asked why the retarded sister, Amy, was not in it, she had revealed that the family always pretended to the world that Amy did not exist. Her mother never allowed her to be seen by strangers. Unbelievably, Jean could not recall one instance of Amy being taken outdoors in her entire lifetime of twenty years. Rather, she had been kept in a crib in a remote room and fed and changed like a baby. Elizabeth realized then Amy's ghostly presence must have been a powerful factor in Jean's early formation. She was a sort of repository of shame and guilt for the whole family.

Elizabeth felt the family's way of handling the situation had created an unusual dynamic, for while Amy was in many ways treated as if she did not exist she was, at the same time, the subject most on the minds of all.

Elizabeth learned that on the very day Jean was born, Amy, then one year old, contracted a severe disease of the nervous system which left her brain-damaged and bedridden. Numerous consultations with specialists were fruitless and now Jean's mother was so distraught with Amy's condition that she was incapable of giving her newborn daughter the attention and love she needed.

Jean's mother's complete preoccupation with Amy only gradually lessened over the years. The highly stressed atmosphere was a poor environment for little Jean who grew up with a feeling of great insecurity and isolation.

Jean's father was an angry but complex man whose frequent outbursts of rage were principally directed against his wife. Because of the unpredictability of the situation, Jean felt fearful and quite alone though she gained some solace from Amy's company.

Amy died of an acute illness at twenty. Shortly before that, Jean had a dream in which she found herself at the center of a slowly revolving hemisphere. She felt suspended and inert. She went through a temperature cycle, from normal to cold and back again. Then she went from normal to hot, finally returning to normal temperature once more. At this point the cycle repeated itself and Jean had the impression that it would go on forever.

Jean believed the dream was a picture of what life was like for Amy. Suspended between life and death, she was stuck in the center of a very small emotional world. The dream showed Jean's abundant empathy for her unfortunate sister.

My colleague had the deepening impression that Jean was experiencing Amy as a living presence within her. While she felt cautious about giving too much weight to such an impression of this kind, Elizabeth had discovered that such intuitions should not be ignored.

With Jean's consent, we set up a series of sessions in which I would participate. In her last session alone with Jean, Elizabeth had actually contacted the presence of Amy. Though little information was acquired in this initial exchange, it set the stage for the work we were now to begin.

The three of us met, and, after a brief talk, Elizabeth placed Jean in a state of relaxation. At that point I began talking to Amy, suggesting that she speak again so that we could all become acquainted. Amy responded immediately in tones very different from Jean's. She talked with a slight lisp and her vocabulary suggested a child of four. Addressing herself to Elizabeth, she said, "You sound different."

"What do you mean?" asked Elizabeth.

"You're too nice. You're going to have to be tough with me."

"Why is that, Amy?" I enquired.

"Because I'm bad. I was bad to Jean."

"What did you do?" I asked.

"I went inside her. I got into her and stayed there."

Amy went on to tell us that she remembered Jean standing by her crib when she was five years old. It had happened then. Jean's need for Amy's company and her guilt about her jealousy of the attention Amy got made her open to possession. To a large extent Amy lived through Jean after that. She could go places and learn things that were otherwise impossible in her condition. And they were both frightened of the volatile feelings swirling around the family home. It was as though together they could resist the forces that were frightening them both.

This information came out over a period of days of intensive work with Jean, though it did not emerge easily. Amy was mischievous and Elizabeth and I would often have to be firm with her to get her concentration. She was obviously enjoying our attention.

When the time came to broach the subject of resolving things between Amy and Jean, I suggested that she start looking beyond the small sphere of Jean's environment. She reluctantly agreed.

As a start, I asked Amy to simply look around in her imagination and see what she could see. The first thing she became aware of were two friendly "presences" standing on either side of her which she called "Left" and "Right." She got a big laugh out of the joke, saying that left could be right and vice versa. It seems that they could somehow exchange places and be each other though just how was never clear to me.

The next thing she saw was an elderly man with a lot of grey hair and a beard. He seemed very wise and was beckoning to her and saying, "Come now. I'll show you the possibilities. The world is bigger than you think." The man seemed to have been appointed to be Amy's teacher and she felt very secure with him.

Though her exploration of broader worlds went on, it did not seem to be producing the desired effect. She was still attached to talking with us and hanging around so that I finally insisted she stop using Jean for living and prepare to move on to the next phase of her existence. She refused. After a rather heated exchange between us, she agreed that it really was time for her to go and said she had just been dawdling. With that, she joined the wise old man who had been instructing her and left.

Throughout these sessions, Jean was fully aware of Amy and what she said. Yet she was never sure if Amy was simply her own unconscious reconstruction of her sister's personality or if she was actually present. While we were engaged in the work, I counseled Jean to leave aside intellectual speculations about what Amy was or was not, but afterwards she realized that she had felt that her sister was in fact present. It was her *mind* that had difficulty with it because she could not fit possession experience into any framework of philosophic or religious thought with which she felt comfortable.

After the sessions had ended, Jean realized that whether she had a ready explanation for the experience or not, there were palpable results. For some time before the emergence of Amy, Jean had felt that she had a kind of alien mass inside her body which she must get rid of. She had tried bioenergetics work to deal with it, but found no improvement. After Amy had departed, however, Jean realized that she was finally free of the feeling. She felt terrifically relieved and now had a sense that her body was her own—a completely new sensation.

Two years after the work with Amy, I asked Jean what she felt about her. She said that once Amy had departed, she had never returned but she felt that her sister was still "around" somewhere. Not as an interfering influence, but as someone near who wished her well. Jean also told me that she had now become more aware of a world of spiritual beings who can affect human lives and that she had at times sensed positive influences from there, aiding her in her creative work. The sessions with Amy had opened up this dimension of awareness.

Section B: Living Family Members

This type of case involves control by a living blood relative. In the examples given here the possessing spirit is the host's mother. Every instance of control by a living family member within my experience to date has involved the intrusion of a parent.

The Complaining Mother

Art was a very successful professor in a small university with a solid doctorate in history. A sophisticated man of the world, he had traveled a great deal.

Art had married at thirty, and two children were born in the first five years. After the birth of the second child, however, signs of serious trouble appeared in his relationship with his wife, Elaine. When I began the work described here, they had been divorced for three years, with Art contemplating marriage to a young woman he had met at the university. But the closer he got to the ceremony, the more uneasy he became. He was growing quite neglectful of his fiance and he was also noticing that a part of his mind and attention was engaged elsewhere, involved in some peculiar inner dialogue. At this point he sought my help.

Art had been experiencing this inner dialogue for many years. He had kept a journal since before his marriage, and in going back over those notes he found his own clear references to a kind of "inner storm." It would last four or five days, during which time he felt that he was not himself, and that he was under great pressure from some inner source that he could not control. He could only weather it out.

While the storm was raging, Art would hear a very censorious voice speaking inside. It would criticize him, and the woman who was head of his department. This woman, Melanie, was a good friend and they frequently got together socially; however, the relationship was not based on sexual attraction.

Although Melanie was the chief object of the derisive remarks of Art's inner voice, anyone who was important to him was likely to be a target. Elaine had received the most criticism. From the very first days of their courtship the voice had found fault with her. While it held sway, Art would fight with all his strength to push it aside, block it from his consciousness, though not very successfully for it always came back, hounding him and robbing his life of pleasure.

Now he was approaching his second marriage and the voice was becoming even more obnoxious. Art had been involved in therapy for some time and had often spoken of this inner influence but he felt that the work done with it had made no difference. Now he was becoming determined to do something once and for all.

In looking back over his journals Art developed a different view of what was happening to him. He had always thought of the voice as an unacceptable negative aspect of his personality that would speak the nasty thoughts that he could not himself own up to. Though he had long ago associated the critical attitude of the voice with his mother's personality, he believed he had incorporated this aspect of her into his unconscious mind. Now, as he reread his journals, he found references to his mother's "long arm" reaching over the miles from her home in Detroit to maintain her hold upon him and to feeling that he was literally "possessed" by her, that she was an entity in him, exercising a direct influence upon his thoughts.

Art wanted to find out if his mother was literally with him—if she was somehow residing in his body even though she was living in another city. He proposed to me that we explore the possibility.

I asked him to become relaxed and then inquired if he could there and then become aware of the voice within and allow himself to enter into its thoughts and feelings. After a brief pause Art said he believed he could.

"Can you hear the voice?" I asked.

"Yes I can."

"Is it familiar?"

"Oh, yes. It's my mother's."

161

"Now stay with this. Can you actually experience the way she is seeing things and the emotions she is feeling?"

"Yes."

"Do you suppose you could let her speak now?"

"Yes, I think so."

"What is your mother's name?"

"Veronica."

At this point I began speaking to the "voice" as if it really were Veronica. I talked about Art's coming marriage and the importance of his making a good start. I said I was sure that as his mother, she wished him all the best, and after going on in this vein for some time, I asked her to respond.

"Can you speak, Veronica?" I inquired.

"Yes, I think so," was the reply.

"What do you think about what I was saying?"

"Art is mine and his life is mine. That's not going to change. I have to make sure Art knows how kooky all these friends of his are. I let him know how silly and stupid they are, especially that Melanie. I don't let anything about her go by."

"What do you mean?"

"Well, she proposed that Art and their friends fix up this cabin to use as a ski lodge on weekends. She got it all organized and they spent three days working on it. Art thought she did such a great job and worked so hard on it. But I told him she couldn't have done all that. She was just making it look like she was working hard."

"You want Art to think badly of her?"

"That's right. And it works. Oh, he thinks he likes her. He admires her professional ability. But then I throw these thoughts in, and before you know it he is doubting himself and his feelings towards her. Also once he starts listening to me, there is no more fun for him anymore. That is what happened at the ski cabin."

"Why shouldn't he have fun?"

"When you have too much fun, you forget what life is really about. It's a burden. Sooner or later everybody has to see that. I helped Art see that sooner. Besides, when he has fun he forgets about me."

Veronica came across as blatantly, almost naively, self-centered, but she was not hostile. She agreed to take up the dialogue at our next session. When she moved back and Art came forward, he remembered everything that had happened during the session.

162

When we next got together, Art and I talked for a while about his relationship with his mother as he was growing up. She had always been heavily possessive and when he entered puberty, she became even more watchful, pointing out the dangers of liking girls too much. They were living in a small town then, so Veronica easily kept her finger on every aspect of Art's social life.

At the same time, she tied Art to her with the double bond of closeness and conflict. Even into his teen years, Veronica would call him into her bed after her husband had left for work. There she would stroke and tease him, creating a high pitch of sexual agitation. Later in the day, however, she would often yell at him about some mishap or other and hit him with kitchen utensils as she chased him around the house.

At the very time when Art should have become more independent of his family, Veronica's tactics helped maintain her position as the central figure in his life. It was with great relief that he finally left home to study in a boarding high school, a step which seemed to Art to be his first chance to develop a mind of his own. Unfortunately, by now the inner possessive bond with his mother was so powerful that it severely limited any independence. This became clear in Art's first serious love relationship—that with Elaine. While courting her, he became consciously aware of an inner voice that spoke distinctly and forcefully, addressing its comments directly to him. It operated most powerfully during the periods of "inner storm."

Elaine was given special attention. Hardly anything she did escaped comment from the voice. As the couple moved towards marriage, the inner complaints grew. After they were wed, the complaints continued, contributing significantly to the trouble that developed between them.

As Art reflected upon things now, he was convinced that the inner voice was indeed his possessive mother at work in him. He was now more determined than ever to bring the matter to a complete resolution.

From the beginning Veronica admitted that in fact she possessed Art. She thought that was the way things should be between a mother and son. Now I asked her in session if she thought such a state of affairs could really be good for either Art or herself. Incredible as it seemed, she had never really considered that question before but as she reflected upon it, her attitude began to change.

She had to admit that it might not be so good for Art after all.

Taking the fun out of his life and blocking him from any significant relationship—even friendships—did not, upon consideration, seem like something he would appreciate her for. She had done these things "automatically," thinking they were "for his own good." In this she had simply been doing what was traditional in her own family. But in thinking about it now she admitted the approach might be wrong.

Also, Veronica started to recognize the effect that the possession of Art was having on her own life, tying up as it did a whole large block of her personal energy. She began speaking of a "Veronica here" with Art and a "Veronica in Detroit," the latter leading quite a drab and boring life. It now dawned on "Veronica here" that perhaps if she paid less attention to Art and more to "Veronica in Detroit" things would be different. This came to her as a revelation and she immediately wanted to see if her hunch was true. So we set up an experiment in which she would start spending more and more time with "Veronica in Detroit" and less and less with Art.

Once this point had been reached in the therapy, things moved steadily towards a resolution. Art noticed that he was hearing less from the inner voice. And even when it was there, he said, it seemed to have lost most of its punch. To all appearances, Veronica seemed to be withdrawing her energy from Art.

As this happened Art was surprised to find that he missed the voice, even the carping and the inner arguments where he would oppose reality and reason to the voice's pettiness and irrationality. He now came to realize what his own important part had been in preserving his neurotic state of possession:

> I saw why *I* allowed those thoughts to go on. They served as a buffer, a way of removing myself from people and from the challenges of life. Those thoughts produced a kind of narcissism in which I became so involved with the action inside of me that I could hardly become engaged in life. It was a way to elude pain and upset and to avoid taking chances. Also it was a way of my not having to admit *my own* feelings about things, a way of avoiding facing *my own* irrationality. Really my mother served as a very convenient buffer against life.

While we were doing the work, Art's mother in Detroit had an operation to remove a cancerous growth of a serious type. I asked "Veronica here" about this and she realized that through her concentration on Art, she had robbed "Veronica in Detroit" of essential vitality. She thought refocusing her attention on her own life might help that.

Here the therapeutic work with Veronica ended. There had not been a dramatic departure of the possessing entity, simply the gradual shifting of the center of gravity from host to self. And the inner voice that had plagued Art for more than ten years had ceased.

I then did a short piece of intensive therapy with Art himself, after which his life began to change dramatically. He now felt ready to enter into the marriage he had been contemplating. In addition, he found his professional life taking a new creative turn, as he embarked on some original research which would bring him broad recognition in his field.

Art also changed in the way he related to his peers. Those who had known him up to this point generally considered him a charming but nonchallenging kind of individual. Now he became much more questioning of people and situations, a transformation which affected both his professional and his personal life. Some who had felt comfortable with the old Art became uneasy with the new one. But on the whole, Art's friends soon welcomed his new assertiveness, and found him a much more interesting person for it.

There was also a remarkable change in Art's mother. Up to the time of the sessions she had been deteriorating physically and emotionally, apparently withdrawing from life. It even seemed that the discovery of cancer might signal the end for her. But after the work with "Veronica here," she started to really come into her own, gradually gathering strength and vitality to the point of being more engaged with people and life than Art ever remembered. She seemed to have gained the proverbial "new lease" on life.

Art gave this piece of therapeutic work its direction. After more than ten years of hearing the inner voice he decided that something had to be done and he had a clear idea of how to do it. For the most part, I simply followed his lead. The resulting changes in Art seem to amply justify the tack taken.

As for Veronica, the improvements in her life started around the time the work with her was completed. Such an alteration could also be attributed to a spontaneous transformation in the face of a life-threatening crisis—the cancer. It is impossible to know for certain. But the possibility of a direct link between the therapeutic work and her improvement is an intriguing one.

A Second Chance

In my work I have frequently come across cases in which a parent regards one particular child in the family as his or her second chance at life. That child is "going to do it right" and fulfill the parent's unrealized personal hopes. As the child grows, the parent makes more and more claims on its life, trying to steer it in predetermined paths. The parent feels justified in doing this, working upon the unspoken assumption that the child is the parent's possession. That intrusion may reach the point where the child truly does appear to be possessed by the parent. The following case illustrates this kind of possession by the living.

Colleen was a young woman in her mid-twenties whose life had not yet taken off. She worked as a graphic artist for a large advertising firm and showed signs of real talent. Yet her performance was lackluster, and she was not progressing in the firm as she knew she could.

Her difficulties at work were compounded by problems with some colleagues. There were a few bright young women who had just come on the job, bringing fresh energy to the work atmosphere. Compared to them, Colleen felt drab and slow. These young women naturally gravitated toward each other and soon formed a clique from which Colleen felt excluded, as much by her own poor opinion of herself as by any rejection on their part. The result was that going to work each day became a misery for Colleen. Colleen's frustration extended beyond her work situation and into other areas of her life. Her attempts to develop her own personal artistic projects were also unsuccessful. She could not seem to find the necessary energy for the consistent effort required, and felt only a numbing passivity.

Between Colleen and her mother there existed an unnatural bond. Her mother lived some two hundred miles away and had no contact at all with the people and situations of Colleen's daily life. Yet her frequent letters were full of allusions which indicated that on an unconscious level, she knew exactly what was taking place in Colleen's life. She was particularly alert to any developments in her daughter's love life. Colleen felt that no matter how carefully she safeguarded information, her mother was aware of all that was happening.

There was, for instance, the time when Colleen had just broken up with a young man and was in a state of grief over the ending

166

of the relationship. Her mother, who consciously knew nothing of the affair, sent Colleen a condolence card with the message crossed out, accompanied by an apology that she did not have any other paper to write her letter on. The front of the card depicted a dark-haired Jesus with an uncanny resemblance to the young man for whom Colleen was grieving.

When her mother spoke of her own life, the effect was depression. She filled her correspondence with news of death and disease. This morbid interest greatly distressed Colleen because she saw in it a sign that her mother was not interested in life. It seemed that she had given up on herself.

I had been working with Colleen for some time when she spoke of a dream that was to lead us in a new therapeutic direction:

> I am at home. My older sister Connie is worried because mother wants to take over her room. I say: "Fine; trade rooms and take mother's room; it's much nicer." Connie says no. She says that what she means is that mother wants to take over something that is in Connie's room—a mahogany chest. I asked Connie if she likes the chest. She says: "It is a very lovely chest, but it needs to be exorcised."

When I asked Colleen what associations she had with the dream, she said that the chest made her think of her mother, that it was actually one that belonged to her mother. It was a heavy, beautiful old chest in which extra blankets were stored. Colleen also connected it with her own body, her own chest. She said she was aware of a continual feeling of heaviness there. Her mother herself seemed to be present in her chest and needed to be got out.

In the next session Colleen brought in another dream:

> I have to move to a new apartment. I have dark heavy furniture, and an awful lot of stuff. But everything is backwards. I have my double bed in the living room and a very ugly copper gothic chest of shelves and drawers that hold a lot in my bedroom. I realize that I never use the bedroom and I haven't been in there for months. My couch is in there and it pulls out into a double bed. A girlfriend tells me to take some time and move the furniture around and get rid of the ugly chest. I know I'll regret that because it holds so much. I figure out how to arrange the chairs in a nice cozy way. Then I realize that all the furniture will need to be rearranged. It's a scary feeling, but I know she's

right. There's no reason why the bed can't go in the bedroom and the couch in the living room.

From this dream, it was clear to Colleen that some serious work had to be done; it indicated that she knew there must be big changes, yet was frightened by them. The reference once more to a chest tied this dream to the previous one, making it seem her mother was the source of the problem.

At this point I asked Colleen to let herself relax so as to make further connections with the dream. She said she felt the heaviness in her chest represented her mother so burdened, so unhappy with her own life. Colleen referred again to her mother's uncanny ability to know everything that was happening in *her* life, and felt that she was actually with her, present in her chest. Colleen believed she could sense all of her mother's thoughts and feelings, and describe them for her. I suggested that she go ahead and do that, and soon, I seemed to be speaking with her mother.

Colleen's mother, Doris, began talking about her feelings of unhappiness. She spoke without hesitation, though slowly, conveying a sense of sullenness and self-preoccupation. She seemed to feel that her life had not amounted to much and never would. As far as she was concerned, it was over.

Then Doris spoke about Colleen. She wanted her daughter to marry and be "happy," to have children and be the perfect mother. She had kept her eye on the men in Colleen's life, and knew all about her boyfriends. Doris said she had remained in the background, while continually applying internal pressure on Colleen to find the "right" man, get married, and be the kind of wife and mother *she* had never been able to be.

As she talked, it became clear that Doris saw in Colleen, her last-born child, a chance to live life again. Through Colleen, she could undo her mistakes and develop the talents she had neglected.

Now we could see the meaning of the two dreams more clearly. Colleen's mother was "residing" in her chest. She needed to be exorcised. Colleen's heavy, dark furniture was the mass of heavy, depressed feelings her mother had about life.

In succeeding sessions I continued to speak with Doris, learning why she was so disillusioned with her own life and so driven to live through Colleen. Doris felt particularly guilty about her children. Because of her husband's powerful influence, she had never been able to have much effect on their upbringing. One son had been permanently institutionalized because of a severe mental disturbance and Doris, keenly aware of her shortcomings as his mother, had been unable to forgive herself.

Doris had tried to be a good mother, investing a great deal of creativity in making a home. As a young woman, she had shown considerable writing and painting talent but had not been able to use these gifts directly while her children were growing up. Then, when her days of raising a family were over, she could not make the transition to a new way of life. Instead of developing her potential as a writer, she remained unhealthily involved with her children. She grieved for her disturbed son, and relied on Colleen as her second chance to correct the failings of her marriage.

My work with Doris had two phases. The first was letting her talk about her marriage and family. She had to make a clean breast of it and squarely face her guilt. As she did so, she began to feel relief. The second phase had to do with having her withdraw her attention from Colleen to focus it on her own life and talents. Once she had forgiven herself, she no longer felt the need to relive her life through Colleen. I spoke to Doris about Colleen's admiration of her talents as a writer, pointing out that now was an opportunity for her to cultivate those gifts which she had put aside when she first married.

From that point on, Doris spoke more often about her love of writing, and how she might resume this interest. As she turned her attention to this, she became less and less involved with Colleen. At the same time her voice took on more energy, and the pervasive feeling of passivity and heavy-heartedness left her.

The resolution of the possession state was not dramatic—simply a gradual withdrawal of attention from Colleen and an investment of that attention elsewhere. The series of sessions ended with Doris taking charge of her life and leaving Colleen to lead her own.

Shortly after this work had come to an end, Colleen told me about a letter which had just arrived from her mother, its tone fresh and optimistic. Doris not only addressed Colleen as an independent person, rather than an extension of herself, but she showed no signs of her wonted psychic awareness of the events of Colleen's life. In fact, she did not seem interested in them.

Through the work with Doris, it became evident just how many of her mother's feelings and attitudes towards life Colleen had been harboring. She had always seen herself as a drudge, passive and uninteresting, believing that life held little promise for her. Now,

169

Colleen's feelings changed, both about herself and about other women. In her own words:

> As a result of the work, I let go of a lot of the resentment I felt towards other women. I didn't any longer feel like a loser compared with them, and was able, for example, to form very good, very warm relationships with two of the women at my job. I had felt horrible and desperate around them before. They seemed like princesses—lovely, creative, independent. I was a drudge. As I overcame these feelings, they began to see me differently. One of them recommended a whole restructuring of our jobs so that I could have a freer hand in artistic productions, do much more creative work, and give up my joe-jobs. Of course, this took months to effect. But I don't believe it would have happened at all without the therapeutic work. Because of the therapy this woman felt much more positive about me and my potential.

Another result was that Colleen lost weight and became more energetic. She began developing her own personal artistic projects, and started to really believe in her future.

In the year and a half since the work was done, Doris has grown even more active socially. The last time Colleen visited her mother, she was astonished to find a vitality that she'd never seen before. Looking back upon the process which took place in the sessions, Colleen remarked:

> What happened was that my mother took her energies back into her own life. The main thing was her being able to talk about her children, her coming to feel that she had done her best and that she was really on her own a lot of the time. She came to accept what had happened. And she realized that it is never too late to make something of your life and enjoy it. . . .

The striking changes in both possessed and possessor after a few sessions of work indicate that the approach used was the right one. The possibility that the living possessor seemed to be immediately affected by therapy taking place two hundred miles from her home seems amazing to me. Unlike the previous case in which the mother had contracted cancer and might be expected to undergo some life change, there was nothing known to be happening in Doris's life which might account for the transformation. Was Doris then really present in Colleen, and did the therapeutic work bring about the changes? That question remains unanswered in this remarkable case.

Chapter 11

Group-Mind Possession

GROUP-MIND

As mentioned in Chapter 5, a group-mind is a collective psychic entity formed when a number of individuals come together to concentrate on a particular idea or task. It functions as a living organism with a mental/emotional life of its own. The quality of thought and feeling of the group-mind may be quite different from that of its members taken individually. Once formed it is strengthened every time the members come together. Its attitudes strongly influence each of them, even when the group is not assembled.

The family is an example of a naturally formed group-mind with its own peculiar characteristics which have been built up over the generations. Its influence on its members is extraordinarily powerful and when so direct as to periodically overshadow the individual and take control of his responses, we may term this group-mind possession.

The first part of this chapter contains a description of two instances of family group-mind possession and treatment. The second part sets forth an unusual case of possession by an individual who seemed to be spokesman for a family tradition.

THE WAY OF THE GROUP-MIND

Group-mind is a common phenomenon which everyone may experience daily in some way. If part of a working staff, the individual will feel the force of that unit's group-mind. If his job is within a large corporation, he will sense its group-mind's mental/emotional attitudes. As he reads the newspaper he will be impressed with how the group-mind of his country helps to shape his own mind about social and political issues. At a sports event he will sense the power of a crowd's group-mind. But nowhere will he feel the effects of group-mind more strongly than from his own family organism.

Group-mind influences are not necessarily bad. A family group-mind may embody a great deal of accumulated practical wisdom. Its attitudes may provide a valuable framework within which to respond to events.

But if the influence of the family group-mind becomes tyrannical, the individual may find himself its unthinking spokesman. Where that attitude is a negative or destructive one, the individual is in trouble.

Marg came from a very clannish East European family with a powerful negative attitude towards life. She was herself a lively, energetic young woman with a great sense of humor. At times, however, she would feel "something" descend upon her, like a "dark cloud," engulfing her in feelings of despair. This would quickly evolve into an overwhelming hatred that could be directed towards anyone. In this mood she felt possessed by some external agency, with thoughts and attitudes not her own in the ascendancy. To some degree she could watch what was happening from the out-side—at least to the extent of knowing that "it" was happening to her again and that she was losing both her usual sense of herself and her own feeling about life. This "cloud" would stay with her for varying lengths of time and eventually dissipate. She would then be her old self again and much relieved to be back in charge.

As we talked about this phenomenon, it became clear that the attitudes Marg evinced during these episodes were identical with the negative qualities of her family's general character. Their chief characteristics were distrust and lack of hope. Life was a burden, hard and heavy. One could not expect to be successful. One could particularly not expect to be happy. This hopelessness was accompanied by an attitude of distrust, first for everyone outside the family: those from a different ethnic group could not be trusted because their ways were different; those from the same ethnic group especially could not be trusted because their ways were the *same.* When not engaged in hostility towards those outside the family, the members concentrated on attacking each other, in-vesting much energy in helping prove the family maxim that no one could get ahead in life.

This attitude was not constantly in operation but it asserted itself in all the crucial matters of life and could thus be considered basic to Marg's ancestral family group-mind. If anyone attempted to free himself from its grip, that grip would be tightened. This was what was happening to Marg, particularly when trying to expand her life and open herself up to broader influences and new situations. At these times, her depressed, hateful attitude was typical of her family.

Therapy for Marg's condition had two main aspects. The first was ordinary psychotherapy, which dealt with attitudes formed early in life and neurotic ties with individual members of her family. The second was the replacement of the negative group-mind with a present experience of a positive group-mind. Experience had shown that if one dealt only with the problematic attitudes, relief was only temporary; the power of the family group-mind would soon enough assert itself again. Marg simply had not yet developed a strong "mind of her own." She needed a surrounding positive influence to counter that of the family group-mind.

The latter was provided by introducing Marg to a household where optimism prevailed and people were well disposed towards each other. Marg began to spend time with this family and as she did, I could see the influence of her own family group-mind diminish. In the process she was growing stronger. Marg eventually married and established a home of her own—another positive stage in her development.

Marg is an example of the type of person who is particularly vulnerable to influence from those around her. Because her particular family group-mind was the first influence in her life, the effect upon her development as an individual was devastating. Yet Marg's vulnerability was a helpful factor in her therapy, the moment a positive group situation became available to her. There she could relax sufficiently to find her own mind and become an established individual.

Maria's case was somewhat different. Her background was Italian. Embedded in her family history were many deeds of cruelty and even crimes of violence. There were also instances of insanity in close relatives. Among many of those who maintained their mental balance was the sense of being unable to get anywhere in their lives.

I became involved in Maria's therapy upon invitation from her regular psychotherapist. She had barely survived a very serious suicide attempt and was now in a state of agitation alternating with indifference. She had felt suicidal often before in her life, but this time had undertaken to kill herself in a state of calm determination, acting without feeling. She felt guided by the firm mental intention of doing away with herself.

Like Marg, Maria spoke of the sensation of being taken over by an external force that did not even seem to be personal. Maria—again like Marg—felt the force come upon her like a "black cloud" which seemed to obliterate all light.

The intruding black force embodied hatred and violence and exuded a sense of contempt for women. It seemed to be the precise manifestation of Maria's family group-mind, especially in the latter trait.

When it took possession of her, everything about Maria changed. Usually a bright, lively young woman, she would become completely negative. The suicidal impulse seemed to emanate from this thing, turning its innate hatred for women against Maria herself. (In male members of the family, the group-mind prompted violence towards the women; in the female members, violence towards self.)

In addition, Maria was addicted to certain drugs, which she would use to obliterate her feelings of misery. This made her situation dangerous, for the drugs were her means of destruction when in a suicidal state.

Maria's therapist and I knew we must act quickly to help her and hit upon the idea of using a visualization technique calculated to counter the influence of the black cloud. A group of people would get together with Maria, enter into a meditative state and visualize bright white light surrounding her and shielding her from the blackness. The white light represented love and positive power and meant that the energy of the whole group was mobilized and directed towards Maria, supporting and strengthening her.

Though Maria felt fortified after each group and in touch with her "true self," the effects were not long lasting. At this time, her addiction would sooner or later drive her back to narcotics, losing for her the positive effects of the group work.

Some years later I spoke with Maria about the treatment that we had used. At this point, she was involved in an intense detoxification regime for her drug addiction and felt she was well on the way to overcoming her problem. Looking back on our work, she stated her belief that it had prevented her from attempting suicide again. Now, as she said, "I'm still around and can do something about the drugs."

As for what can be said about the inner nature of her experience and the methods used to help her, I do not feel prepared to give a final answer. Whatever interpretation one might want to give to such elements as "black clouds" and "white light," it seems to be productive to treat them on their own terms and accept the positive results that accrue.

THE FAMILY SPRITE

I closed the door behind Mike Doan as he left the session. Turning to Catherine, his therapist, I asked, "What have we got here?"

"I don't know what to make of it," she answered, looking both puzzled and amused.

We had been working a number of sessions with Mike in connection with his feelings towards his mother, when we were suddenly confronted by an elflike character with a strong Irish brogue who called himself "Shamus." Speaking "through" Mike (who was in a state of deep relaxation), he had such charm and wit that Catherine and I were soon enthralled by him.

Shamus made a few very humorous remarks about Mike, and his family and some of Mike's recent activities. His Irish accent and peculiar phrasing sometimes made him difficult to follow. Truly one with the "gift of the gab," he gave every indication that he had not been able to exercise it lately.

That was Shamus's first appearance. In the next session, the insights about Mike's family history continued to flow freely but when we questioned Shamus about himself, he indicated that "they" wouldn't let him talk. He showed a marked fear about going any further but we persisted with our questions, and he began to loosen up.

I asked, "Who are these people you are so afraid of?"

"Ah, it's the women," Shamus answered. "They have the power. They tell me to say nothing. They say it must all be kept in the darkness."

"Who are these women? Where are they?"

"They're all around here. Surely you see them. They are in the darkness. If I talk, they say the devil will get me; they'll see to that."

We tried to find out who these "women" might be and as Shamus slowly and reluctantly began to yield to our questioning about them, he revealed his own antiquity. The women, it seems, were the

175

ancestral women of Mike's family line. They were the guardians of the family secrets and the custodians of the family tradition, keeping each generation in line and making sure no outside influences for change penetrated the family core.

At the time of this work with Mike, the concept of guardians of family tradition was unknown to me. But about a year later I came across a fascinating statement by Dr. Titus Bull (whom I have already mentioned in Chapter 8) in an obscure pamphlet called *Analysis of Unusual Experiences in Healing* (1932). Writing from his own clinical experience with disturbed individuals, Dr. Bull, Director of Research for the James H. Hyslop Foundation, claimed that the thoughts of departed ancestors can influence the mind of a living family member:

> In other words, some departed ancestors attempt to mold the lives of those incarnated who are akin. Their right to do so is never questioned. It is bred within them. It is the right . . . which family ties have engendered and can do great harm and injustice to the victims.

Dr. Bull further asserts that this ancestral mental influence can in some cases become outright possession:

> The primary obsessor [possessor] in this case would likely be one who claimed the right by ties of blood, who had no desire to do anything but keep the mortal in line with family ideals.

There is one "primary" possessor, and other departed family members may exert their influence on the victim through him. In Mike's case, Shamus would seem to have been the primary possessor, and the women those who exerted their influence through him.

It was clear to us that he was certainly vulnerable to the suggestion of the women. And, as we began to observe, he did contribute to preserving the traditional family mentality in Mike.

Shamus, it turned out, had been subject to the power of these guardian women for a long, long time. How long, he was not sure, but his personal memories went back through many generations, and he also seemed knowledgeable about family history prior to his own life. Shamus was a kind of family chronicler who had witnessed the fateful unfolding of many generations.

I had never before encountered a sort of *family sprite* entity, by which I mean that Shamus had his own definite personality but at the same time embodied the spirit of the family. The notion of a being who observed the comings and goings of a family's generations, who could remain in existence within some family member in each, was new to me. I knew of no reference to such an entity in the literature of possession, multiple personality or hysteria. Though I would later stumble upon a similar entity in a member of another Irish family, at the time of Shamus's first appearance, I had no comparison.

Nevertheless Catherine and I realized that we must first deal with Shamus's fear of the women. We pointed out that of themselves, they were not powerful, but depended on his terror of them. We suggested he use the simple white light technique of imagination to protect himself against them. When he did so, he felt a considerable lessening of fear and we were able to continue.

As he grew more confident, Shamus revealed more and more about the family history, with its cycles of fortune and misfortune. Its early history had apparently been one of prosperity and success, the family behaving with magnanimity towards their neighbors who, in turn, held them in high esteem. Next came a period of rising avariciousness among the women of the family, their former generosity replaced by a narrow, grasping attitude which led to downfall and poverty. The men blamed the women for this outcome. Their resentment grew and one day their pent-up rage broke out in terrible sexual violence. They first stormed the church (their "holy mother") and desecrated a statue of the Virgin Mary. Then they attacked the women with a frenzy and subjected them to violent sexual humiliation. The children witnessed this crazed scene and were severely affected. When it was all over, the men were overwhelmed with guilt. From that time they looked upon themselves and the whole family as cursed and expected the most severe punishment to ensue.

As Shamus told it, the punishment did follow, largely self-inflicted by the men of each generation after that. Though the violent event was soon erased from the conscious memory of the family, it left in its wake the feeling that they were fated. Tragedy after tragedy occurred, and the Doans came to accept the curse as their lot without knowing how it came about in the first place.

Shamus brought out the memory of the family's day of violence with great difficulty. Not only had there been an unconscious conspiracy in the family to keep it in the "darkness," but Shamus himself had been alive at the time and a participant in the crazed violation of the women. As a result he carried a terrible guilt and believed he could never be forgiven.

Because Shamus seemed to identify with the family as a whole, his guilt was more than personal. When he was alive, he may have served as a *seannachie*—a story-teller who passes on family history and speaks with the wisdom of its tradition. When he died, he apparently succeeded in passing into a member of the next generation, thereby beginning a series of possessions. But with each new generation, Shamus passed on not only the traditional wisdom but also the family's sense of sinfulness. Because he promoted in the minds of his hosts a compulsion to self-destructive acts, he became an instrument of the family's bad fortune. Only by facing squarely his long-standing guilt could Shamus free both himself and the family from its self-fulfilling curse.

The final piece of work with Shamus accomplished just that. In the therapeutic process the memories came back and spilled out in an agony of regret. Once freed from his tie of guilt, he could cease inducing self-punishment in his host. After only a few more sessions Shamus left Mike and moved on to whatever phase was next for him.

Many months later I spoke to Mike about the experience. He told me he still did not fully understand it, though he knew it was something he had to go through.

"It was like a record in me that had to be played," he said. And when it was played out, Mike could respond to people more freely. In the past, he had found himself always bringing out the worst in the women in his life—fulfilling the traditional antipathy of his family group-mind. Between the completion of the work and the time I spoke to him, Mike had married, a step he believed possible as a result of the work with Shamus.

At the end of it all, Mike did not know what to make of the Shamus persona. Was he a real individual who had existed centuries ago as he claimed? Mike was not sure though some things favored the notion. For instance, when Shamus spoke through him, Mike felt as if he was standing off to the side, listening to someone else. Mike experienced him like a separate individual. He commented:

> I developed an affection for Shamus. I had a respect for him. He had a terrific sense of humor. . . . At times when I was very

depressed and feeling self-destructive, Shamus's energy and sense
of life prevented me from doing myself harm. . . .
Even as we are talking here I have a feeling Shamus is very
interested in the conversation. He is like an old friend who drops
by. This is the first time he has returned. He is listening. He
wants to see that we get the whole thing right.

I share Mike's questions about the independent reality of Shamus. While a therapist is doing this kind of casework, he must
accept things as they present themselves. That happens quite
naturally. During the work I had no difficulty in treating Shamus
like a being, distinct from my client Mike. Shamus "felt" like another
person. But as distance from the work increases, the doubts grow.
The evidence of the data has not changed but the passage of time
of itself makes the extraordinary more unbelievable. This appears
to be a universal experience. However, I think it would be a mistake
to believe that because the doubts grow one is moving closer to
the truth. Rather, what apparently happens is that time creates a
space within which the natural human tendency to discredit the
unusual has more room to work.

The question of Shamus's independent existence is an important
one. It is a question I will never be able to answer. But as far as
Mike's life goes, it is an irrelevant question. Mike's life is better
as a result of the work with Shamus. That is enough satisfaction
for both therapist and client.

Chapter 12

Possession Puzzles

This chapter includes some unusual cases of possession which do not fit neatly the principal categories of the foregoing. Although each contains puzzling elements, they nonetheless offer interesting perspectives on the possession phenomenon.

THE COACH

John Tandy, a colleague and friend, had been working for about a year with a young woman who was part of a group that had engaged my services as a therapist.

She now seemed to be undergoing a breakdown of some sort. His client was both talented and sensitive, but subject to attacks of extreme depression during which she would become very distrustful of everyone around her, including John himself. She would withdraw into a hard, protective shell which made communication with her nearly impossible; at the same time she would emit dark feelings of anger and contempt. John told me that she was now alternating between this closed state and attacks of utter panic which made her beg for help for her condition.

John had decided that the best way to treat her was to work intensively with her for a short period of time in a different setting; he thought The Willow, a country estate kept specifically for such projects, would be the ideal place. He was not sure how long this special treatment would take but stressed the urgency of the situation and asked me to join him and half dozen assistants there.

When I arrived at The Willow, the others were already there. Trudy, John's client, was seated at the kitchen table trying unsuccessfully to join in the general conversation. She was clearly in a state of terror. Her eyes shifted quickly from face to face as she rubbed one hand in the other. Periodically her whole body would tremble convulsively.

After we retired to the large room used for therapeutic work, John spoke about what Trudy had been going through. He said that he had asked me to join the project because I was acquainted with her through my work with her therapeutic group and might be able to provide a helpful perspective on her condition. As John talked, Trudy looked at me suspiciously. She had agreed to my being a part of the therapeutic project—even welcomed it—but now that we were all together and beginning to concentrate on her, her mood was shifting from vulnerable panic to contemptuous distrust. And judging from her expression, I was the person she considered the greatest threat.

When a group of people come together to work therapeutically with one individual, that person's disturbance often manifests itself more vividly than usual. The concentration of attention and energy upon the individual draws the symptoms forward. That was happening to Trudy now. As John talked and others responded, her face took on an expression of utter disdain, as though she had erected a powerful emotional barrier and was now daring anyone to try to penetrate it.

Luckily, however, her mood was still vacillating so that when I began to question her about what she was experiencing at that moment, she could respond. She said she was hearing words inside her mind, like a voice speaking to her. It was advising and coaching her, telling her to keep away from all these people—especially myself—and that we were liars. It said she must resist all feeling but that above all, she must keep her mind closed and not allow anything we were saying to reach her.

As Trudy spoke, I could feel two powerful warring forces within her: the contemptuous person in the voice, and a frightened young woman begging desperately for help—even now. Speaking to the latter, I asked Trudy to sit back and relax. I then suggested that rather than fighting the contemptuous voice within, she should allow it to speak freely. I said I believed she had been fighting it for a long time, but that approach had not been working. She had simply been getting worn down. I assured her that in the safe context of the therapeutic project she could let the voice speak without fear. After a few moments of inner struggle Trudy relaxed, and soon we were listening to "the voice."

"Leave the girl alone," it began. "She is in my control."

The voice was steady, almost quiet. It gave the impression of perfect self-confidence. It spoke with an utter lack of feeling.

As it continued, the voice assured us that it would do with Trudy as it wanted. There was to be absolutely no discussion. It did not care who we were. It did not care what happened to Trudy. It feared nothing. I attempted to taunt it, tried to get any kind of emotional response. But nothing made the least impression.

The peculiar feelingless quality of the voice was rather disconcerting to me because I could not sense in it any opening for exchange or discussion. In any previous possession work I had done, I'd always had the impression of making *contact* with the entity, even if only by being the object of its rage. There had always been some feeling that the entity and I had at least a common humanity that provided a basis for discussion. But this voice gave no such impression. I felt puzzled and a bit worried. What would I do if I could not establish any basis for communication? If the entity was beyond reach—if it operated on a basis different from that of common humanity, what could be done to free Trudy of its influence?

I decided that I must get it to tell me what it was and what purpose it had in being with Trudy. Perhaps it would show some opening.

"Who are you, anyway?" I asked.

"I am the one in control of the girl," it replied.

"Yes, but are you a person? Have you ever had a human life?"

"No."

"But where do you come from?"

"I've been around a long time. But I don't want to talk about this."

"What about Trudy? What are you doing with her?"

"I have my purposes. She does what I tell her to. She is useful."

"Do you have a name?"

"No."

"What am I going to call you?"

"You can call me 'the Coach'. After all, that is what I do."

"Well, listen, Coach. You are taking unfair advantage of Trudy. You are treating her like your property. This is cruel. You don't know what it is like to be used that way."

"I do know what it is like."

"What do you mean?" I asked. This seemed to be an opening. The Coach was a bit uneasy when he made that last statement. Some kind of vulnerability was showing through. "What do you mean?" I repeated.

"It seems as though there is someone after me."

"What are you, anyway? What is this thing that is after you?"

The Coach now admitted that he really did not know what he was. As I continued questioning him along the same lines, he became more accessible, finally agreeing to continue at another time. With that we ended the exchange, and I asked Trudy to come forward.

In talking about her subjective experience of the possession, Trudy revealed that just before she relaxed, she felt as if she were driving along a road. Suddenly it was as though a shock of electricity went through her and someone wrenched the wheel from her hands, pushing her out of the driver's position and saying, "Obviously she's going to botch things up. I'd better take over." From that point on she was like a nervous passenger; she had neither the strength to take back the wheel herself, nor any certainty of what the usurper would do with it. Upon reflection Trudy realized she had often experienced this but it had never before been vivid enough to come fully into consciousness.

Trudy said she had felt present through the whole exchange, but she was also aware of the Coach's thoughts as he was speaking. It was as though he had known her family for generations, but she felt his actual presence in her had begun when she was about two years old. Until now her awareness of him had only been subliminal.

Trudy also had a vivid impression of the "thing" which was threatening the Coach. She could feel his fear of this creature which seemed stronger than he and very dangerous. It did not seem to be human.

The Coach was a surprise to both John and me. Its discovery made it difficult to contemplate moving on to any other kind of therapeutic work, so we decided to leave the "retreat" of The Willow and carry on with this specific work in daily sessions back in the city. I agreed to help John as best I could since I had been involved in the initial confrontation with the Coach.

In the next session with Trudy, the Coach continued to talk about himself, first of all about the creature that was after him. He spoke of a feeling of wandering in "space." There he had encountered the dangerous creature which had been on his tail ever since. How he came to be wandering in space and for how long, he could not answer. But he remembered how he had taken over Trudy when she was little. This had given him a respite from his wanderings and had somehow provided protection from the threatening creature. But he could remember nothing of an existence before his wanderings.

We held a few more inconclusive sessions before the Coach had an experience that would open the way for all the work to follow. It began with a vision of a bush burning. As he watched it burn, it seemed to grow into a tree. Then he was drawn to the vision. There were burning buildings all around. The Coach then realized that he was himself being engulfed by fire. He was burning; he was going to die in the fire. A pair of arms came down and carried him away. But his body stayed in the fire.

Now the Coach realized for the first time that he had lived the life of a man. More emerged about the life in the form of impressions. He felt that he had left behind a wife when he died but that he had lived his life in great inner isolation and treated her very badly. He realized how much he loved her only when he was dying; he had had very little to do with her sexually. He felt he had not used his body well. There was the impression of impotence.

The Coach had a sense that all this had taken place in the eastern Mediterranean. (Trudy later looked at a map and pointed to an area near Antioch.) He had lived inland, in a very dry area. The Coach also had a vague memory of stealthily scaling a very thick wall with a group of men at night. He was not sure why.

This was the first of three lifetimes he would recall over the next few sessions. The second was less vivid and started with the feeling of being cut adrift and falling. As he fell he had the sensation of ripping into another world. This world was being deluged with water—not from above, as with rain, but from below. It was rising and covering everything. Water was crashing everywhere. Buildings were going under. He was aware of one building in particular. It had many arched windows without glass. That was the extent of his impressions.

The third lifetime was the most striking and significant of the three; its details unfolded in a series of visual impressions, sometimes accompanied with strong emotion.

It started with an image of a cobra's head. The cobra was guarding a woman. The setting was near India. (Trudy later pinpointed it as Burma.) He saw many people, most of them dark-skinned. There were large crowds. Then there was a switch to a set of people who were above the masses.

In the next scene the Coach could see a courtyard garden; the air was heavily scented and very humid. Lush vegetation grew all

around. There was a luxurious residence with many windows opening onto terraces. An important local ruler lived there. He had a
daughter.

There was another man whom the Coach felt to be himself. He
was a merchant—young, vigorous, very passionate—something of
a Don Juan. He was having a secret, forbidden affair with the ruler's
daughter. They had met often. Then one night, while they were
making love, he suddenly realized that she was no longer his. He
could see it in her eyes. Engulfed both by his sexual feelings and
by his rage, he seized her neck and began to strangle her. At this
point he blacked out.

He came to in a basement prison room. Though he could not
remember, he realized he must have killed his lover. Next there
was a brief trial or judgment. He felt great remorse for what he
had done, but there was no compassion for him.

He was knocked out again and regained consciousness in a pit.
He looked up to see faces lining its rim, jeering at him. Then he
saw a huge constrictor-type snake. After a waiting game the snake
seized him, encircling his body with its powerful coils. The Coach
blacked out from terror and left his body. He looked down upon
the gruesome scene. Death had actually come from a crushed
spine.

All through the description of this scene, the Coach was going
through agony. His screams were shattering, and went on inter-
mittently over a period of two hours.

When it was all finished, he felt he knew much more about
himself. He now felt like a person with a history. He believed he
had carried the feelings of betrayal (the girl's change of heart) and
guilt (for his murderous act) into the life where he had died in the
fire. His unresolved state had led to his wandering for centuries
in some misty, limbolike world—where he had come across the
dangerous creature. During that time of wandering he had forgotten
or deliberately blocked out all memory of having lived human lives,
so that by the time he got involved with Trudy's family, he was
operating instinctively. Having reclaimed his history, with its pain
and guilt, the Coach felt human again.

The work with the Coach was now basically finished. His state
of mind had altered so radically that he could express gratitude for
our assistance in finding himself. His attitude with Trudy had evolved
from domination to friendliness and during the final few sessions

he actually gave her some shrewd advice about the conduct of her personal affairs from which she profited greatly.

Trudy's own experience of these sessions was interesting. As she described it:

> Things came to me as pictures and feelings, not words. I was and was not connected with what was happening. *I* would experience it, but it was not *me* to whom the experiences belonged. I was like a record player playing the song.

Trudy said this experience of separation was especially noticeable when the terrifying snake pit incident was being recalled. During that session she cried and screamed continually. To the observer it was a racking experience. Yet, Trudy was herself partly observer:

> In that session of terror in which I could not stop crying, it was my body . . . crying. At the end I felt completely worn out, but it was more as if I had listened to somebody else going through something really upsetting. I felt separated from it. . . . It was more the way you would feel hearing something that had happened to a friend. From the power of it my chest hurt, but that was all. It was my body which was crying, but the tears were not mine.

Describing her early impressions of her connection with the Coach, Trudy would put it this way:

> It was like it gave me somebody to talk to. Not that I ever did talk consciously with him. . . . But there was a feeling of companionship. I was little and unhappy. I felt entirely alone, cut off from both my parents. I was open to any kind of companionship. He could take control. He could say, you do this and you do that. That's where he started coaching. But as a result I carried his burdened feelings. I felt heavy and sad.

As to what eventually happened to the Coach, Trudy saw it this way:

> There was never a feeling of departure, as though he went forever. It was much more like a friend whom you might see once in a while. But there was no more interference in my life or my feelings.

The main body of this work lasted approximately one month. When we started, Trudy was in a state of emotional breakdown. When we finished, she could carry on with her life very effectively. She felt much lighter and more optimistic. I observed in her a remarkable new openness. Although Trudy still had states of depression, anger and distrust, she never again exhibited that cold hardness that she could unpredictably show before. Previously, when she entered those encapsulated states, she was unapproachable. The condition seemed to have to just wear off. Now with a little effort, Trudy could always be reached. This alteration in her personality was permanent.

In the four years since this work was done, there was no recurrence of interference by the Coach and no further breakdown. Trudy says that her sense of lightness and feelings of optimism remain. She is now considered to be a dependable source of cheer and good feelings at her job and has also started to develop certain creative interests.

There is one further peculiar change. Throughout her life, Trudy had an utter terror of snakes. It significantly diminished after her recounting of the snake pit episode, and while she is still not a lover of snakes, she no longer goes into a state of paralysis at their mention, as she once did.

This case is full of puzzles. I find it difficult to arrive at a firm conclusion about the reality of the Coach and his various former lives. Trudy herself has never come down firmly on one side or the other of this question. At times she feels it was all an allegory of some inner transformation; at other times she feels there may be something more objectively factual about it.

I do know that our approach led to good results. By taking the Coach seriously and allowing him to tell his story like a real person, we helped prompt changes in Trudy that were beneficial and lasting. I am not confident that the inner settling which occurred as a result would otherwise have taken place.

HANS AND HORST

From the first time I met him, Charles struck me as a highly intelligent and sensitive young man. A writer by profession, he seemed to have strong intuitive power—a gift that proved to be a problem, for he often expected other people to show an equal awareness of the unconscious dimension of things. Not surprisingly, he frequently felt himself out of synch with the ordinary processes of everyday life and much of his therapy with me involved his coming to terms with his nearly clairvoyant perception of the world. He had to learn to distinguish clearly between the conscious and the unconscious workings of other people's minds.

I had been seeing Charles for some time. A good deal of the personal material to be dealt with concerned his mother's emotional smothering of him throughout his childhood. She had been the German war bride of a British serviceman whose business concerns took him away from their home in England for long periods of time. Charles, her first child, became the companion she longed for and this led to an emotional devouring of the boy and a strong love-hate dependency on his part.

During the course of his therapy Charles had at times mentioned fantasies, feelings or compulsions that were not easy to explain in terms of the family drama that was unfolding. Early in 1981 these odd remnants were becoming more and more of a preoccupation for Charles.

There were first of all a number of elements connected with World War II Germany. Most often repeated was Charles's experience of seeing a building with a particular architecture and slipping immediately into a "dreamy" state resembling a light trance. In that state he would "remember" having seen a similar building in Dresden, Germany, during the war. When this happened he would feel in danger of "losing control," of entering into another dimension of time and losing touch with his present self—a particularly frightening experience. He could not fathom how he, born years after the war ended, could have "memories" of that period. To his best recollection, these dreamy "feelings of familiarity" began when he was about eighteen.

Charles recalled too that as a child accompanying his mother on brief visits to her homeland, he would feel a terror of the train stations there. He also had a paralyzing fear of German officials who would board the trains asking for identification. We could discover nothing in his own or his mother's experiences in Germany to account for these reactions.

Very recently, Charles had been badly shaken by something else. Lying in bed one night, he had not yet fallen asleep and was quite alert when suddenly he heard the sound of marching jackboots. They seemed to be coming closer and closer. For all the world it was as though a troop of goose-stepping soldiers were tramping through his room. As the noise grew in volume, terror seized Charles who leapt up and looked all around his apartment trying to discover the source. He also checked the hall and the street, but could find nothing to explain what he had heard.

Other distressing symptoms were also growing more pronounced. For example, the fear of dying young had been plaguing Charles for some time but now it was haunting him day and night. He felt that death was imminent and that he would have to end his life without having accomplished anything really worthwhile. Another symptom was a sensation of pressure in the center of his chest—as though something were pushing physically from the inside, trying to get out.

Though Charles had for years accepted his odd experiences, some of which dated from his earliest childhood, as just part of life, it was clear that he could no longer tolerate the distress they were causing nor leave the puzzling questions they raised unanswered.

Charles believed that there was something in him on the verge of revealing itself. When he relaxed, thoughts would come to him that seemed to be bits of a story out of context. Strangely, they were in the German language. Although he had learned to speak a little German during his trips there with his mother, Charles was not very fluent. He had the impression, however, that whatever was going to be revealed would be in German. I knew a little German, but thought it best to bring in someone fluent to assist with the work. Charles agreed and so I asked Monica, a colleague who was born and raised in Germany and now working as a psychotherapist, to join us.

In the first session, I put Charles into a deeply relaxed state and told him to talk about whatever first came to him. He began talking about his latest experience of a "feeling of familiarity" and as he did so, had the urge to speak in German. I told him to go ahead and that Monica would ask him questions when appropriate.

Charles now began relating the life experiences of two separate individuals named Horst and Hans. He spoke in each case in the first person—sometimes as Horst and sometimes as Hans. The setting was wartime Germany. Over the next five sessions, the stories of their lives there in the 1940s unfolded. Typically, Charles would begin with some "memory" image that had spontaneously come to him during the previous few days. That would lead into a new section of the narrative.

Charles spoke entirely in German. According to Monica the form of the language was unusual, being fluent "high German" but with the accent of a local dialect. We could not explain this in terms of Charles's experience with the language.

After the work had been completed, I asked Charles to give a brief summary of the events of these two men's lives as he had described them in the sessions and I am inserting Charles's response here. Although written a year after the session took place, it still conveys something of the flavor of the work:

Horst was the stronger of the two. From Dresden, a Jew, son of an intellectual—in many ways, not much of a Jew at all. Family spoke German and didn't practice Jewish customs. A rather irreligious upbringing. During our sessions, I remember him as a frightened man, frightened of the times, of dying. It all happened in the mid-40s (1942–1945). Transported to a camp and then to Theresienstadt. He was something of a physical weakling. His father's influence had helped him get to Theresienstadt since he wouldn't have survived a work camp. [Theresienstadt was an internment camp for Jews, mainly artists and intellectuals; although considered by the Jews of the time to be less brutal than the others, it was in fact the scene of many atrocities.] He weakened there. He aged from late teens to early twenties during the experience. He kept to himself. He hated himself for not wanting to be a Jew. And on seeing others die, he felt frightened of death. Horst was shot in the head after collapsing while being forced to march along a railway track, and I remember it as the first moment of peace in years. In revealing Horst, I remember how vividly his dialect came to me. Also his feelings towards his father whom he did not particularly respect but who in the moments before death, he wanted. . . .

Hans was a naive young German from the south of the Sudetenland. He had a father, but his mother had died earlier. Hans worked as a guard on the railroad. His curiosity about the freight cars carrying Jews and others north finally got him stationed at Theresienstadt towards the end of the war. He was horrified and guilty but intellectualized about the necessity of it all and on being German. I remember him as always wanting to say, "I'm sorry for all of this." He knew Horst to see him in the camp, and Hans was part of the group that led them along the railway. It was Hans who went up to Horst and demanded and then pleaded that he get up. When Hans didn't shoot him, another older officer did. I don't know what happened to Hans but I have a vision of him snapping, running into the woods and himself being shot.

It took five sessions for Horst and Hans to tell their stories. As the narrative unfolded, Charles experienced a feeling of relief. Although he could not understand why or how Horst and Hans were present in him and speaking through him, he was not upset about that. It seemed enough that their stories were finally coming to light.

By making their stories known through Charles, both Hans and Horst came to terms with unresolved elements in their lives. The culmination of this resolution was the narrative of the death of Horst.

A young man with a great deal of artistic promise, Horst had had high hopes about his life. The events of the war destroyed those hopes. He feared death and when it came, did not want to admit that it was happening. He died but because he could not accept the fact, he seemed to be suspended in a limbo between the point of death and the afterdeath world. The work in these sessions brought about Horst's liberation from that state. He fully experienced his death through Charles and to his relief, discovered that it was not as bad as he had feared. Death had not annihilated him. Rather, at the moment of death, he experienced a sudden feeling of peace.

Hans, too, came to a personal resolution through Charles. As he spoke, he acknowledged his guilt about participating in the persecution of the Jews. He realized that his act of kindness to Horst in his last moments was atonement for his wrongdoings. Most important of all, he was able to forgive himself.

The completion of the work brought about some notable changes in Charles' life. He no longer had the fear of imminent or untimely death. He lost his preoccupation with details relating to wartime Germany and his compulsion as a writer to concentrate on the period. Now he began to write stories and plays about present issues.

Charles also noted the disappearance of a peculiar habit that had been with him since his early childhood. From the age of about two, he would always try to put things together in pairs—rocks on the beach, for example. This pairing activity was prominent in his life, eventually becoming a preoccupation to bring pairs of people together. While he would remain aloof from human interaction, he would study those around him and attempt to make couples of them. This habit completely disappeared after the work with Hans and Horst. Instead Charles found himself wanting to mix with people and develop much more of a social life. When he looked back, Charles related his obsession to the unconscious desire to bring Hans and Horst forth and resolve things between them.

A year after the last session with Hans and Horst I asked Charles what he thought about the experience. He said that, although he was very reluctant to admit it, he actually believed that Hans and Horst were real persons who existed when and where they said they did. He noted that there were both Jewish and German elements in his own background and that perhaps these men were attracted to him for that reason. Charles said that in any case he did not feel dogmatic about the explanation. He was simply interested in trying to make sense of an experience that did not seem to yield a conventional explanation.

The case of Hans and Horst is one of the more puzzling of my experience. It has some of the characteristics of a subconsciously elaborated "romance" such as those sometimes produced by mediums. But the comparison to this or other types of secretly incubated fantasy material breaks down. Such fantasy constructions are produced to fulfill some unconscious need and are signs of a hidden conflict.

The case of Hans and Horst has characteristics of a different kind of phenomenon—one that I have come across in a number of other cases. It seems best described as an "inner recording" that needs to be played out. The "inner recording" resides on some unconscious level deep within the individual and slowly works its way to the surface. Eventually it pushes at the gates of consciousness with an urgency that cannot be ignored. Once the inner recording has been played out through the consciousness, the individual feels a great sense of relief. Afterwards, changes take place in the individual's life and in Charles's case, they were striking and lasting.

A FORCE FROM BEYOND HUMAN EXPERIENCE

Marius had a doctorate in history, had taught in a university and at the time I first saw him, held a good position with a government health agency. He had a gift for astute socio-political analysis of current events. He was also an individual who inspired confidence and trust in people and had accordingly been appointed to an influ-

192

ential office in a large voluntary community organization. He was married and the father of a beautiful daughter. By all ordinary standards, he would have been considered fortunate.

But when Marius came into my office one particular December day he was a tortured man, dangerously near collapse. He believed he was on the verge of killing his wife. This was not a passing angry mood; he was deadly serious. He said he could feel no love for his wife; he experienced not the slightest compassion for her as a human being. All he wanted to do was to kill her with his bare hands, enjoying the satisfaction of seeing her die slowly and agonizingly.

Marius knew that he must not do it because of the consequences, but he could feel no sense of conscience about the matter. He felt driven by some relentless inner compulsion to see blood. He felt like an animal, engulfed by primitive impulses, oblivious to reason.

There had been warning signs over the previous year and a half of my therapy with Marius. Now and again there would be a flash of something extremely primitive and dark lurking in the background of his mind. For instance, he had dreamt of himself crouching in a crude hut, staring at strips of raw meat hanging to dry from the ceiling. He had another dream of dwelling among people who lived in shallow caves—like holes—in the hillside and wore animal skins for clothes. And there were dreams of ancient landscapes peopled with savages on the move through bitterly cold weather, looking for food. These dreams yielded little in terms of associations.

There was another dream—a very recent one—that haunted Marius. In it, he is going downstairs to his basement when he meets a man coming up. The man looks at him and Marius feels icy terror. Powerfully built, this stranger has an extremely primitive appearance. A few days after this dream Marius was checking a collection of coins he kept in his room and found that one had been removed from the box and placed on a shelf. He could find no explanation for this. About the same time he noticed that a window screen he had repaired had been torn in a very peculiar fashion. Again he could find no explanation. In a session following these occurrences, Marius went into a state of relaxation and heard a voice speaking from deep within himself saying that he (the voice) was the man he had met on the stairs in his dream. He was present inside him always and could come out any time he wanted to. To prove this, he had twice taken possession of Marius's body, first shifting the coins and next, tearing the screen. The possession had been so complete as to produce total amnesia in Marius. This man, whoever he was, claimed he was going to become more and more dominant.

Other signs of real trouble were the sudden urges Marius would feel to see blood, hear bones cracking and feel them crunching in his teeth. These impulses would come out of nowhere and as quickly disappeared—until recently. The desire for blood had suddenly escalated so that whenever Marius saw his wife, he wanted to rip her flesh with his teeth and crush her skull. He was in an extremely dangerous state.

I had known Marius for a number of years. He was a sensitive man with a capacity for great human sympathy and though he had a fiery disposition and could get very angry on occasion, this would quickly blow over.

I also knew that Marius truly loved his wife. But the murderous impulses he was now experiencing had suppressed that love. The humane aspects of his personality seemed to have been almost completely swept away, replaced by a frightening viciousness.

At the same time his state was trance-like: his eyes were glazed and he seemed like someone surrounded by a dense fog. When I spoke to him, the glazed look would clear somewhat and he would ask me to help him. Could I not do something to bring things to a head? He could not go on this way.

As we talked, I went back over his therapy in my mind. In his sessions and groups Marius had uncovered painful memories of sadistic treatment from his father. His mother had let him fend for himself in that situation, rather than try to protect him. Over the years he had resolved much; he had stopped hating his father, who was now dead, and was on good terms with his mother. So many things had been dealt with and yet here he was, ready to murder, his life on the verge of utter ruin. I could not account for his state in terms of any of the standard therapeutic frameworks.

Marius himself believed there was an entity present in him that had periodically taken him over and was now ready to possess him completely. Marius told me that the first time he ever sought therapeutic help (before I knew him) it was because he felt the existence of a monster inside.

As Marius continued to talk, it was clear how uncomfortable he felt with his own description. It seemed too fantastic to believe. He was describing an experience that amounted to possession by some kind of spirit—an entity with a mind of its own that had taken the form of the sinister man on the stairs. Since Marius was not a religious man in any conventional sense, the notion that a spiritual entity could take over his body and control his mind was not easy for him to accept. And yet that was what he was experiencing and he could not put it in any other terms.

Because of the urgency of the situation, a few days away from the city at The Willow, the country property available to us for special therapeutic work, seemed to be the answer.

I contacted five colleagues to assist with the project so that we could do intensive psychotherapeutic work, day and night, to get to the bottom of the disturbance. Marius knew them and felt he could be very open in their presence. It also seemed important to have several strong men involved because of the amount of violence seething just below the surface. Although Marius was a big man, I had never feared harm from him, even in his worst moments. But I knew that if violent feelings needed to be expressed, he would be inhibited in doing so unless he knew secure physical restraint was available. So about a week after that dramatic session in December, the seven of us set off for The Willow.

Among other things in that last session, Marius had spoken about something in him called "the Bear." Though it seemed to be an animal presence, nothing else was clear and I was puzzled by this reference. I had come to accept as a working hypothesis the notion of the sinister man possessing Marius, but the introduction of the Bear was a further complication.

From the beginning of our therapeutic project, Marius had strong ideas about how we should proceed. His picture of the Bear was clearer now and he believed it had to come out of him first. The sinister man would be next. Marius suggested that if he lay in front of a very hot wood fire and absorbed its healing warmth, he would be strengthened to the point of allowing the Bear to show itself. Once the Bear had revealed itself, it would leave.

That night we built a roaring fire in the fireplace and Marius lay in front of it, shirt off, absorbing the warmth and brightness. After about half an hour he began howling and tearing at the floor. This went on for another half hour. At the end of that time Marius relaxed and began talking. He said the Bear had emerged and had left him. He now knew more about it: that it *was* an animal and it was ancient. It had been killed long ago by a group of hunters who worshipped some evil force. Marius called them the "half-humans."

195

They had acted sadistically: Marius had a vivid impression of the scene when they found the Bear asleep in a cave, and attacked it with rocks and clubs and finally with fire. No matter how many of them the Bear killed, more came with fire sticks. He was twice their size and could clearly remember their bones cracking in his teeth as he killed them.

The Bear was made to die slowly and its spirit then went into one of the hunters and lived there, passing from father to son, down through generations, until it reached Marius. The Bear spirit was filled with feelings of rage and revenge but it was not evil. Its removal had not touched the source of evil that was torturing Marius. However, according to Marius, while the Bear was being tortured and killed all these generations ago, there was an entity—a "round hole in space"—suspended in the air nearby. It was feeding on the energy being released in the violence. The Bear sensed it, for it, too, had entered the hunter. The Bear spirit had been waiting all this time to avenge itself on this entity and this thing—whatever it was—had to be dealt with next.

The next morning, with Marius in a deeply relaxed state, I asked him to allow the evil thing inside of him to come forth and speak. Marius shuddered, his eyes flickered and he moaned a few times. Then his expression changed and an arrogant look came over his face. He began laughing, a low amused chuckle.

"This whole thing is laughable," he said, seeming to look around at us all, though his eyes were closed.

"What do you mean?" I asked.

"You are all pitiful children," he replied.

"Who are you? Are you Marius?"

"That is for you to find out—if you can."

Then he winced and said, "Stop with that light. I don't like it."

To give Marius a feeling of security for the work, I had arranged the six of us in a circle around him and had asked everyone to concentrate feelings of affection and support upon him in the form of "white light" protective energy. The entity was referring to this "light."

"No," I replied, "we will not stop the light. The light cannot harm you. And it is necessary for Marius."

The entity continued to argue about the light. It said the light burned. It begged that we stop it at least for a minute to let it have some rest. It threatened and cajoled, but we took no notice

196

of its arguments. Finally it gave up the dispute and we moved on to other things.

"Who are you?" I asked. "And where are you from?"

"My name is Morlac. I have always been."

"Have you no beginning?"

"No."

The entity went on to boast of its power and antiquity. It had been worshipped, it said, under various forms over the ages. It had been sacrificed to as a goat and a stag. It had fed off the life and energy of those who worshipped it. Its power derived from the fear and awe it inspired.

As we talked, it was clear that Marius was growing very exhausted. I brought the session to a close, asking that he take over his body once more. He came back slowly. When his mind was clear again I asked him what he remembered of the session. He had complete amnesia.

In the sessions that followed over the next three days we continued our confrontation with the entity. It was not human and could remember nothing of its beginnings—only that it claimed to have been worshipped by people, under various guises, for thousands of years. It detested affection and love but it prospered in an atmosphere of violence and fear. It had been a god for the hunters who killed the Bear and had come down the generations with it.

The entity described itself as a kind of "shimmering" in space, a sort of vortex, completely dark, with a "rim" of some kind. It needed the energy of other beings for nourishment. It considered itself to be totally superior to human beings and basically alien to this world but it felt helplessly imprisoned by the white light as we worked.

The therapeutic project ended after four days of steady work and we returned to Toronto with some concerns about what was to happen next. Clearly, the work was not finished. As the sessions had progressed during the project, the entity had seemed to become more cooperative but it was still there, and no one felt it could be trusted. We would have to continue our sessions in the same fashion.

As we proceeded, Marius began to retain a memory of what was taking place. Though for a long time he could not piece together a complete picture, he did sense the general tenor of exchanges. He attained complete recall only in the last few sessions.

After a number of city sessions, something new entered the work. The entity began to recall its origins. It realized it had come from some other place and had a history that preceded its Earth experiences, though it could not remember that history.

Then one day the entity realized something about itself: that it was not totally dark, as it had always thought; in fact, its "rim" had a tinge of light. From that point things moved quickly. The entity recognized that it did not have to fear the white light, that it had long ago in some other place lived in the light. Next came the recognition that it must leave the host it was possessing. At first the entity feared starvation without a victim to feed upon, but when it realized that the light would nourish it, it left.

By this time Marius was experiencing total recall of the material of the sessions. He felt tremendous relief at being free of the possession, but somewhat dazed and confused as well. As we talked it became clear that before anything else, he must set in order his badly shaken family life.

With the departure of the entity, Marius's feelings of love for his wife returned. We had a number of talks with both of them to help her understand what he had been going through. They re-established their neglected sex life and set about to build a future together.

Marius soon became involved in a business where he could invest his immense energy. He and his wife worked on it as partners and soon turned their enterprise into a striking success.

Marius's desires for violence and blood disappeared totally when the entity left. A year and a half after the project there has been no recurrence of the trouble. Marius looks upon the transformation of his life as truly remarkable and to this day, considers the project as the turning point of his life.

He does not try to convince anyone that what he experienced was real, for he does not know what to make of it himself. He knows only that this is how he experienced it. By our letting the experience speak for itself and following through as though it were real, his life was saved from ruin, and he has moved into a far more creative phase than any he had previously experienced.

But I cannot explain the phenomenon. Was there actually present some animal spirit called "the Bear?" Did a nonhuman entity with a sordid ancient history really take possession of this young man? I do not feel comfortable about answering either of these questions with an unqualified yes. Because the case seems so odd, I find myself reluctant even to write about it. The fact remains, however, that it occurred as I have described it (if anything, I have toned down some of the more dramatic elements of the experience) and the transformation of Marius's life was real. I believe that had I not taken seriously his description of what he was experiencing there would have been disastrous consequences. As a therapist, that is good enough for me. As a philosopher, I remain puzzled.

Chapter 13

A Note on Reincarnation

In cases of possession, as has been seen, the subject repeatedly emphasizes the alien quality of his experiences. The personality that is revealed is *not* perceived as himself. In contrast to the possession victim, the subject of reincarnation feels the central figure in the dramatization or memory definitely to be himself, although in another identity. Because the experiences of possession and reincarnation are not the same, this chapter is included here by way of a note. The examples given may, however, provide useful data for probing the central question posed throughout this book: the problem of the nature of human multiplicity.

Two Dreams

It sometimes happens in the course of therapy that a dream will be presented which the client experiences as having a quality entirely different from the usual. Though one may apply therapeutic analysis to it, that procedure turns out to be quite sterile. One ends up feeling that what is needed is not so much analysis as a new perspective on the client's inner life. The two dreams that are given here had that "different" feeling about them. Both of them appeared to be instances of reincarnation-type memories.

The first dream was that of a client named Darlene, a very astute therapeutic worker in her own right. She had the dream some years before my work with her. One day the dream came back to her in connection with certain therapeutic material. She then recounted it to me:

> I watch as a woman who lived many centuries ago keeps being reincarnated. It is like watching a book of her lives. She usually had a pin in her hair, a hat, or somewhere on her person in each of the scenes which pass before me. She is evil. Somewhere in

a previous life she had killed a child. This had to be avenged. A man was showing how this was to be done. If you looked straight into her eyes or held something there her face would show her guilt—it would blacken. Then she had to be stabbed. I believe this actually happened in the dream—in fact, it may have happened first and then the history of her lives flashed by. I remember clearly how in her lives certain things always repeated themselves. When she appeared in a room, for instance, it didn't matter whether the room was very primitive or more modern, *the basic structure was always the same.* The phrase remained with me very clearly when I awoke.

Darlene told me that the dream had an unusual feeling about it. It seemed like a good idea to let the meaning of the dream emerge from Darlene's own unconscious, so I asked her to relax and place herself back in the environment of the dream. She did so and found she was able to elaborate considerably on what she had first recounted. She said,

> I see the woman in the room. She is very distraught and keeps wringing her hands and pacing the floor. She is restless and upset. There is a large piano in the room and a photograph of a child on the piano. I can't make out who the child is or whether it is a boy or a girl, just that the child is fair-haired. . . . I can't see what the child died from, but I do have a feeling it was through some neglect of the woman.

Later, Darlene expanded further on the dream. There were two elements of continuity: the pin that the woman wore in different places in the various scenes or lives, and the room itself, the structure of which was always the same. This continuity of structure seemed a central point for Darlene. She was especially aware of one wall in the room that went through a number of transformations from life to life, being at one time plain stone, at another time plastered, and at yet another time finished and painted. She said she did not believe the wall was a particular physical structure that had existed, but rather a symbol. The significance of the symbol was that throughout the woman's various lifetimes, *her* basic structure was always the same. That is, it was always essentially the same self that was being reincarnated, although her physical and personal characteristics would vary.

The mention that the woman was evil did not imply that she was basically bad but referred to the evil deed she had perpetrated in killing the child. The evidence of that deed would show up in each lifetime—as symbolized by the blackening of the face. The fact that the woman would then have to be stabbed indicated that she could not escape her guilt. Retribution was demanded in lifetimes subsequent to her evil deed.

Darlene could see implications in the dream for her present life experiences. She could see the woman as herself. The dream had come to her mind when we were exploring her feelings of guilt concerning the handling of a child in her care. She had been drawn to help the child because he had seemed to be lost and in need of love and protection. She now believed it possible that she had become involved primarily to attempt to undo her former abuse of a child. Although she did not feel absolutely certain of this interpretation, it seemed plausible to her.

One further matter of interest. Darlene had always been fascinated with the piano though she had never taken lessons or learned to play. When she saw the woman pacing restlessly in the room, she noticed the piano and had the feeling the woman could play it. She thought that her desire to play the piano might have been connected with having had that skill in a previous lifetime.

Moving on from Darlene's experience, we find a somewhat different attitude in the second dream. While Darlene felt uncertain about the reincarnational aspect of her dream, another client, Ruth, who had the second dream, felt an inner conviction that a former lifetime was involved. Here is Ruth's dream:

> I was traveling in dank old trains through what appeared to be Eastern Europe with my sister. The atmosphere was furtive and shadowy. I arrived at a train station where I knew I was going to meet my death. Men who allegedly were allies were trying to kill me, and I was filled with a sense of inevitability, mingled with an unquestionable knowledge that I had already been through the experience and therefore knew precisely what was about to take place. The scene at the train station was crowded—people seemed homeless, confused and desperate. A bunch of us were herded into a large room with a high ceiling, where a film was going to be shown. Both I and my sister knew that this was a ploy to set up murder. I could see men at the back of the room loading up cannons and guns, and I was certain that they were getting prepared to kill me. As we waited for the film to begin,

my sister squeezed behind me and whispered that I should huddle close and tuck my body in front of hers so that the guns would have to go through her before they could kill me. Somehow we both knew that for some reason these men would not kill her and I would therefore be safe. The film ended, and as we left the room unharmed, I was puzzled—I had been certain that I was going to die there.

The scene switched and I was ushered into a small office or doctor's examination room. Immediately I knew that this was where I would die. The doctor in the office got up, came over to me and said in unconvincing sympathetic tones that I was gravely ill and my only hope for survival was a shot of serum he was about to give me. My sister, who was still with me, seemed to know that he was lying. We both knew he was about to kill me, but even attempting to escape was totally futile, so strong was the knowledge that there was no escape—that this was simply my fate. The man took a huge vial of yellow serum and shot it into my anus. I knew immediately that it was cyanide and very suddenly the whole scene looked like a film of a scientific experiment. I could see the poison traveling up through my spine and entering my bloodstream, and I watched it slowly kill me. I was conscious of dying.

The scene switched once again. I was still alive but the time period seemed modern and I appeared to be in North America. I was walking along a street with my lover feeling happy and somewhat carefree. I was aware of what I had been through. I said to my love, "You know, now I know that reincarnation really does exist." When he asked me how I knew this, I replied, "Because I watched myself die, and here I am."

Ruth told me that reincarnation had been an ongoing issue for her from the age of fourteen. She had felt drawn towards the idea but had never been convinced. The dream seemed to be the answer to her question. Her dream, like Darlene's, had the air of being "different" in quality from other dreams. The last section of the dream seemed very vivid to Ruth. Her sentiments in that episode were continued into waking life: now she knew that reincarnation really did exist.

Ruth's parents were Polish Jews. Although they had been in Poland during the Second World War, they had never been interned in concentration camps. The war nonetheless had made a deep impression upon them. Ruth was born many years after the war, but she could feel its shadow hanging over the family as a very

real influence. Was the dream the product of an unconscious synthesis of information and feelings she had absorbed from her parents about their wartime experiences mixed with her own subjective
material? Though she realized that one could make a case for that
theory, her intuition told her it was not so. She was convinced the
experience was what it claimed to be: a recounting, in somewhat
confused form, of real events in another lifetime which she had
lived.

When I asked Ruth whether she felt her present life had been
influenced by this earlier one, she said:

> Yes. The notion of reincarnation involves the belief that the soul
> chooses its parents. I feel I have something to work out with
> the parents I have. A lot of the work of my therapy has been to
> shake off the persecution, life-is-death attitude which character-
> izes my parents. I believe that in working with this attitude of
> my parents I was also dealing with my feelings from the lifetime
> described in the dream. . . .
> I have had a strong reaction to war all my life. As I was growing
> up, my awareness that war was going on in some part of the
> world would affect my ability to have fun. I would become aware
> of it and then would stop having a good time. I feel this is also
> related to that former life.

Neither of the two dreams described is very dramatic or striking.
To the outsider they are not convincing proof of the reality of
reincarnation. They do not contain compelling evidence that these
young women had indeed lived other lives. The dreamers themselves had two quite different attitudes on this score: Ruth was
sure her dream portrayed reincarnation; Darlene was not.

The value of the dreams—for our purposes—is not that they
provide some proof of reincarnation. It is that they are examples
of a type of experience of multiplicity which is fairly common. The
subject experiences himself as having in the past had one or more
personalities other than his present personality. The experience
of these alter personalities takes place within a dream or dreamlike
context, which has a "different feeling" from other experiences in
that state. The person may or may not end up convinced that those
other personalities are "real," but the dream experience stands
out in the subject's mind as unique.

In the following case the reincarnation-type experience was much
more vivid and detailed. Also, the apparent present-life effects

were more palpable. Because of its highly dramatic character, the case is more striking. Nonetheless it leaves unanswered the basic question of the reality of reincarnation.

A LEGACY OF GUILT

It sometimes happens that a client who has been involved in therapy for a time becomes unconsciously constrained by the framework that that therapy employs. If, for instance, the emphasis of the therapeutic work is upon pinpointing the emotional patterns of the client's early family life and seeing how those patterns are repeated in present neurotic reactions, it may become difficult for the client to discover other possible sources of present difficulties. However, should those built-in limitations on the client's imagination be removed, new avenues of exploration can be opened up. Such was the case with a young man I worked with some years back.

One day Will Davis, a colleague, invited me to sit in on some sessions with a client of his. Will had for some time felt there was an elusive element in this man's therapy that he had not been able to pinpoint. He thought that perhaps the two of us could better discover what it might be. I accepted his invitation. Will's client agreed to this arrangement and we set up a series of five sessions.

The client, Bob, had for years been plagued by a powerful feeling of guilt for which there was no definable object. This guilt could attach itself to any person or event in his life. But although the situation itself might eventually be resolved, the objectless feeling of guilt would always remain. Painstaking examination of Bob's life had yielded nothing to explain how such guilt could have originated. Bob was beginning to fear there was no answer. He thought he might have to resign himself to accepting this state of affairs as a fact of life. Will hoped this would not be the case.

In the first session Bob started to speak about what was most on his mind: a relationship between himself and a young woman, Susie, that had recently come to an end. There had been a great deal of good in the relationship and he was naturally feeling grief about the loss of that. But while they were involved, Susie had also become the object of Bob's haunting guilt. Now that things had ended, the combination of grief and guilt was very disturbing to Bob. He believed he was in danger of becoming bitter about Susie, and felt he had to do something about it.

Bob then went on to speak of other things, but later in the

205

session, in a state of deep relaxation, he returned to the matter of Susie. He felt his grief and guilt far exceeded anything justified by the events of their relationship. Although the feelings were directed toward Susie, he could not see how she could be their actual source. I asked if he could make any other connections with them. He said he could not. It seemed that we were up against the same dead end he had met so often before.

However, without realizing it, Bob had been searching for *specific types* of associations—those connected with childhood or adult traumatic experience. And he was coming up empty. I believed that if Bob could allow himself to move outside that usual therapeutic framework, we might be able to get somewhere. I asked him to see if he could discover any other associations with the feelings—anything whatsoever. He was silent for a while. Then he mentioned something new: "The feeling seems very ancient."

It seemed to me we had to follow any lead we could get, so I encouraged him to elaborate on that impression. "Let your imagination go," I suggested. "You say it seems ancient. Try to place yourself in its original setting."

Bob hesitated for a moment and then seemed to move into a more deeply relaxed state. When he did that, out poured a whole new set of impressions:

> I am watching a woman from a distance. It looks like she is a priestess of some sort. It seems like this is ancient Greece. We are in a temple. The priestess has her left hand on a column that comes about to the top of her thigh or slightly lower. She is dressed in a robe—white or very pale blue. She is full-breasted. I can't see her face.

Neither Will nor I understood what Bob was talking about. But we both thought he should be allowed to follow his train of images wherever they might lead. We asked him to continue.

> The priestess and I are on an island. It seems like there is a special relationship between us. There are many other people about. Now a group of soldiers comes to the island in a large military ship. They land and rush ashore. They move towards the temple, killing people as they go. I am crouching, waiting for them to enter the temple. They come in and seize the woman. They stab her through with a sword and the blood rushes out. She falls slowly, and as she does she transfixes me with her gaze. I feel an agony of grief—and guilt.

The reason for the guilt which he experienced here was then revealed:

> It seems that this woman had specially chosen me. I had been a slave to a Greek thief. She bought me and took me away to train me to help her in her work. She was teaching me how to be a magician or priest. But I wanted power. I wanted to hold her place and rule the island. So I made a pact with a political faction that they would deliver the island and her to me. But they wanted the island, so they killed her. I think I fainted. Perhaps I was killed too, but I don't think so. I think I became an outcast.

Then another scene came to Bob as he continued to relax:

> I am in a cave. It seems like the cave is in France in an early Christian period. It is the autumn of the year. A woman is standing in the center of the cave and I am a little distance from her. This is essentially the same woman as before. There are many people—men, women, children—standing around. Men rush into the cave. They are fanatical Christians. They hold on to me while they grab the woman and stab her. We had been engaged in a magical rite and were deeply connected when the stabbing took place. A shock goes through me when she is stabbed, as though what is happening to her is happening to me because of our connection. I feel tremendously guilty, like before.

Again the guilt. In this case the reason for the guilt was somewhat different. Bob continued:

> I was boasting to people about what we were doing in the cave. The woman had chosen me to be her priest and I was both happy and frightened about that. I bragged to people about what we were doing in the cave and this led to being discovered by the Christians. I was frightened about being her assistant and so felt somewhat relieved by her death. But I also felt grief-stricken and guilty.

In the next session Bob recovered more of this episode. It seems that when the Christians moved in on the group in the cave, they killed not only the woman, but also the participants in the rite who were standing around—men, women and children indiscriminately. Fires broke out in the cave as torches fell. Somehow Bob, in the personality of the woman's assistant, escaped and ran through the woods. He was eventually caught and killed. This was his description of what followed his capture:

> I am in what looks like a cell. Torturers come and take me out of the cell. I am strapped to a table and tortured. A red hot iron is thrust under my right rib cage. I am castrated and disemboweled while still alive. I don't seem to feel much pain. I am in shock. I am floating above and to the right of the table, watching what is being done to me.

All of these scenes were described with a great deal of emotion. Bob sometimes sobbed and moaned as he was speaking. He was particularly agonized at those points where he acknowledged his treachery, in one case, and his foolishness which led to the murder of the woman, in the other. Upon emerging from relaxation in the first session, Bob immediately associated the woman in both scenes with Susie. He felt that he had been connected with her in these other lifetimes and had, in his present life, carried the guilt of those former relationships.

It seemed that with the recounting of the French scene, the material was exhausted. Nothing more of significance was revealed in the three sessions that followed. Once the series of five sessions was over, I ended my involvement in Bob's therapy.

Some years later I had occasion to speak with Bob about those sessions and the effects they had had on him. I asked him if that objectless guilt had abated afterwards. He said that it had, and continued:

> Life got much lighter. From those sessions I understood why my life had been as it was. Now I was free. The knowledge freed me.

Bob told me that the realizations he reached at that time had made a great difference with regard to his life direction. He said:

> Before that time I would try one thing and then try another. Nothing would fall into place. Afterwards I was able to focus my efforts. The understanding of those other lifetimes did not of itself change everything. I still had to work to make things different. But that knowledge lifted the weight which had been on me, and I was able to move ahead.

Bob felt that he still had more to learn about his past lives. Since his first realizations, he had experienced spontaneous flashes of other connections from former lives. He hoped to be able to follow through on those flashes at some point.

Chapter 14

The Therapy

Over the years, I have discovered certain basic elements that tend to appear consistently in the course of therapeutic work with possession. These elements have proven themselves cohesive enough to justify speaking of a "therapy for possession." It was not possible, in describing some of the individual cases on which I have worked, to give an adequate outline of the main components of this therapy. For that reason, a separate treatment of the subject seems in order.

I must emphasize once again that my experience with possession cases is principally of the type involving possession by human beings— usually related to the victim by blood—and possession by family group-minds. I have already described the principles for treatment of group-mind possession. What follows, therefore, is an exposition of therapy for cases of possession by human spirits, living and discarnate.

EXPLORATION

Possessed individuals frequently come to the therapist complaining of certain specific symptoms. Most frequent are: (1) hearing voices; (2) a sense of something alien residing in a specific location within the body; (3) a feeling of regularly not being oneself. When symptoms such as these are spoken of, the therapist might well undertake a period of exploration with the client to discover precisely where the work needs to be done.

The process of exploration involves four important steps: (1) exhaustion of conventional therapeutic possibilities; (2) alteration of the therapeutic expectation-framework; (3) amplification of weak signals; and (4) discovery of the elusive element. Each of these steps needs further elaboration.

EXHAUSTION OF CONVENTIONAL THERAPEUTIC POSSIBILITIES

Symptoms such as those described are not unfamiliar to the psychological worker and do not of themselves indicate a possession experience. For that reason, the first line of approach for the therapist must be to see if such symptoms are manifestations of well-known syndromes of mental disturbance. In most cases, such symptoms will yield to conventional psychological analysis. The condition is then cleared up by ordinary therapeutic means and there is no need to look further for explanations.

In the majority of cases on which I have worked, the client had already spent a fair length of time in some more conventional form of therapy. Therefore, this step did not take as long as it would in the case of someone who started without such background.

ALTERATION OF THE THERAPEUTIC EXPECTATION-FRAMEWORK

Although a conventional therapeutic approach will usually be sufficient, there are times when it does not produce the expected results. Despite the most assiduous application of the best techniques, the voices persist, the alien mass remains or the sense of not being oneself lingers. At that point one should consider altering the framework of expectation within which the therapeutic work is taking place. This suggestion requires a bit of explanation.

Every therapist has a certain theoretical/practical framework within which he approaches his cases. That framework will have been built up from a combination of factors—not the least of which is the original training received. It consists of a set of expectations about the type of material that the client will produce and the nature of the underlying causes that will be discovered. These expectations are influential in determining the way the therapist speaks to the client and the techniques he uses to elicit material from him. The expectation-framework serves a useful purpose in the therapeutic process. It brings to bear a tried and proven approach that represents decades of collective psychological wisdom together with the particular experience of the therapist himself. In that way, it gives a solid rule-of-thumb starting point for the therapy. But the expectation-framework also has a negative effect: it limits the imagination of both therapist and client in the therapeutic encounter.

When a client walks into the therapist's office and sits down, the expectation-framework of the therapist immediately comes into

211

play. It may never be explicitly spelled out, but the client soon senses what it is. He comes to recognize what the therapist is looking for, what type of material he believes important and what is irrelevant. The client automatically starts responding to that expectation-framework and, where his attitude is positive, produces the material that he believes will be useful for the therapeutic process while ignoring everything else. The client often becomes so immersed in the therapist's way of seeing things that it is virtually impossible for him to speak about matters that do not fit into that expectation-framework. He will consciously dismiss those renegade thoughts, attitudes or experiences as irrelevant nonsense. Perhaps he will actually become blind to the existence of such material within himself. Or he may retain a consciousness of the material, but that consciousness will only come into play in other contexts and not in the presence of the therapist. In these matters, one must never underestimate the power of the therapist's expectation-framework to censor the client's thoughts.

I must emphasize that all of this takes place outside the awareness of both client and therapist. The client does not intend to withhold important information. Neither does the therapist intend to suppress the client's thoughts. Unfortunately, it is precisely because neither is aware of what is happening that certain crucial factors may never be discovered.

If, therefore, the therapist is getting nowhere with his usual approach, he may find that by deliberately altering his normal therapeutic expectation-framework new material will surface.

Altering the therapeutic expectation-framework may be very difficult. The therapist will first have to see clearly the extent to which his peculiar expectation-framework has been absorbed by the client. He must then find a way to make the client become aware of those thoughts, feelings or attitudes that, because of the framework, have been generally dismissed. However, since these thoughts, feelings and attitudes are usually at some point *conscious*, since they *do* flit in and out of the client's conscious thinking, he may—with the right encouragement—be brought to pay attention to them and speak of them. Once that difficult task has been accomplished and the client has allowed his own peculiar way of experiencing things to come forward, the therapist can make some surprising discoveries.

212

AMPLIFICATION OF WEAK SIGNALS

To do so, however, the therapist may have to help the client make the internal experience strong and clear enough to work with. Sometimes the client's relevant inner sensations are feeble or indistinct. The inner voice may be shaky, the feeling of an alien substance vague or the sense of not being oneself confused. These weak signals need to be amplified.

Often the client will recognize that he had "always" or "for a long time" been aware of the symptom. But he reveals that he has tried hard to ignore it or has even carried on a continual battle to suppress it. The therapist must now help the client to approach the symptom in an entirely new way. Instead of trying to dismiss it or fight against it, the client must actually give it *more* energy, *more* force. Put another way, he must approach this process with the same attitude used by a practitioner of judo. The judo expert does not oppose force with counterforce. He does not try, for instance, to halt the charge of an opponent rushing towards him. Rather, he allows the opponent to drive right on through and throws him over as he does so, thus making use of the opponent's momentum. It is the same with those voices, feelings or sensations that are disturbing the client. Instead of opposing them and trying to force them out, the client must use their power in his favor. He must help them build up to the point where they can no longer hide in the background. Given more energy, amplified, they become more obvious and so available for the first time to be dealt with directly.

The therapist can allow his client to do this only if he has judged that the client is able to take it, that his ego is strong enough to remain intact while allowing other egolike elements to express themselves. This is a judgment that the therapist will have made when carrying out the first step—the exhaustion of conventional therapeutic possibilities.

If the therapist judges the client capable, he will then need to reassure him that it is beneficial to let it all happen, that he can safely let those weak, nagging impulses grow strong and clear. The client will also need to know that the therapist will stay with him and see him through the process.

As the therapist assists the client in making the inner signals stronger and clearer, there may be a breakthrough of new material.

213

The client may suddenly be flooded by a host of vivid impressions. He will need to speak about them and allow them to take him where they will. He may discover from those impressions that he is undergoing an experience of an unusual kind. This brings us to the next step.

Discovery of the Elusive Element

Discovery is the simplest step. If the therapist has succeeded in altering his expectation-framework and has worked to help the client amplify weak signals, he will be ready to pay attention to whatever the client brings forth. Discovery is simply recognizing the nature of the client's experience *as he is experiencing it.*

The client may be having any of a number of different types of experience. He may feel he is being controlled or influenced by an inner presence, an entity other than himself. In other words, he feels possessed. Or the client may be flooded by "memories" of a life in another time and place. Such reincarnation-type experiences are not rare. Then again, the client may turn out to be having some unusual inner experience of a kind not treated here. It is important that no matter what the experience described, no matter how unconventional it may seem, it be allowed to manifest fully and be recognized on its own terms. Only then can the full extent of the client's experience be appreciated. And only then will the therapist be in a position to gain new information about the nature of inner human experience.

Here it may be profitable to reiterate a point mentioned in an earlier chapter. Neither therapist nor client need be convinced that the experience is in reality what it seems at first glance. All that is necessary is that they are willing to allow the experience to evolve completely and become clearly defined. This will permit a suitable therapeutic approach to be developed.

At this juncture we move from the explorative phase to the therapy proper. In the description that follows I will be dealing only with therapy for cases of possession-type experience. Instances of reincarnation experiences are, for the most part, easily handled: all that is needed is that the "memories" be recited and any connection with the client's present life explored. As to other types of unusual inner experience that may be discovered, they are beyond the range of this book.

THERAPY INVOLVING A HUMAN POSSESSOR

The majority of the possession cases I have dealt with involved possession by a human spirit, either living or discarnate. I discovered that when the possession experience was treated *as if* it were exactly what it appeared to be—invasion and control of the client by another human spirit—the condition could almost always be cleared up. Success did not depend upon my conviction or my client's that the experience corresponded to a metaphysical reality; it was only necessary for us to accept the *experience itself* as valid and worthy of serious attention.

In the description of the therapy to follow, the *as if* attitude that I adopted towards the possession phenomenon will be assumed throughout. The possessing entity will be described as a separate person, and the relationship between possessed and possessor will be treated as occurring between two individual people.

Since it is not necessary to come to a final conclusion about the metaphysical nature of the possession experience in order to deal therapeutically with it in an effective manner, I will reserve discussion of that issue for the last part of this book.

MAKING CONTACT

Once a possessing entity has been discovered through the exploration process, it is necessary to make effective contact with it. That may not always be easy. Sometimes the entity will be reluctant to talk to the therapist. Or if he does talk a bit, he may refuse to cooperate.

The therapist must find out how to "hook" the entity. He must discover a way to get his attention and eventually, his willing participation in a solution. He must, in other words, draw the entity into the therapeutic process. Unfortunately, there are no general rules to guide the therapist in this matter; it is almost entirely a matter of intuition and ingenuity.

Interestingly, every case of possession in my experience has had the possessor speaking through the possessed. The vocal apparatus used was that of the client. I have never encountered a paranormal manifestation of a possessing spirit. That is, I have never seen a case that involved "direct voice" (where a voice speaks from somewhere outside a human organism) nor any other psycho-kinetic communication. Although there was often a pronounced alteration in vocal quality and sometimes a dramatic change in facial features, I do not consider these to be paranormal phenomena. One need not move beyond ordinary explanations to account for them.

EXPLORING THE POSSESSION RELATIONSHIP

Once the therapist has an exchange going with the possessing entity, he can start to gather information about the possession state. He will attempt to discover whether the possessor knows where he is and what he is doing; the time and circumstances that lead to the possession; why it happened in the first place; and the reason for its continuing.

I have found that the answers to these questions vary greatly. Sometimes the entity does not know where he is. More frequently, he knows that he is somehow involved with the client, but does not at first recognize that he is exercising control over him and interfering with his life. There are cases, however, in which the possessing entity knows exactly where he is and what he is doing.

As to time and circumstances of original entry, there are as many answers as there are individual cases. Occasionally, though, the entity does not know how and when it first happened and cannot reclaim the memory. As a rule this information is useful but not crucial.

Of great importance, on the other hand, is information about the *reason* possession originally took place and the purpose it continues to serve for the possessor. This knowledge will provide the key for the therapy work that follows.

POSSESSION AND FAMILY DYNAMICS

Most possession cases in my experience have involved invasion and control by the spirit of someone related by blood to the host. In such situations it will be necessary to explore the basic dynamic of the client's family constellation in the process of reaching resolution of the possession.

The power of family influence in these cases is hard to overestimate. Often it is felt that the rights of the individual member are subordinate to those of the family as a whole. In these instances, the "good of the family," the "way of the family," the "custom of the family," the "reputation of the family," the "preservation of the family," the "protection of the family," et cetera are of supreme importance. If necessary, the individual family member must be sacrificed to preserve them. Dr. Titus Bull addresses this subject and its relevance to possession in *Analysis of Unusual Experiences*:

> The premise is that there is an influence which can be exerted upon the mind of mortals by ideas embodied in thoughts from their departed ancestors. In other words, some departed ancestors whenever possible, attempt to mold the lives of those incarnated who are akin. Their right to do this is never questioned. It is bred within them. It is the right only which family ties have engendered and can do great harm and injustice to the victims. . . . It would not be fair to say that all ancestors are unwise nor all mortals influenced in this way. But there is a type of mortal whose mind is easily influenced by the stronger minds of the family group. We observe this influence all about us. The more clannish the family group, the more likely is this to be true on both sides of the veil. It is, however, not to be considered as a spirit obsession [possession] in the true sense. The idea to be conveyed here is that thoughts from the discarnate, readily acceptable to the incarnate, would be those ideas embodied in the general outlook of a particular family group. We find this idea demonstrated in a family line whose members are overproud of their lineage. It seems inbred and persists and is not easily scattered; but beyond this general theme, the members of the family would not be easily influenced, as long as each member remained in normal health. The intervention of shock, however, or anything that could upset the nerve balance of a member of such a family group, would place him in actual danger of becoming a victim of true spirit obsession [possession]. . . . The primary obsessor in this case would likely be one who claimed the right by ties of blood, who had no desire to do anything but to keep the mortal in line with family ideals.

In this framework, the family operates like a unified living organism that survives from generation to generation. The organism has a mental and emotional life, imbued with certain attitudes and a character that have been formed through untold generations of family experience. The individual members exist to preserve and transmit the family ideals. They must not defy those ideals, nor even change them in any substantial way. The individual members are, therefore, subservient to the good of the whole, and considered the possessions of the family organism.

The reason discarnate spirits of relatives sometimes feel it their *right* to possess and control a family member seems to be that they consider themselves representatives of the family organism itself. As such, they are its spokesmen and feel justified in exerting pressure to bring the victim in line with traditional family attitudes.

Special consideration must be given to those cases in which the possessing entity is someone upon whom the host had a great dependency in life. In these instances it is often easy to trace a progression from possessiveness to possession. The most common example of such an evolution is that of possession by a parent. The child is naturally open to the parent in every way, and if the parent exercises too great a possessiveness, there is little that the child can do to resist. It is sometimes difficult to determine at what point the parent's possessive invasion becomes possession. However, if it has not happened before, it may very well occur upon the death of the parent.

The mother is in a unique position with regard to the issue of possession. Right from conception, mother and fetus form a single symbolic unit. After birth, the symbiosis continues for some time. While this condition exists, the mother treats the infant as an extension of herself, attending to his every need, caring for him as she would for her own body. In a normal development, the infant moves through various states of greater independence while his mother's possessive attitude towards him is correspondingly mitiated. As the child grows into adulthood, he approaches full independence from his mother. She, in turn, prepares to let him go, to live a life completely separate from hers. Trouble occurs in this process when the mother does not relinquish control of her offspring's life to a degree corresponding to his burgeoning independence. She is reluctant to give up a role that has been outgrown. She begins to act in ways that—in the old circumstances—were natural, but now can only be called invasive and possessive. Many cases I have worked with showed clear evidence that such possessiveness can result in a state of possession. This was true, for instance, in "The Second Chance" (where the possessor was living).

Therapy for possession by family members must deal head-on with the issues that have traditionally been considered parental or family prerogatives. It will have to indicate where these prerogatives are simply the enshrinement of family structures designed to control individual members rather than free them. Both possessor and possessed will benefit from such an analysis.

Having made this special note on possession by family members, let us return to the subject of therapy for possession in general.

THERAPY FOR THE POSSESSOR

In the course of my work I discovered it was seldom a good idea to try to be rid of the possessing entity quickly. It is usually better for both possessor and host that the entity be helped as much as possible to understand the possession situation and eventually leave it for something better.

If the situation is to be understood, one crucial question must be answered: what is the purpose of the possession as far as the possessing entity is concerned? There seems to me to be three possible answers: (1) there is no particular purpose; (2) there is a positive or helpful purpose; or (3) there is some selfish purpose.

Sometimes the possessing entity does not have any special purpose in being there. He is simply confused and has entered into the host almost accidentally. Usually, in these cases, the therapy for the entity is brief; it amounts to enlightening him about his condition, much as Wickland did, and helping him to move on. Occasionally, however, once the confused entity does discover where he is, he realizes that he has some unhealthy attachment to the host. Therapy is necessary to free him from that neurotic bond. This was the situation in the example of "The Confused Father."

In other cases, the possessor is present in the host to assist him in some way. Although the motive is basically positive, the method is not. Instead of helping the host, the entity causes confusion and distress. An example of this is seen in the case of "The Helpful Grandmother." This case also illustrated the fact that even where there are fundamentally good motives, there may be unhealthy elements in the possessor that have to be treated therapeutically.

Where the purpose of the possession is basically selfish, a great deal of therapy needs to be done with the possessing entity. The case of "The Complaining Mother" is an instance of this kind of condition.

When therapy is undertaken with the possessing entity, the therapist works as he would with any flesh-and-blood person. This proves to be surprisingly easy once things get started. The possessor responds as a person quite independent of the host. He speaks of the host in the third person and is capable of any emotion towards him. He has his own personality with its unique characterological traits, his own set of life memories. Through the therapeutic process, he will uncover his own neurotic life patterns based upon his personal life history. He will eventually come to his own therapeutic resolution of those problems, often after recovering painful, repressed memories.

In dealing with cases of discarnate possessing entities, the therapist will generally find that this work proceeds more swiftly than does therapy for the living. Relevant repressed material is recovered more quickly, and progress towards resolution is more rapid.

Therapy with living possessing entities, however, is more slowly paced. In that respect it is similar to working with a normal client. A peculiar thing about working with living possessing entities is that the therapist often has the impression that he is not dealing with the entity's complete personality. Instead, it seems like a fragment of the person which, while remaining connected to the whole, has split off to be with the host.

It is usually necessary to do therapy with the possessor before he can move on. The reason is that full dissolution of the possession involves a *resolution* of the relationship between possessed and possessor. That resolution can be attained only when the possessor has come to terms with his unhealthy attachment to the host.

RESOLUTION

Resolution between possessor and possessed is the same as resolution between any two individuals in a relationship. Both must take part in the resolution process. Each must come to terms with the other. They must learn to see each other realistically and come to a mutual agreement as to how they want to be involved with each other.

As the possessor gains understanding of the neurotic nature of his tie to the host, he will desire to end his unfair usage of him. He will give up his possessive attitude towards the host and allow a relationship of independence and equality to develop. As he relinquishes his possessive *attitude*, he will also be ready to leave behind the *state* of possession itself. A question then arises whether there is reason to continue a relationship of any kind at all.

In most of the possession cases in my experience there is a

family connection between possessor and possessed. Often there have been feelings of affection and love between them in life, and those feelings are evident in the therapy process. Sometimes such natural feelings of attachment were not present in life (the two may not even have known each other), but have developed in the course of the possession relationship. Resolution of the relationship between possessor and possessed must take into account positive feelings of this sort.

It is important to note that in the kinds of cases I have encountered, the possessed often—almost always—has a hidden attachment to being possessed. This hidden attachment must be uncovered and openly recognized by the possessed. Otherwise he will unconsciously hinder the resolution process and not allow the possessor to go.

MOVING ON

When resolution between possessed and possessor has been reached, the possessing entity will naturally desire to move on.

For the living possessor, "moving on" is simply a matter of becoming wholly present to himself. He realizes that much of his energy has been siphoned off into preoccupation with the host. Now that this is about to cease, he looks forward to having all of his resources available to do whatever he wants to do with his life. This will happen when the split-off fragment of his personality, which has possessed the host, returns home.

The discarnate possessor, on the other hand, experiences moving on in quite a different way. He realizes that he has been living a very limited existence and is interested in having a fuller life. He feels ready to enter into the "next phase of existence." Just what that is for a discarnate spirit is not clear. There are indications that it involves being with other discarnate spirits and learning and growing in some unknown way. In any case, as the possessor becomes more confident through the therapeutic process, his curiosity about that phase grows. He often undertakes some initial exploration and thereby usually gains some notion of where he is going before he leaves.

Two principal kinds of relationships are possible between possessing entity and former host after the entity moves on. The entity may retain a friendly connection with the former host, perhaps assisting or advising him later on in life questions. Or the entity may sever all connections with the former host. He is simply gone, and apparently has no inclination to be further involved in the life of the client.

FAILURES AND SUCCESSES

Failures in the treatment process can happen at two stages: there can be failure to discover or failure to resolve. I have had both.

In a number of instances I found that even though I applied the exploration procedure described above, I was unable to discover any new material or a new view of what was happening with the client. Although the client complained of symptoms typical of possession victims, neither conventional techniques nor alteration of the expectation-framework led anywhere. In some cases, relief was found in therapeutic work done at a later time.

Failure to resolve could happen in two ways. In the first, there is simply an exchange with an entity or a recovery of reincarnational material which is inconclusive and eventually fizzles out. The result is that the client leaves no better than he came. In the second, the client ends up in worse condition than when he started. Fortunately, this second possibility has not yet occurred in any of my cases.

Failures in which there is no conclusive resolution are more likely to happen where the possessing entity is still living. I have encountered a number of instances in which the living possessor just did not want to give up his hold on the host. The entity seemed afraid to have all of his attention focused upon his own life; that was too dreary a prospect. The only spice in his life seemed to be derived from the vicarious living carried on through his victim. Incidentally, with this kind of failure, the possessor was in every case a parent.

Luckily, such failure does not mean that the host is doomed to lasting possession. Even though the possessor never accepts an honorable solution, the victim can nonetheless free himself. He can learn to close himself down to the possessor's presence and effectively eject him.

I consider successes to be those cases in which there is some change for the better. That change may vary from slight improvement to a radical, positive alteration in the personality. The cases described in the previous chapters present a variety of positive outcomes which range across the spectrum. Occasionally, the change in personality was not dramatic, but the voice, the alien mass or the feeling of not being oneself was removed—or at least drastically diminished. A strange phenomenon occurred at times: the client had a story that had to be told—like a phonograph record that had to be played out—and once out, it was finished. In these instances, clients invariably were relieved to have the thing brought out, though some did not, at first, feel any personal changes. Then, after a period of time, they did notice change and a perspective on their lives that they had never before possessed.

For some clients there were striking positive changes. The case histories provide sufficient examples of such notable improvements. It is my estimation that approximately two-thirds of the fifty cases of possession by human entities with which I have worked fall into this category.

Positive results are tricky things to evaluate, particularly in the realm of therapy. When working with possession cases, one is tempted to think that positive results indicate that possession is an objective reality. This conclusion would not, however, be justified. It has been shown again and again that, when it comes to healing emotional ills, widely differing techniques based on radically opposed metaphysical systems can produce equally good results. The positive outcomes, therefore, are obviously due to some factor other than the philosophical beliefs of the therapist.

The most one can say in the case of my work is that the *as if* approach is fruitful. If the therapist accepts the client's experience on its own terms and proceeds *as if* it describes an objective reality, he is likely to meet with success. As a worker interested in relieving emotional ills, the therapist can rest content with that. As a philosophical thinker he is likely to feel unsatisfied. He wants to know the nature of the reality behind appearances. Part Four of this book will attempt to wrestle with that metaphysical question.

Can "Possessing Entities" Be Created by the Therapeutic Process?

Nearly one hundred years ago, Pierre Janet clearly pointed out that a secondary personality could be induced in a patient by merely suggesting it was there. His creation of such a personality in his patient Lucie was described in Chapter 2. In this instance he was communicating with her subconscious and succeeded in giving the communicating part a name. From that moment on, the new personality, "Adrienne," began to exist as a clear-cut individual. This demonstrates, among other things, the tremendous susceptibility of the client to the suggestions of the therapist.

Now, Janet created the new personality in his hysterical patient deliberately, in the course of researching the nature of the subconscious. Suppose, however, the therapist introduces such a suggestion into the subconscious of his client without realizing that he is doing so. Suppose that because he expects to find a possessing entity in his client, he unwittingly provides the client's subconscious with enough indications about what he is looking for to induce the creation of a possessing entity. The possibility of such unconscious suggestive activity on the part of psychological workers has frequently been pointed out in the literature over the past decades, and should be considered here.

Should such an accidental creation of a possessing entity occur, the therapist would be placed in a rather ironical position. He would himself be contributing to the client's disturbance by creating a new full-blown entity which would then have to be got rid of. He would end up going through a futile therapeutic exercise with an entity which he would appear to have discovered, but had actually produced. For a worker whose main concern is to alleviate the ills of his distressed client, such a situation would be a nightmare.

The client's subconscious is extremely alert to all signals received from the therapist. As mentioned earlier when we dealt with therapeutic expectation-frameworks, the client can respond to inhibiting messages that escape even the therapist's detection. If this is true of negative or inhibiting suggestions, it is equally true of positive or eliciting suggestions. For that reason, the therapist must guard against subtly suggesting to the client that he has possessing entities within him, and in that way inducing his subconscious to create them.

When I am working with a client who exhibits symptoms often associated with possession, I endeavor to carry on the exploration process in such a way that there is as little chance of suggestion from myself or the situation as possible. Where the client already has a feeling of inner presences, the problem is greatly lessened. It then is simply a matter of exploring what he already feels. However, where the symptoms are more vague, such as the experience of an inner voice, the presence of some alien "thing" in the body, or the feeling at times, of not being "oneself," greater caution is required. When the expectation-framework has been altered and an attempt is being made to amplify weak signals, it is essential to let the phenomenon manifest *in its own terms* and not subtly steer it towards some predetermined outcome. The therapist must not, in other words, hint that he expects to discover other presences within the client. For if he does, he is sure to "find" them, whether they were there originally or not.

Naturally, the therapist will encounter cases in which the client already is aware of inner presences before he comes for help. Those entities may have been produced through suggestion received from elsewhere in the client's environment, it is true. But one would hope that if this were the case, that fact would be discovered in the process of applying conventional therapeutic approaches to the client's condition.

The problem of suggestion-pollution from the client's environment is a real one, however, and must be given serious consideration. It is particularly difficult to avoid when clients come to know each other, as they would in, say, a group-therapy situation. When this happens, they can easily influence each other's expectations and create powerful suggestions in the subconscious mind. For example, if a client who has undergone therapy involving a possession experience discusses this with another client, he may very well sow the seeds of suggestion which could later bear fruit in the subconscious creation of a "possessing personality." The therapist must be aware of such a possibility and treat the situation appropriately. This would ordinarily involve bringing the suggestive factor to consciousness so the emotional material associated with the personification can be dealt with directly.

One final comment. In writing about his work with multiple personalities, Dr. Ralph Allison indicates that a patient will sometimes creatively produce a new personality for himself. The new personality is manufactured by what Dr. Allison calls the *inner self helper* (ISH), an entity within the client which promotes his welfare. In *Mind in Many Pieces* he describes such a creation of a healthy personality in a disturbed individual who could not function well in day-to-day life. The healthy personality took control and assisted Allison with the client's therapy. It is my opinion that it could conceivably be therapeutically beneficial to assist the creation of a full-blown personality that embodies mixed elements already existing within the individual in a disorganized way. In this case, the personality would—in a sense—be there in a latent form. Binet spoke of such a possibility when commenting on Janet's creation of "Adrienne." He said:

> It should be carefully noted that if the personality of "Adrienne" could be created, it is because the suggestion met a *psychological possibility*; in other words, there were disaggregated phenomena existing there apart from the normal consciousness of the subject. This disaggregation prepared the unconscious person, and in order to [bring about] the collection and crystallization of these scattered elements very little was needed.

Perhaps this sometimes happens in working with what appear to be possessing entities. Perhaps these entities have, on the occasion of some suggestive influence, been created from the latent elements of "mother," "father," "grandmother," et cetera residing in the client's unconscious. If this were the case, we might consider the possibility that their becoming personified and vividly embodied may be doing the client a service. It may provide a means of working more effectively with those latent subconscious elements and bringing them to resolution. It may, in other words, offer an opportunity for those elements to be seen clearly for the first time and integrated into the individual's ego. It is doubtful that the therapist would be justified in deliberately setting out to personify these elements, containing as they do a mixture of positive and negative aspects. But there may be a good argument for using such personifications, once produced by suggestion from environmental sources, to further the client's therapeutic work.

Part Four
Coming to Terms with Multiple Man

INTRODUCTION

There are three principal approaches that can be taken to explaining the phenomena of possession and multiple personality. The first is to see both as instances of intrusions of an entity or influence from without. The second is to regard both as manifestations of unintegrated elements from within the psyche of the subject. The third is a combination of the first two. All attempts to expound the causes for multiplicity conditions reduce themselves to one or other of these approaches.

INTRUSIONS FROM WITHOUT

Put simply, this approach sees a multiplicity of consciousnesses within an individual as a sign of possession by an outside agency. The subject of the multiplicity is being interfered with, and the extra consciousnesses are being imposed from without. In this picture of the situation, it makes no difference what the intruding consciousnesses may *claim* to be. Whether they know it or not, they come from elsewhere.

According to this view of things, the intruder may or may not make his presence known to those around the subject. When he does, the situation is recognized for what it is: invasion by an entity from outside the subject. This is clearly the case, for example, with mediumistic and demonic possession. But often the presence of another independent being is not clearly manifested in the con-

227

duct of the subject. This is what happens with many instances of multiple personality in which the alter personality does not claim to have any life apart from the host. In this case the intruder may, for a long time, escape detection. However, if one digs deeply enough, say the exponents of this theory, one will discover that there is indeed an invading entity who has either forgotten who he is or is deliberately concealing his identity.

On the other hand, we are told that sometimes the intruding being will not have a specific identity. The reason is that it is a psychic creation produced by an outside agent—either deliberately or unconsciously. However, in this case, too, the influence is external and must be treated as such.

UPRUSHES FROM WITHIN

This attempt to explain the phenomenon of multiplicity sees it as a purely private affair. The victim himself has created the alter personalities who, at first glance, appear to have an independent existence. A thorough investigation of the unconscious realms of the victim's psyche will reveal how and why he has produced these troublesome inner residents.

In cases of multiple personality, the scenario is clear enough. The subject experienced traumatic situations of a kind that were beyond his ability to bear. Under such pressure, he manufactured a personality that was able to handle the situation where the original personality could not. An analysis of the personalities will reveal their original purpose and function.

Possession is explained similarly. The victim's unconscious mind forms a personality that claims to have an existence apart from that of the host. That personality serves a specific function for the host. It may be there to draw concern and attention to the host. It may embody certain feelings that are unacceptable to his conscious mind and thus provide a guilt-free outlet for the forbidden emotion. Or it may serve to promote certain religious ideas of the host—being the fulfillment of a kind of spiritual wish. Whatever the purpose, the phenomenon is the creation—albeit unconscious—of the host's own psyche.

A COMBINED EXPLANATION

There are many researchers who have not been able to simply come down on one side or the other in this matter. They believe that both points of view have validity and that the investigator must keep his mind open to either kind of data. After all, they say, there is nothing intrinsically contradictory in holding that in some instances, the alter consciousness or personality is merely the product of the subject's unconscious mind, while in other instances it derives from without. The danger, they point out, is in trying to force all the data to fit one framework of thought. This can lead to a distortion of some facts and a disregarding of others.

Those who take this position emphasize that there is not yet sufficient knowledge to allow a well-formed judgment one way or another about the matter. Certainly the evidence that all multiplicity phenomena are the result of the intrusion of some agency from outside the subject is flimsy indeed. On the other hand, there are many facts that will not submit to the usual reductive analysis of those who hold the second view. It seems much more prudent, say the exponents of a combined explanation, to keep an open mind on the matter as relevant data continue to accumulate.

Although attempts to explain the phenomena of human multiplicity may be reduced to the foregoing three categories, a reading of the relevant literature reveals that the approaches devised within these categories exhibit the greatest possible variety. Human inventiveness seems to be especially active when it comes to constructing systems to make sense out of this mysterious aspect of human personality.

It is possible, however, to discern two great historical traditions which have struggled with the problem of multiple man: the occult and the psychological. The following chapter examines these two approaches.

Chapter 15

Two Approaches to Multiple Man—
The Occult and the Psychological

Men have been trying to understand the data of human multiplicity for a long time. Any effort to fathom the mystery of multiple man must take note of previous attempts. However, the explanations which have been devised over the centuries are so numerous that it is impossible to give an adequate account of their diversity. Fortunately, the task of attempting to grasp the essential import of these explanations can be simplified. The efforts to synthesize human experience of multiplicity fall into two great categories: the psychological synthesis and the occult synthesis. The best way to tackle the problem of understanding multiple man is by beginning with an examination of these two approaches.

The occult synthesis is ancient, its beginnings predating written human record. It embodies a world view that explains all mysteries in terms of an understanding of the intrinsic metaphysical nature of the universe. It proceeds deductively, moving from an intuitive view of the inner structure of reality to an explanation of the data of human experience. It is, at bottom, a spiritual philosophy of the nature of the universe.

The psychological synthesis, on the other hand, has only in the last two hundred years really come into its own. Its approach is to attempt to explain human personality in terms of scientific models. It proceeds inductively, beginning with the data of experience and generalizing from there. The laws and theories that derive from its investigations are considered to be imperfect and in need of constant revision. Although it does not of itself rule out the possibility that man has a spiritual dimension, the models it constructs to account for the data of human experience tend to be mechanical. This follows from the fact that its concerns are primarily pragmatic—discovering what model produces the best results. It does not attempt to provide metaphysical answers about the nature of reality.

These are the two great synthesizing traditions, often portrayed in the modern world as warring against each other. The occult tradition tends to view the scientific as unacceptably analytical, reducing all of life's mysteries to mere mechanics. The scientific tradition tends to see the occult as both naive and dogmatic in its approach to explaining human experience. The conflict between the two traditions has not been absolute, however. There have been men in each camp who have recognized value in the perspective of the other and taken that into account in their own synthesis.

These traditions have had a tremendous influence upon everyday thinking about human multiplicity in the modern world. The average man is, in the conduct of his everyday affairs, both occultist and scientist. Both traditions have formed his thinking, and each holds a powerful attraction for him as he searches to understand himself. Neither can be ignored if we wish to better comprehend the nature of multiple man.

THE OCCULT VIEW OF MULTIPLE MAN

The term "occultism" covers a vast array of religio-philosophical traditions. It includes everything from the ritual practices centered around the oracular cults of ancient Egypt and Greece, through the development of "natural magic" in the late Middle Ages and the Renaissance, up to present-day movements such as spiritualism, theosophy and the Golden Dawn. Under its heading we also find the ancient traditions of witchcraft and the multitude of magical practices associated with so-called primitive cultures all over the world. Its forms are so varied that one almost despairs of giving an adequate impression of its dimensions.

However, despite the tremendous variety of forms, it is possible to speak of an occult world view that is common to all. For that reason, the best approach to describing the occult view of multiple man is not to enumerate the specific doctrines of a number of schools of occult thought, but rather to present the general outlines of the occult view of the nature of reality.

Although the occult world view I present here is that which, in its main points, is common to all traditions, I have taken the more

231

refined elements principally from the esoteric tradition as it developed in the Western world, particularly in Europe and England. I have done this because on some points, this tradition has well-developed teachings about which primitive traditions are silent, having not yet brought their assumptions to consciousness.

THE OCCULT WORLD VIEW

"Occult" means "hidden" or "concealed." Occultism basically involves a belief that: (1) there are hidden or unseen forces in the universe; (2) these forces exist whether we acknowledge them or not; (3) these forces operate according to well-defined laws; (4) there is thus an overall *meaning* inherent in the universe; and (5) the purpose of life has to do with fathoming that meaning and getting in tune with those forces.

Central to this view of things are the concepts of "life-force" and "thought." The occultist holds that there is a universal life force that manifests itself in everything that exists. Everything is alive, even so-called inert objects. Also, every living thing has a mental dimension. Some form of mentation is believed to be present even in matter. For that reason everything that happens in nature is part of a rational process. Consciousness and purpose are present even in those events that appear to be the result of chance. Natural law, which one can see operating on every level of existence, shows that there is a rational motivation behind all that happens.

For many occult traditions, this rationally functioning universal life-force is called "God." In their view, God is immanent in the world, present in all of the manifestations of life. But he is also transcendent, beyond and greater than what he has created. Since there is one divine mind behind all that is and all that happens, the occultist possesses a unitary view of nature. The occultist makes this universal unity and meaning in the universe the object of his study and research.

All the creatures of the universe are given their character and form by the mind of God. Also, they are held in existence by the life-force that comes from God. "Thought" and "life-force"—these, says the occultist, are the basic constitutive elements of the creative action of the divine.

But according to the occult view man, too, is a creator. He has a unique position in the world, being something of a little god. His mind generates thoughts that give form and character to his creations. And the life-force emanating from him gives them existence. When his mind gives form to sounds, he is a creative musician. When his mind gives form to building materials, he is an architect. Man, therefore, creates his own universe, populated by the creatures of his mind, just as God created the great universe. Man is thus the microcosmic image of the great macrocosm of God.

But man not only creates physical artifacts, he also creates psychic artifacts. His thoughts themselves, when charged with sufficient energy, become substantially existing entities. These substantially existing "thought-forms" have power. They can produce palpable effects both upon himself and upon others. Those effects can be constructive (when one generates thoughts of healing and encouragement, for example) or destructive (when the thoughts are of psychic attack, domination, draining of vitality, possession or similar things).

According to occult teaching, human beings can learn not only to develop the powers latent within them but also to tap into the immense forces of nature. These forces have been personified in the traditional gods, goddesses, angels and demons. The different divinities represent the various aspects of basic natural forces, such as growth, strength and conservation, as well as decay, war and destruction. Someone who wishes to make use of these cosmic powers puts himself in tune with them through ritual acts and calls upon them to manifest through him. When he does this he becomes a channel for divine power. He is thereby enabled to do marvelous things. As he mediates this potent energy, he may use it to see the future, gain knowledge of hidden things, alter the course of events, or transform himself into a stronger, more complete, more divine person. The power itself is neither good nor bad. The intention of the user determines whether the effects will be constructive or destructive.

As the occultist develops a deeper knowledge of the inner nature of things, he is able to make use of a part of himself built up in the nonmaterial dimension called the "astral world." The occultist can learn to transfer his consciousness to this astral body, something that happens spontaneously in sleep. The astral body survives death. When a person dies, his consciousness passes once and for all from the physical body to the astral. Thus the personality survives death intact, and the individual continues to function on the astral plane, now in a new phase of existence.

Survival of death is a tenet held by virtually *all* schools of oc-

233

cultism. Reincarnation is held by most. It involves the belief in an eventual return to earthly life. If the individual still has lessons to learn in this world, he is born again to live in a new body and form a new personality.

For all occultists, whether or not they believe in reincarnation, the goal of life is to live in tune with the laws of the universe and to be transformed more and more into the likeness of the gods or God, eventually to be united with the divine in some ineffable spiritual life.

HUMAN MULTIPLICITY

While practically every occult tradition believes in possession and has ways to deal with it, there are only a few that speak about multiple personality. This is true because multiple personality has been recognized as such chiefly in the Western world, and even that recognition has occurred only in the last two hundred years. However, occult philosophy has the principles to explain the mechanism of multiple personality and some of its modern exponents have done so. I rely on their writings for the treatment of multiple personality given below. But first I would like to look at the occult view of possession.

POSSESSION

For the occultist, possession is simply explained. The astral body, bearing the "spirit" or center of consciousness, leaves the physical body of the host. The physical body is then vacant and the "spirit" or center of consciousness of another entity may move in and take over, controlling the host's physical functioning.

Where withdrawal of the host's consciousness is complete and the invading spirit takes full control of the organism, there is total possession. In these cases the host will usually have no memory of what takes place during the period of possession, for his consciousness is occupied elsewhere.

In cases where withdrawal of consciousness is only partial, the takeover of the possessing entity may be incomplete. Then the two consciousnesses, that of the host and that of the invader, coexist simultaneously within the one organism. These instances of so-called lucid possession are more common in civilized societies than in primitive ones. Here the host may actually converse with the possessor while in the possessed state. Afterwards, the host will usually have a full memory of what took place while possessed.

Even in cases of complete withdrawal of the host's consciousness from the physical body, the "spirit" or "soul" maintains a connection with that organism to preserve its vital functioning. Without this connection the organism would die.

In the occult view of things, possession is not so extraordinary. Full or partial withdrawal of the consciousness from the body is happening all the time anyway—in sleep, for instance. Given the proper conditions, any entity may very well intrude. For that reason, most occult traditions have developed specific means of guarding against possession. These include everything from amulets and rituals to protective visualizations.

Although the basic nature of possession is agreed upon by most occult traditions, the identity of invading entities is not. However, most hold that possession can be perpetrated by both living spirits and artificial psychic creations. The living spirits may be either human souls or nonhuman beings. The artificial creations are considered ordinarily to be produced by an individual or group who set out explicitly to manufacture an entity. But most traditions recognize the possibility that such invading thought-forms can be produced without the conscious or explicit intention of the individual or group.

The state of possession may be a violent intrusion into an unwilling victim, or it may be sought out by the host. Most occult traditions have some provision for voluntary possession. Some even include possession as a principal element in their day-to-day practices. Thus, spiritualists have their mediumistic seances, voodoo societies their trance-inducing dances and cabalistic magicians their invocations of the gods.

MULTIPLE PERSONALITY

As mentioned above, cases of multiple personality have only rather recently been noted—principally in Europe, England and America. One does not, therefore, find much discussion of the matter in occult literature. However, the phenomenon holds no surprises for the occultist. He has a ready explanation for what is occurring. He simply sees it as a special kind of possession.

The personalities that come and go in a multiple personality subject are generally seen as spirit presences which periodically invade and leave the body of the victim. In this interpretation, when a person speaks with an alter personality, he speaks as an individual totally distinct from the subject. If the multiple personality condition is to be cleared up, the alien personality or personalities must be removed from the host through whatever means seem appropriate.

The occultist also holds that the invader may not be a spirit at all but rather an artificially created psychic entity. In this case the possessing entity is a highly charged thought-form produced by some outside person or persons. That thought-entity will most likely be demonic since it so forcibly intrudes into a person's psychic space.

The notion that multiple personalities are the manifestation of invasion by some outside intruder is by far the most common explanation employed by occultists. There is, however, a subtlety that many occultists introduce into this view of multiple personality as possession. They hold that while it is sometimes a case of possession resulting from invasion by an outside influence, it may just as often be a matter of possession by a fragment of the individual's own psyche unconsciously crystallized around some thought-form. The victim may have given some interiorly produced thought a specific personification and charged it with such energy that it has the power to periodically break through into consciousness and take control of him. Since the personality fragment is unconsciously formed and charged, he does not recognize himself as its creator. So while it has a kind of objective existence, as all thought-creations do, it is nonetheless subjectively produced.

In most cases, the individual has no awareness of those periods when the unconsciously produced, thought-form shaped psychic fragment is manifesting in the world. His normal consciousness is withdrawn and the fragment is in control.

The thought-form shaped fragment may be helpful or harmful, depending upon the quality of the thought involved. If the thought was hateful and destructive, the fragment appears as a negative personality, capable of harmful acts towards both the host and others. If the thought was positive in character, the fragment appears as a helpful personality, sympathetic to the needs of the host.

Whenever the multiple personality is the result of such unconsciously produced thought-form personifications, it is necessary for the host to be directly involved in removing those creations if any permanent relief is to be obtained. For if occult methods are utilized to dissolve the thought-form without the participation of the victim, he will simply unconsciously recreate the situation in a short time. Only if the victim recognizes his part in their production and claims the hidden thoughts which were the seeds of their formation can the personalities be prevented from reforming.

If the occultist believes the alter personalities are possessing entities who have moved in from the outside, he approaches treatment differently. Where the invading entities are spirits, they must be removed. Where they are artificial psychic creations produced by someone other than the host, they must be dissolved or sent back to their maker.

There is yet another occult explanation for cases of multiple personality which is of interest. Some occultists believe that at times, manifesting alter personalities are in fact personalities from former lifetimes of the individual. In other words, they are personalities developed in previous incarnations of the subject's basic self. The individual does not, however, recognize them as such; neither do the personalities themselves realize that they have lived before. But they do strongly claim to be the subject, while at the same time firmly denying that they are the other personalities. Occultists point out the fact that some personalities in multiple personality cases show signs of belonging to another culture and/or another age. What is lacking is specific memory of their former existence. This reincarnational explanation for some alter personalities may at times be combined with a possession explanation to account for the various personalities in a multiple.

The occult tradition is a venerable one. For unknown ages it has given people a way of understanding human experience. Its dependence upon intuition as the basis for knowledge is both its strength and its weakness. The development of the scientific method in more recent times has provided a valuable new approach for gaining knowledge of the world. Some of those who place themselves in the scientific tradition have made significant contributions to the understanding of human multiplicity. Next, we will deal with a few of the more important attempts to arrive at a psychological synthesis of the data of multiple man.

THE PSYCHOLOGICAL VIEW OF MULTIPLE MAN

We now move on to see what the psychological synthesis has to say about multiple man. The treatment will necessarily involve the recapitulation of some of the material already presented in various sections of the book. However, we now have sufficient background to describe in concise form the evolution of ideas about human multiplicity in the psychological tradition.

DIVIDED CONSCIOUSNESS

When, as described in Chapter 1, Puységur put the peasant Victor into a state of magnetic sleep, he opened the door to a whole new line of inquiry into multiple consciousnesses in human beings. His discovery of artificial somnambulism showed that there is much more to the human mind than that aspect which functions in everyday awareness. It was now seen that there are two parts to the mind, two streams of consciousness quite separate from each other, each having its own train of memory. The newly revealed second consciousness could be brought forward at will through the application of mesmerism and studied at leisure. The implications of this discovery of "divided consciousness" were vast. Over the past two hundred years they have been gradually drawn out and become the basis for the formulation of great psychological systems.

One of the first things that happened was that a connection was made between the second consciousness or second self and the phenomenon known as "dual personality" (later to be called by the more generic "multiple personality"). Although there is reason to believe that this phenomenon was not something new to the human condition, it was only first recognized by the general public around the time that divided consciousness was becoming known. The earliest well-known case was that of Mary Reynolds (described in Chapter 3), which was first written about in 1816, only thirty years after Puységur's discovery. In such cases of dual personality, the second personality was frequently described as a "somnambulistic self," and it was often believed that when the subject alternated between personalities, he was actually entering and leaving a state of somnambulistic trance.

With the rise of Spiritualism those who were studying divided consciousness tended to see in the phenomena of mediumship and spirit possession a striking application of what they were learning. Some of them explained what was happening as the second self impersonating a departed spirit. Others, who accepted the possibility of intervention from the discarnate, likened it to hypnotically induced somnambulism in which the ordinary consciousness moves aside and one's second consciousness comes forward. In the case of spirit possession, they maintained, one's ordinary consciousness moves out of the body and the consciousness of some departed soul is able to move in.

THE SUBCONSCIOUS

In the latter decades of the nineteenth century, the psychological understanding of human multiplicity took a further step forward with the work done by investigators of the condition called "hysteria" (discussed in Part One). Among the most important of these researchers were J.M. Charcot, Alfred Binet and Pierre Janet. These men attempted to understand the origin of this strange disorder which can cause such symptoms as paralysis, convulsions, blindness or numbness without any discernible physical cause. They were aware of the work of the magnetizers and the reality of the phenomenon of divided consciousness. They also knew of experiments done with posthypnotic suggestion upon individuals in the state of somnambulistic trance. These revealed that an idea implanted in the mind of the second self would act like a seed growing there, eventually materializing in the accomplishment of the previously suggested action. This caused them to look to the somnambulistic self as the hidden source of hysterical symptoms.

The notion they developed was that small split-off fragments of the personality could secretly develop within the individual's second self and eventually manifest in the symptoms of hysteria. Janet gave this view its most cogent formulation in his concept of "subconscious fixed ideas." He said that some disturbing idea, such as a frightening experience, could be cut off or "dissociated" from the conscious awareness of the individual and continue to live a life of its own in the "subconscious"—that region which lies "below" our ordinary consciousness and which corresponds to the second self of the magnetizers.

In this, Janet was formulating a scientific model for understanding the human mind. That model divided the mind into two regions: the conscious and the subconscious. By tracing the hidden evolutions of painful or disturbing ideas which had been banished to the subconscious mind, the investigator would find that they had shaped themselves into remarkably developed autonomous mental units. These could then force themselves to the surface and manifest in the physical symptoms of hysteria. These subconscious fixed ideas were thus seen to be endowed with an autonomy and life of their own which was carried on simultaneously with the ordinary waking life of the individual.

It is clear that for Janet, the existence of these hidden constellations of fixed ideas showed that the subconscious mind possessed thinking ability. This subconscious intelligence could appear to be rather rudimentary if one were to simply look at the physical symptoms of hysteria. But the subconscious also showed its mental ability in other ways which Janet called "psychological automatisms." These were defined as actions performed without the subject's ordinary consciousness being involved, and included such phenomena as posthypnotic suggestions and automatic writing.

Also included under the heading of psychological automatisms were manifestations of multiple personality. Janet saw the various alter personalities as distinct somnambulistic states, each with its own memory chain. These somnambulistic states could coalesce to the point of being true personalities through various means, but one of the factors that would greatly facilitate the process would be to give it a name. When coalesced, the personality would not only develop its own individual set of memories but also manifest characteristic attitudes, likes and dislikes.

Janet explained the phenomenon of possession as an example of being controlled by a subconscious fixed idea. Also, he saw mediumship and the other aspects of spiritualistic manifestation as examples of psychological automatism, eruptions of hidden material from the subconscious without the conscious participation of the subject.

All in all, Janet's formulation of the subconscious origin of multiple personality and the possession experience became the ruling attitude of those who subscribe to the psychological view of multiple man. Those who fall into this tradition tend to agree that the subconscious mind (1) has various levels or states; (2) shows the capacity to reason, plan and formulate; and (3) can secretly incubate a complex of ideas and emotions for a long period of time, and then allow those ideas and emotions to suddenly manifest full-blown in the individual's life.

FURTHER DEVELOPMENTS

Virtually everyone who accepts multiple personality as a genuine phenomenon and works with it therapeutically is employing the principles of subconscious formation as developed by Janet. If there are differences of opinion among modern workers, they arise mainly on the level of *how* the subconscious does what it does and what forces compel it to action.

Moving from multiple personality to possession, one finds a much greater diversity of opinion among members of the psychological tradition. Some insist that the possession experience can always be fully explained in terms of the subconscious productions of the victim. Others believe that although this is often the case, at times the evidence for some kind of external intrusion is strong enough to deserve serious attention.

It is not possible to describe here the main psychological formulations concerning multiple man which have developed since Janet. For those interested, the references in the bibliography for Part Four can serve as a starting point for further investigation.

Chapter 16

An Integral View of Multiple Man

In this final chapter I will be taking a tack different from that of the rest of the book. Up to now, my approach has been what could be called "phenomenological"; it has consisted largely of describing experiences and the participants' interpretations of those experiences. I have attempted to make as clear as possible the nature of the multiplicity experience in its own terms, and in the terms of those who have treated it. In Chapter 15, I went further and presented the interpretations given by those who have made a special study of the phenomena. Now I would like to move on to exercise a bit of speculative imagination and give you an idea of how I myself have come to interpret the phenomena of human multiplicity. At times I will go beyond the realm of psychological speculation and touch upon that of metaphysics. I trust that this intrusion can be forgiven, however, since we all have our philosophical leanings and need to air them now and again.

Before beginning, I would like to emphasize three things. First, a therapeutic consideration. As I have mentioned before, I do not hold that therapeutic effectiveness is dependent upon, or even related to, the philosophical beliefs of the therapist. I do not, therefore, consider agreement with the philosophical conclusions reached here to be a prerequisite for doing good therapy with multiplicity disturbances. In my own case, the therapy preceded the conclusions. Second, an organizational consideration. This chapter is not a summing up of what has been presented in the earlier parts of the book, nor is it a treatment intended to give validity to material already presented. The rest of the book stands firmly on its own ground. And third, a caution. In this chapter I will be talking about how I see things now. I have not always seen things this way; my views have evolved to this point and I am sure will continue to evolve. Also, they do not constitute anything like a complete system for understanding the inner nature of multiple man. Rather, they are reflections on certain aspects of his inner constitution. It is hoped that these reflections will be a stimulating addition to the discussion of the nature of human personality.

THE PROBLEM

In ordinary life we tend to make certain assumptions about each other. When I meet George or Mary, I see each as a single physical organism and expect to be dealing with one individual. What at one moment that individual consciously thinks, feels, experiences or does, I expect him to remember and own up to at a later moment. I expect continuity and unity of memory as well as continuity and unity of identity.

If, however, I encounter George one day and he assures me that he is *not* George but rather Harry, a very different kind of personality who claims to share the body with George, I may be somewhat taken aback. Or if I am talking to Mary, and her voice changes and she asserts that she is Aunt Hilda who died when Mary was two years old, I might find that a bit odd. For this kind of behavior violates the conventions of unity and continuity which we take for granted. It causes confusion, and we tend to feel there is something terribly wrong.

But these more dramatic violations of the conventions are not the only ones. There is more and more evidence that even "normal" people are multiple. Hypnotic research on "hidden observers" (already mentioned in Chapter 2) indicates that there is reason to posit any number of individual hidden personalities within the ordinary human subject. Psychiatric workers such as John Beahrs are saying that people function like an orchestra—made up of multiple selves—rather than like solo instruments. The more one finds out about human multiplicity, the more one wonders whether the continuity and unity conventions are not really a simplistic misreading of the human situation, based upon the naive assumption that one body means one person.

The question of whether that assumption is really naive or, in fact, based on some higher awareness will be left aside for now. Before examining the problem of unity further, more needs to be said about the phenomenon of multiplicity.

MULTIPLICITY

Most of us experience ourselves to some degree or other as multiple. We have our "moods" and "changes of mind." I might, at times, find it hard to identify with an emotional reaction I experienced or a course of action I took last week or last year. On the odd occasion I might not even be able to remember some important thing I said or did, and express surprise when someone points it out to me. These are common examples of multiplicity—the kind one does not ordinarily become alarmed about.

There is no alarm because, by and large, I feel that I possess a basic personal unity which provides a sense of oneness and continuity in my life. When using the pronoun "I," I believe that it refers to a single center from which all of my feelings, thoughts and actions derive.

However, by glossing over these experiences of multiplicity, we are deprived of a deeper understanding of the nature of our inner selves. So let us now consider an example of multiplicity different from those mentioned so far and see what it may have to show us.

DRAMATIC PERSONATION

In the course of my work as a therapist, I have made extensive use of a technique that is usually called "psychodrama." This is a dramatization carried out for therapeutic purposes. A scene is devised and enacted which, it is hoped, will have a helpful, emotional impact upon the client. The scene may be the recreation of something that actually happened in the client's life, or it may be an imaginary situation concocted to bring hidden elements to light. I have found the technique powerfully effective. Over the last fifteen years, I have used it on literally hundreds of occasions.

It is largely the circumstances of my practice that have made it possible to use the technique frequently. I have often taken care of therapeutic groups of various kinds, and these have provided an excellent context for psychodrama. The dramatization would be set up with group members playing the roles needed. Sometimes the client himself would be engaged in the drama. The scene might, for instance, be that of a drunken father abusing the mother in the presence of the children. An actor would be chosen for each member of the family with perhaps the client playing himself as a child. The scene would then be dramatized with as much emotional power as possible. The enactment might induce an abreaction in the client, or it might simply clarify hidden emotional dynamics of the family never before seen. When the psychodrama was finished, the implications could be further explored both by those engaged in the acting and those viewing the scene.

From using this technique for many years, I have noticed two remarkable things. First of all, I have been surprised at the fine acting job done by individuals who have shown no particular talent in that direction in other circumstances. And second, I have been struck by how little information the actors seem to need to perform their roles. Each of these points needs a bit of elaboration.

While I have, at times, had individuals participating who were either professional actors or had a penchant for that art, the great majority of dramatizers have had no such inclinations, and often were reluctant or even frightened to try. Frequently they were individuals singularly lacking in a dramatic flair in the conduct of their daily lives. Nevertheless, I have found in people a widespread ability to effectively portray a characterization, even when they were given little instruction about what to do. There seems to be within people a natural ability to take on a personality other than their own and to act from within that assumed personality. They appear to actually *become* that personality and to some extent, leave their own personality behind. The English word which most closely expresses this phenomenon is "personation." My experience with psychodrama shows me that human beings may be said to have the *innate capacity* to "personate," to take on full-blown personalities and act from within them. It is my belief that everyone has this ability, although certain individuals have severe blocks against using it.

Usually an individual who has agreed to perform a role in psychodrama at first feels stiff or self-conscious. However, that is soon left behind. The actor enters more and more into the "spirit" of the situation, forgetting that there are people watching, responding spontaneously to developments taking place within the drama. Sometimes the actor becomes so involved that, according to his own description, he temporarily forgets that he is acting. He begins to "believe" he is the personality he is portraying and enters so deeply into the situation that when it is over, it takes some time for him to "recover himself." I have seen individuals so taken over by their acting part that for an hour or more afterwards, they had confused impressions of still being the person portrayed.

Such extreme reactions could be interpreted as a sign of disturbance within the actor. However, I have often seen this happen to very stable individuals, and believe it to be an indication of the great malleability of the human psyche.

As to the second point, I would like to simply mention it now and return to it later. It amounts to this. The actors in these dramatizations often have little information to rely on when they are performing their roles. In some instances, they might have gleaned certain details from being in the same therapeutic group as the person for whom the drama is being performed; most often, they have only a few words from the coordinator who sets up the drama to guide them in presenting a personality entirely unknown to them. Yet sometimes the allusions they make, the movements they execute and the peculiar phraseology they use are remarkably accurate. The person for whom the drama is being performed may actually think the actors are intimately acquainted with the individuals being portrayed. I believe that this is a sign that an unconscious connection has somehow been established with the personality being portrayed. I will discuss a little later how such a thing might be possible.

For the moment, there is one main point I would like to make in this discussion of dramatic personation. This type of therapeutic dramatization provides striking examples of the human being's amazing capacity to create and enact personalities. The presence of this ability in the human psyche has important implications which will be discussed next.

PERSONALITY AS A TOOL

Human beings are sometimes characterized as tool-making animals. Although there are many examples of lower animals using simple devices to accomplish some end (such as the ape that reaches food with a stick or the bird that breaks a clam's shell with a stone), man is different in that the whole of his practical life seems to be centered around the invention and utilization of tools.

This human characteristic has more far-reaching application than is ordinarily recognized. I think there is reason to believe that the whole of man's *emotional* life is centered around the invention and utilization of those tools that we call "personalities." And I believe that the remarkable facility that he possesses to create them is an indication of that fact.

At this point I would like to introduce a working definition of the term "personality." Usually the word "person" simply means an individual, a human being. "Personality" correspondingly means the complex of characteristics that distinguishes that individual from others. However, since it is now recognized that there can be more than one personality within an individual human being, the meaning must be further defined. I will call "personality" that complex of characteristics that has a completeness and cohesion sufficient for one to think of it as distinguishing an individual human being, even though it may not be the sole "inhabitant" of a human body. Only by expanding the definition of "personality" in this way can it be applied to cases of multiple personality and other multiplicity phenomena.

Many "I's"

In a lecture related in *Views from the Real World*, G.I. Gurdjieff (1873–1949), the great Russian mystical teacher, agrees that such ingenuity is not limited to those subject to multiple personality "disturbance":

> Man is a plural being. When we speak of ourselves ordinarily we speak of "I." We say " 'I' did this," " 'I' want to do this"—but this is a mistake.
>
> There is no such "I," or rather there are hundreds, thousands of little "I's" in every one of us. We are divided in ourselves but we cannot recognize the plurality of our being except by observation and study. At one moment it is one "I" that acts, at the next moment it is another "I." It is because the "I's" in ourselves are contradictory that we do not function harmoniously.

P.D. Ouspensky, who worked with Gurdjieff from 1915 to 1918, in his book *In Search of the Miraculous* quotes Gurdjieff elaborating on this point:

> "It is the greatest mistake," he said, "to think that man is always one and the same. A man is never the same for long. He is continually changing. He seldom remains the same even for half an hour. We think that if a man is called Ivan he is always Ivan. Nothing of the kind. Now he is Ivan, in another minute he is Peter, and a minute later he is Nicholas, Sergius, Matthew, Simon. All of you think he is Ivan. You know that Ivan cannot do a certain thing. He cannot tell a lie, and you are surprised he

could have done so. And, indeed, Ivan cannot lie; it is Nicholas who lied. And when the opportunity presents itself Nicholas *cannot help lying.* You will be astonished when you realize what a multitude of these Ivans and Nicholases live in one man. If you learn to observe them there is no need to go to a cinema."

In the book *Mysteries* (1978) Colin Wilson further develops Gurdjieff's theme. He states that an individual's selves are arranged within him like the rungs of a ladder. The bottom rungs of this "ladder of selves" are wide, for our lower selves are characterized by a feeling of diffusion, lack of focus and low intensity. They are robotic in character. But as one moves up the ladder, the self-rungs become progressively narrower, being characterized by a greater concentration. The higher selves, therefore, operate under increased pressure, with greater intensity and more of a feeling of being alive. One moves *up* the ladder through purposeful activity or through a heightened awareness brought about by life-crises. One moves *down* the ladder through depression and fatigue. *What* moves up and down the ladder of selves is *consciousness.* The individual identifies with that self where his consciousness happens to be at that moment.

It is an interesting fact that those who have worked with or studied multiple personality cases often refer to that condition as a "creative illness." They mean that when an individual is confronted with a problem or conflict, he solves the difficulty inventively by creating a personality suited to handle the troublesome situation. This solution is certainly preferable to other possible approaches such as schizophrenic withdrawal, paranoid projection or manic flight. Instead of relying on these escapes the individual creates a *tool*, a personality designed precisely for the need confronting him. In that way he is able to continue functioning in the world. Often the personality-tool he fashions is so well designed that everyone assumes it is the primary personality; indeed it may be considered a definite improvement over the primary personality. In any case, a tool should be made to fit the task, and multiple personality subjects show themselves to be particularly deft at this kind of invention.

There is a remarkable study by Reima Kampman of the University of Oulu in Finland, which indicates that creative inventiveness is not limited to multiple personality cases. In her article appearing in the *International Journal of Clinical and Experimental*

Hypnosis in 1976 and entitled "Hypnotically Induced Multiple Personality: An Experimental Study," she concludes that subjects capable of producing secondary personalities are "clinically healthier and more adaptive" than those who cannot. She further suggests that responding to the suggestions to develop multiple personalities is a "creative activity of the ego." This gives us a strong indication that the greater the ability to create personality-tools, the healthier and more adaptive the individual.

As Colin Wilson says, as a person's consciousness moves from self to self, his sense of who he is changes. These changes of identity are happening to people all the time, but they are seldom reflected upon.

Similarly, the great American psychologist William James wrote in his *Principles of Psychology* that as we live our ordinary lives we are "seized and possessed" by a multitude of selves which constitute the "empirical me." He, like Wilson, sees these selves as arranged in an ascending hierarchy. He places the "bodily self" at the bottom and the "spiritual self" at the top. All of these selves serve specific purposes and together form the cohesive whole we call an individual.

Gurdjieff, Wilson and James are describing a condition they consider to be common to all human beings. They start from their own experiences and similar events in the lives of other "normal" people. It is their contention that, whether we realize it or not, we all experience ourselves as multiple. I agree with this view.

The multiple selves within human beings all have their uses. We need our more robotic selves to plug away at routine tasks. We need our higher selves for creative undertakings. In between there are all sorts of important functions to be carried out by whatever selves are suited to the purpose. Wilson gives a good example of such a middle personality when he describes the experience of a "schoolmistress" personality within himself. This personality was able to step in at a crucial moment and bring order when, under work pressure, a dangerous panic was being induced by a lower level of his being, just as a schoolmistress would walk into a noisy classroom and bring the students to immediate attention with a clap of her hands.

Looked at from this point of view, man's ability to make personality-tools to deal with the challenges of life is a great strength. It allows him a versatility in coping with the many facets of human existence.

A great philosopher once said, "Man is infinitely malleable." In no aspect of human nature does this more truly apply than in regard to his ability to create personalities as needed. It is as though the subconscious is composed of a highly plastic "substance" which is available to be shaped into any form of personality required. Speaking about this remarkable malleability in terms of a plastic substance is, of course, only figurative of a quality that remains mysterious as to its essential nature. However, if we are going to discuss it at all, such figures of speech are unavoidable.

As mentioned before, man's subconscious malleability gives him a great advantage in dealing with the challenges of life. However, not everyone makes full use of this ability to respond inventively to situations. In fact, it would probably be true to say that for the majority of people, their personality-tool making power is largely in abeyance. They might find one or two serviceable personality-tools and leave it at that for the whole of their lives. This has the advantage of simplifying things, but the disadvantage of affording little flexibility in coping with the changing vicissitudes of life.

But if inner malleability and the capacity to create personality-tools are a great advantage for human beings, they also have their problematic side. This must be considered next.

EVENT AMNESIA AND IDENTITY AMNESIA

A client of mine—not a multiple personality—once told me that he sometimes felt he was a multitude of selves. These selves, he said, were like straws loosely bundled together within him. As different straws were drawn out and put back, he would be now one self, now another. He never knew which self he would be at any moment. Neither did he know who or what it was that determined which straw would be chosen, though he knew the selves were all his. He was aware of what his different selves were doing as they were doing it, and afterwards he could remember all that had happened perfectly well. But when thinking back he found it hard to *identify* with those other selves. He had great difficulty in claiming their feelings and actions as his own when he was not actually "being" them.

This client was suffering from a kind of amnesia, but of a sort different from that ordinarily recognized. The term "amnesia" has long been used in a rather uncritical fashion in connection with multiplicity of consciousnesses. Its basic meaning is "lack of memory" and assumes that there is *one* consciousness which *knew* and then *forgot* something. I will further examine this confusing use of the term later. For now, however, I will pass over that issue and use the word in the way it has been traditionally employed—that is, to emphasize the experience of discontinuity.

To return to my client's description, it is clear that in cases like his the subject does not lack knowledge of an event; rather, he lacks connection with an identity. He knows *what* he has done or undergone—the event—but he does not feel that it was *he* who experienced it. He does not feel that other personality to be himself as he *now* experiences himself. It seems appropriate then to speak about two kinds of amnesia. I will call them *event amnesia* and *identity amnesia*. With event amnesia, the individual lacks knowledge of an experience; with identity amnesia, he lacks connection with the subject who had the experience. My client was describing lack of connection with an identity, not with an event, and so was suffering from identity amnesia only.

Identity amnesia exists in its extreme form in cases of multiple personality. It is, in fact, the distinguishing mark of that condition. The assertion "I am not he and he is not me" is always present when one personality of a multiple becomes aware of another. Event amnesia, on the other hand, although generally a part of multiple personality, is not one of its essential characteristics. This is demonstrated by the fact that two personalities can exist side by side in one individual, each completely aware of the actions of the other, and still consider themselves entirely distinct. In his *Outline of Abnormal Psychology* (1926), William McDougall pointed out a number of such cases of "coconscious" personalities. Here there is no event amnesia. There is only identity amnesia, the inability of one personality to identify with another. That is the essence of multiple personality.

Identity amnesia can, however, exist in different degrees. My client was not, as I mentioned, a multiple personality. Yet he described a certain amount of this kind of identity discontinuity. I believe that everyone, to some extent, experiences identity amnesia. It is so common that we toss it off with phrases such as "I was not myself" or "I must have been out of my mind." As a therapist, I often come across this kind of identity disowning in statements like "The way I was shows there is a lot of my mother in me" or "That was my superego talking." A similar identity discontinuity may be seen in the attitudes of those who have just

251

joined or left cult-type situations: they tend to disown their previous personality state.

Because there is no forgetting of events, this experience of discontinuity is usually not given sufficient attention. This is shown by the fact that the issue of multiple consciousnesses is too often linked with event amnesia. However, as I have pointed out, that is not the essential issue even for full-blown multiple personality cases.

Part of the problem is in the terminology itself. "Amnesia" means loss of memory. If you forget what you did, you suffer from event amnesia. If you forget who you were, you suffer from identity amnesia. But the term itself implies that there is a single person or self who forgets. If the person *now* is sufficiently distinct from the person *before* to say that the event was not experienced by him or the identity was not experienced by him, there is actually no "forgetting" involved at all. There is simply change of identity. In that case, the distinction between the two amnesias is simple: with identity amnesia the facts of the experience become available to the new personality, whereas with event amnesia they do not. Obviously, the question finally reduces itself to this: is there a rock-bottom unity behind the changes of identity? I will take up this question presently. But first there is something else to consider.

OPERATIVE SELF, LATENT SELVES AND PERSONETTES

The personality operating at any moment in an individual may be called the *operative self.* That is the personality in which, for the moment, *consciousness-in-the-world* dwells. All other personalities are at that moment latent with regard to functioning in the world. As consciousness-in-the-world moves to another personality, the identity to some extent changes. The extent to which it changes depends upon the degree of evolution that personality has reached— that is, how much character and inner cohesion it has developed. If it is somewhat undeveloped, it might better be called a "personette." It will, in that case, have only a partial sense of self-identity when partaking of consciousness-in-the-world. It will also share in the stronger sense of identity of the developed personality with which it is associated. All of these points require elaboration.

The operative personality is the one which at the moment possesses the individual's consciousness-in-the-world. This notion agrees with that of F.W.H. Myers, who saw the "supraliminal conscious-ness" as the one developed to deal with existence on this planet. Consciousness-in-the-world is the active functioning of that su-praliminal self. I have developed Myers's picture further with the notion that the supraliminal self has available to it a number of personalities suited for the job of functioning in the world. These personalities have been developed for very specific tasks in that functioning, and the individual's consciousness-in-the-world moves from one to the other as each is needed. Each of these personalities takes on the individual's consciousness-in-the-world, much as the personalities of Billy Milligan would take "the spot" when neces-sary, and as "consciousness" would move up and down Colin Wil-son's ladder of selves as the individual altered the quality of his engagement with the world.

I have said that when the consciousness-in-the-world dwells with one self, that self is operative and the others are latent *in so far as consciousness-in-the-world goes*. This does not mean that the selves cease to have *any* consciousness. The discovery of multiple hidden observers within the individual, all of whom have conscious-ness simultaneous with the operative consciousness, would lead us to think that one's many selves may retain a type of conscious-ness of their own when not operative in the world. That is the way Billy Milligan described the situation with his many personalities. They continued to perform certain mental tasks when they were not in "the spot."

As consciousness-in-the-world moves from one personality to another, identity changes. That is because the sense of self-identity of each personality resides with that personality. Each personality is, from that point of view, a self.

When the personality is very unformed, it may be called a "mood" or "frame of mind" or "mental state." These have a certain amount of individual character and inner cohesion, but not enough to de-serve the name "personality." But to highlight the personalitylike nature of these states, I would like to call them "personettes." A "personette" would be a complex of characteristics which attaches to a temporary but repetitive emotional state, has a degree of complexity and cohesiveness and is subject to identity amnesia.

The sense of identity of a personette is not strong enough to stand on its own. It associates itself with one of the subject's well-formed personalities and partakes of the sense of identity of that personality.

I would like to note that among those personalities latent within the individual there may be some which seldom or never take on the consciousness-in-the-world. It seems to me quite possible that some latent personalities may be very well developed and yet never come to light, never become the operative self. Certain work with hidden observers seems to point in this direction. The question would then have to be posed about how and when such personalities would have been formed. Should the hypothesis of reincarnation prove to have validity, past lives might be one source of such well developed but latent personalities. Another possibility is that the subconscious mind is capable of forming and honing hidden personalities for some purposes which completely escape our present body of knowledge.

UNITY

Although some degree of identity amnesia is simply part of the human condition, having too much of it can mean trouble. For if an individual's life is to be productive, it must have running through it a sense of oneness and continuity which comes from the awareness that, in the last analysis, all proceeds from one coordinating source. It must, in other words, be characterized by an intrinsic unity which transcends the multiplicity.

But since human beings are so malleable and creative in terms of making personalities, the problem becomes one of establishing unity. And the problem of *unity* is ultimately the problem of *meaning*, for without a sense of unity in one's life, without the feeling that the *many* are working together for *one* purpose, that life will seem chaotic and senseless.

So if we are, as Gurdjieff says, hundreds of thousands of "I's," and if we move through these multiple selves as needs require and invention allows, what provides the essential unifying structure? If we are personality-making beings, precisely *what* or *who* is doing the making?

I alluded to this question earlier in pointing out that the terms "identity amnesia" and "event amnesia" are to some extent misleading. It is not as though someone forgets who he is or what he has done; there is, instead, a succession of "someones" who may or may not have access to the memories of the others. Nevertheless, the use of the term "amnesia" does have a certain validity if there is an overall unifying subject to whom all these various selves belong.

So we return now to the question posed at the beginning of this chapter: when we encounter one human organism, is it naive to suppose that we are dealing with one human subject? Or, put another way, is there an essential unity of the psyche which corresponds to the singularity of the body?

If there is not, if the only unity for an individual is the simple fact that he has but one body, then each human being is merely a loosely bound collection of consciousnesses operating within the single organism. There is, then, no metaphysical unity behind the multiplicity. That in fact seems to be the view of John Beahrs given in his *Unity and Multiplicity*. He agrees that we are all multiple, that "there can be an unlimited, potentially infinite number of hidden observers or 'personalities' within a single human individual." He also posits a kind of unity, consisting in something he calls the Cohesive Self. But the unity of the Cohesive Self in this schema seems rather weak, being brought about by one of our many personalities or part-selves taking up the position of coordinator of the others, much like a conductor takes up the baton to lead an orchestra. In this view an individual is a conglomeration of disparate elements, held together in uneasy cooperation under the leadership of one coordinating consciousness which can easily be replaced by another. While I believe this view has validity and throws much light on the nature of human psychological functioning, it does not, in my opinion, give a satisfactory answer to the question of the rock-bottom unity of the individual.

Is there, then, another source of unity besides the body or some temporarily coordinating personality? Is there an agent that is the unique origin of the inventive and rich multiplicity that the human personality manifests? Is there one unseen center that coordinates everything an individual is and does?

I believe there is such a unifying agent. I believe there is, at the core of each human individual, a single toolmaker which produces his array of selves, personalities, personettes or whatever one may wish to call them. That source of unity I call, for want of a better term, the "ultimate self."

What can be said about this ultimate self? First of all, it is clear that it is not directly knowable. It can only be sensed by the individual, never directly grasped. The tool is not the toolmaker. We can know directly only the personalities or lesser selves that

255

the ultimate self fashions. These lesser selves are known through their emotions, thoughts and actions. They have a character which can be identified. Not so with the ultimate self. For if you could describe it and thereby set it off from other selves within the person, you would then have to look for another yet more ultimate self which would be the source and unifying principle of the selves described. So the self being considered would not really be ultimate, not that core element that gives the whole its intrinsic unity.

I might look at myself and ask: which of my personalities is the "real me?" I would then have to choose one from among the many and invest it with that preeminence. But I believe that would be a mistake. As I mentioned in Chapter 3, such an approach was taken by some of the earlier workers who dealt with multiple personality. They made a judgment about which personality was the "real self." This led to confusion and suffering for the patient. The problem was that in artificially elevating one personality to the status of the "real" self, they were simply choosing one from among basically equal partners. What needed to be seen was that if there is a "real" self, it is not one of those vying for control of the consciousness. It is something beyond that. This holds true not only for multiple personality cases, but also for "normal" individuals.

The nineteenth-century philosopher Carl Du Prel also addresses this question of the "real me." In his *Philosophy of Mysticism,* Du Prel talks about the fact that we discover in ourselves a multitude of "personifications" of ourselves. We are always splitting ourselves up, for example, in the personifications of our dreams or in the secondary consciousnesses discovered in somnambulism. None of these personifications, says Du Prel, is our rock-bottom self. The ultimate self is called by Du Prel the "Subject." It is the Subject that does all the personifying. And this Subject is unknowable.

When writing about his "ladder of selves," Colin Wilson asks the same question about the ultimate self beyond the many selves. He frames the question in this way: what lies at the top of the ladder? As, when moving up the ladder, the rungs become narrower and the sides converge, we experience higher and higher selves. Eventually we come to a single ultimate point: the "real me." How can one characterize that point? It cannot be identified with any of the self-rungs of the ladder, not even the highest. What then can be said of it? All that Wilson can affirm of this "real me" is that it is identical with the Spirit, the Oversoul which presides over all.

Many philosophers who write about the nature of the ultimate self reach the same conclusion. They say that in the last analysis, there is no way to distinguish it from the ultimate foundation of all that exists—the One at the source of all being. I am not, at this moment, prepared to follow to these dizzying heights of metaphysical speculation. However, one correlate of this conclusion would be that the consciousnesses of all intelligent beings are somehow ultimately *connected*. This correlate would have important practical consequences for the understanding of the phenomenon of possession. It is to that fascinating subject that I now turn.

POSSESSION

I have earlier defined possession as the invasion of an individual by an alien intelligent entity. Sometimes the presence of the possessing entity is perceived by observers. At other times it is experienced only internally. Sometimes the host's personality is absent during the intervals of possession (trance possession). At other times the two personalities are there simultaneously (lucid possession). In the latter case, there is almost always some kind of moral or emotional influence exercised by the possessor upon the possessed.

Trance possession is analogous to multiple personality in that usually the main personality of a multiple is absent when the other personalities manifest. Also, complete identity amnesia and some event amnesia are present in both conditions.

Lucid possession, on the other hand, exhibits only identity amnesia, and that in an extreme form. Lucid possession does show some similarity to less dramatic instances of identity amnesia, however. Individuals may describe carrying out some act, producing some response, or being overcome by some feeling while their ordinary consciousness looks on "from a distance"—with interest or horror. The analogy of this type of experience to lucid possession seems quite close.

Where the comparison between possession and other multiple states breaks down is in the fact that with possession, an *alien* entity is involved. "Alien" means that it is neither the individual himself nor a repressed or split-off part of him that takes possession. If there is indeed such a thing as possession, this is its distinguishing mark: the invading entity is *not* the host.

Following upon the earlier discussion of personality as tool, it is

257

now possible to introduce a new definition of possession. Considering that the ultimate self can create within the individual whatever personalities it requires to deal with living in this world, the new view of possession which emerges is this: possession is the creation of a personality within an individual by an ultimate self other than that of the individual himself.

With possession, the malleable "substance" of the host's subconscious is used by an alien self to mold a new personality which becomes the vehicle for the presence of that alien self. So the personality-toolmaker is an entity other than the host. Since it is created by another self and a bearer of its presence, the new personality is under the domination of that alien self.

It makes little difference what type of being that alien self is. It may be a human individual—living or dead—or it may be nonhuman. The essential element is that it is a personality-toolmaking self other than that of the host.

Possession by group-minds, thought-forms or other psychic creations originating from without is a somewhat different matter. In this case, the molding influence does not carry the presence of its maker. For that reason it is intellectually rudimentary and does not strike one as possessing that indefinable quality associated with persons.

A word could also be inserted here about the tangentially related matter of reincarnation. Should the ultimate self of the individual continue to exist after death and repeatedly enter and leave this world through multiple lifetime experiences, it would seem possible that it could recreate or reassert those former personality constellations in the conscious experience of the present individual. Conceivably, a personality formed in a previous life could intrude into present consciousness in various degrees—even to the point of appearing to be a case of full-blown possession.

I would like to return now to a matter mentioned earlier: the information used in the enactment of psychodramas. As I said, I have often seen actors in a psychodrama, operating from very little information, "become" the person that they were portraying to such perfection that they even used that person's characteristic gestures and peculiar phraseology. How is such a thing possible? One could suppose that the actor was picking up information telepathically from the subject for whom the psychodrama was being done. That seems a plausible supposition. But one must also consider the *way* the actor experiences the enactment. Often he has the sensation of being *taken over* and losing himself during the dramatization. Taking that into account, I do not feel satisfied with a telepathic explanation. There seems to be something more, some further element which involves another *presence*: the *presence* of the person being portrayed.

This may, at first glance, seem a rather extreme position to adopt in an attempt to explain the matter. But if we look into it a bit deeper, it might not seem so farfetched.

Carl Jung speaks of the fact that we have not only a personal unconscious, with memories and complexes formed from our own personal life experiences, but also a collective unconscious. On the level of the collective unconscious we are connected to all other human beings, not only in the past, but also the present. These collectivities are layered. There is, on the deepest level, the great human collectivity to which we all belong. On that level we are connected with all humanity past and present. Then there are smaller collectivities, such as nations or ethnic groups. Here the connections are closer because there are more specific experiences held in common.

Although Jung does not develop the details of the nature of collectivities of the smaller more concentrated kind, I believe there is a continuous progression of collectivities from the whole of the human race right down to the individual family. It is my view that the connections on the level of the collective unconscious of the smaller groupings are more complex and contain more detail than those on the level of the collective unconscious of the whole human race. In other words, as one moves down the continuum from the collective unconscious of humanity to the collective unconscious of the family, connections between the individual members become closer and more enriched with the contents of specific experiences of the members.

The implication of this view is that all people are intrinsically connected, partaking of a common substratum of some unknown kind. The smaller the collectivities, the more particularized and immediate the connections between the members, to the point of actually feeling the collectivity as a grouping of *presences*, past and present. There is no reason to suppose that some of these presences may not impinge upon one individual more than others, using channels formed by the connections of the collectivity. When a particular presence impinges on another individual so powerfully as to manifest in him concretely, there exists a state of possession.

Using the new definition given above, a state of possession exists when one individual within the collectivity uses the channels available within that collectivity to impinge upon another individual and create in him a new personality. That personality is under the domination of the impinging individual and is a vehicle for his presence.

This implies that since connecting channels already exist within a small collectivity, possession is more likely to occur between members of that collectivity. This suspicion seems to be borne out by the fact that I have come across so many cases of possession of individuals by someone who is a member of their ancestral family.

SELF-POSSESSION

The ultimate goal of multiple man is complete *self-possession*. This is a state which, it seems, we are not destined to experience in its fullness in this life. Yet we do experience it in degrees, and at times get a glimpse of what the ideal is like.

I would describe the self-possessed person as an individual who is able to so shepherd his being that none of its elements move completely beyond his embrace. This means that when a person is completely self-possessed, the many facets of his being, the many personalities of his creation, are fully unified from that core which is his ultimate self. This also means that the self-possessed person cannot be possessed by another.

In the state of self-possession, multiplicity holds no threat. The self-possessed individual realizes that having many personalities available to him is an indication of the array of tools at his disposal. He does not feel alienated from them. He claims them as his own and appreciates them for what they really are.

Self-possession is brought about not by "fusion" of the many facets, but by consciously linking them to his ultimate self from which they come. As the individual's consciousness residing in each of his personalities becomes more and more aware of his ultimate self as a presence, that connection is strengthened.

The self-possessed person *knows who he is*. He knows he is at bottom, his ultimate self. He recognizes his many facets as tools which he, as his ultimate self, has formed. The infusion of each of those facets with this awareness is the essence of self-possession, for only in this way can his ultimate self fully possess its creations.

Summing Up

Possession involves the invasion of a person by an entity from the outside.

Multiple personality involves the spontaneous emergence of a personality manufactured within.

The *hidden observer* phenomenon involves the manifestation of personalities normally concealed within the ordinary individual.

Basically these terms describe *experiences*. How one *explains* these experiences is another matter. The challenge to anyone dealing with this field is to refrain from too facile interpretations. The Caribbean spiritist believes he *knows* what these things are. So does the American psychoanalyst. Each uses his interpretation to treat those plagued by forms of disturbing multiplicity, and each has his successes. But I believe that at this stage of things *all* speculation about what is behind these experiences must be considered provisional. Otherwise the explanation becomes a screen that sifts out facts of experience which do not fit in, a censoring device that deprives us of the information needed to gain a deeper understanding of the nature of multiple man.

Bibliography

This bibliography is meant to serve two purposes: (1) to give complete information about the sources directly quoted in the text and (2) to provide a selection of works which can serve as a starting point for further study of the matters dealt with in the book. It is not intended to be an exhaustive listing of relevant writings.

PART ONE

Allison, Ralph, *Mind in Many Pieces*. New York: Rawson, Wade Publishers, Inc., 1980.

Azam, Eugene, *Hypnotisme, Double Conscience et Altérations de la Personnalité*. Paris: Librairie J.B. Baillière et Fils, 1887.

Barrucand, Dominique, *Histoire de l'Hypnose en France*, Paris: Presses Universitaires de France, 1967.

Beahrs, John, *Unity and Multiplicity*. New York: Brunner/Mazel, 1982.

Binet, Alfred, *Alterations of Personality*. New York: D. Appleton and Company, 1886.

——————— , *On Double Consciousness*. Chicago: Open Court, 1980.

Boor, Myron and Philip Coons, "A Comprehensive Bibliography of Literature Pertaining to Multiple Personality." *Psychological Reports*, 53 (1983), 295–310.

Bramwell, J. Milne, *Hypnotism, Its History, Practice and Theory*. New York: Julian Press, 1956.

Buranelli, Vincent, *The Wizard from Vienna*. New York: Coward, McCann & Geoghegan, Inc., 1975.

Carlson, Eric, "The History of Multiple Personality in the United States: I. The Beginnings." *American Journal of Psychiatry*, 138 (1981), 666–68.

——————— , "The History of Multiple Personality in the United States: II. Mary Reynolds and Her Subsequent Reputation." Paper delivered at the 55th annual meeting of the American Association for the History of Medicine, April 30, 1982.

Chastenet de Puységur, A.M.J., *Mémoires pour Servir à l'Histoire et à l'Etablissement du Magnétisme Animal*. Paris: J.G. Dentu, 1820.

Colquhoun, J.C., *An History of Magic Witchcraft, and Animal Magnetism* 2 Vols. London: Longman, Brown, Green, & Longmans, 1851.

——————— , *Isis Revelata*, 2 Vols. Edinburgh: MacLachlan & Stewart, 1844.

Cory, Charles, "A Divided Self." *Journal of Abnormal Psychology*, 14 (1919), 281–91.

Darnton, Robert, *Mesmerism and the End of the Enlightenment in France*. New York: Schocken Books, 1970.

Deleuze, J.P.F., *Histoire Critique du Magnétisme Animal*, 2 Vols. Paris: Mame, 1813.

Dessoir, Max, *Das Doppel-Ich*. Leipzig: Ernst Gunthers Verlag, 1896.

Dingwall, Eric, *Abnormal Hypnotic Phenomena*, 4 Vols. New York: Barnes & Noble, Inc., 1967–1968.

Duoptet de Sennevoy, Jean, *An Introduction to the Study of Animal Magnetism*, London: Saunders & Otley, 1838.

———————— , *Traité Complet du Magnétisme Animal*. Paris: Germer Bailliere, 1856.

Ellenberger, Henri F., *The Discovery of the Unconscious*. New York: Basic Books, Inc., 1970.

Elliotson, John, *Numerous Cases of Surgical Operations Without Pain in the Mesmeric State*. Philadelphia: Lea and Blanchard, 1843.

Esdaile, James, *Mesmerism in India*. London: Longman, Brown, Green, and Longmans, 1846.

———————— , *Natural and Mesmeric Clairvoyance*. London: Hyppolyte Bailliere, 1852.

Freud, Sigmund and Breuer, Josef, "Studies on Hysteria," *The Complete Psychological Works of Sigmund Freud*, Vol. II. London: Hogarth Press, 1964.

Goldsmith, Margaret, *Franz Anton Mesmer: The History of an Idea*. London: Arthur Barker Ltd., 1934.

George Greaves, "Multiple Personality 165 Years after Mary Reynolds." *The Journal of Nervous and Mental Disorders*, 168 (1980), 577–96.

Gregory, William, *Letters to a Candid Inquirer on Animal Magnetism*. London: Taylor, Walton, and Maberly, 1851.

Gurney, Edmund, "The Stages of Hypnotism," *Proceedings of the Society for Psychical Research*, 2 (1884), 61–72.

———————— , "Stages of Hypnotic Memory," *Proceedings of the Society for Psychical Research*, 4 (1887), 515–31.

Haddock, Joseph, *Somnolism and Psycheism*. London: James S. Hodson, 1851.

Hilgard, Ernest, *Divided Consciousness: Multiple Controls in Human Thought and Action*. New York: John Wiley & Sons, 1977.

Inglis, Brian, *Natural and Supernatural*. London: Hodder and Stoughton, 1977.

Janet, Pierre, *L'automatisme Psychologique*. Paris: Félix Alcan, 1889.

———————— , *Nevroses et Idées Fixes*. 2 Vols. Paris: Félix Alcan, 1904.

———————— , *The Mental State of Hystericals*. New York: G.P. Putnam's Sons, 1901.

———————— , *The Major Symptoms of Hysterics*. New York: Macmillan Company, 1907.

Jastrow, Joseph, *The Subconscious*. London: Archibald Constable & Co., Ltd., 1905.

Keyes, Daniel, *The Minds of Billy Milligan*. New York: Random House, 1981.

Mayo, Herbert, *On The Truths Contained in Popular Superstitions*. Edinburgh: William Blackwood and Sons, 1851.

McDougall, William, *Outline of Abnormal Psychology*. New York: Charles Scribner's Sons, 1926.

McKellar, Peter, *Mindsplit*. London: J.M. Dent & Sons, Ltd., 1979.

Mesmer, Franz Anton, *Le Magnétisme Animal: Oeuvres Publiées par Robert Amadou*. Paris: Payot, 1971.

——————— , *Mesmerism: A Translation of the Original Scientific and Medical Writings of F.A. Mesmer*. (ed. George Bloch). Los Altos, California: William Kaufman, Inc., 1980.

——————— , *Mesmerism, by Doctor Mesmer* (ed. Gibert Frankau). London: MacDonald, 1948.

Myers, Frederick W.H., *Human Personality and its Survival of Bodily Death*, 2 Vols. London: Longmans, Green, and Co., 1903.

Northridge, W.L., *Modern Theories of the Unconscious*. New York: E.P. Dutton & Company, 1924.

Osty, Eugene, *Supernormal Faculties in Man*. London: Methuen & Co., Ltd., 1923.

Plumer, William, "Mary Reynolds: A Case of Double Consciousness." *Harper's New Monthly Magazine*, 20 (1860), 807–12.

Prince, Morton, *The Dissociation of a Personality*. New York: Meridian Books, 1957.

——————— , *The Unconscious*. New York: Macmillan Company, 1929.

Psychiatric Annals, Vol. 14, No. 1 (January, 1984): whole issue is devoted to articles on multiple personality.

Putnam, Frank, "Traces of Eve's Faces." *Psychology Today* (Oct., 1982), 88.

Rausky, Franklin, *Mesmer ou la Révolution Thérapeutique*. Paris: Payot, 1977.

Richet, Charles, *Thirty Years of Psychical Research*. London: Collins, 1923.

Rochas, Albert de, *L'Externalisation de la Sensibilité*. Paris: Chamuel, 1895.

——————— , *Les Etats Profonds de l'Hypnose*. Paris: Chamuel, 1892.

Schreiber, Flora Rheta, *Sybil*. Chicago: Henry Regnery Company, 1973.

Sidis, Boris, *The Psychology of Suggestion*. New York: D. Appleton and Company, 1911.

Sizemore, Chris and Pittillo, Elen, *I'm Eve*. Garden City, New York: Doubleday & Company, 1977.

Taylor, Eugene, *William James on Exceptional Mental States: The 1896 Lowell Lectures*. New York: Charles Scribner's Sons, 1983.

Tinterow, Maurice, *Foundations of Hypnosis*. Springfield, Illinois: Charles C. Thomas, 1970.

Tischner, Rudolph, *Franz Anton Mesmer*. Munich: Verlag Der Münchner Druke, 1928.

Townshend, Chauncy Hare, *Facts in Mesmerism*. New York, Harper and Brothers, 1844.

Watkins, J.G. and Watkins, H.H., "Ego States and Hidden Observers." *Journal of Altered States of Consciousness*, 5 (1979), 3–18.

Whyte, Lancelot, *The Unconscious Before Freud*. New York: Basic Books, 1960.

Allison, Ralph, "The Possession Syndrome on Trial." Paper read at the American College of Forensic Psychiatry Second Annual Symposium in Psychiatry and Law, April 25–28, 1984.

Beard, Paul, "How to Guard Against Possession." *Spiritual Frontiers*, 2 (Autumn, 1970), 224–28.

Brennan, J.H., *Experimental Magic*. Wellingborough, Northamptonshire: Aquarian Press, 1972.

Brittle, Gerald, *The Devil in Connecticut*. Toronto: Bantam Books, 1983.

_____ , *The Demonologist*. Englewood Cliffs, New Jersey: Prentice-Hall, Inc., 1980.

Brown, Rosemary, *Immortals by My Side*. Chicago: Henry Regenery Company, 1975.

_____ , *Unfinished Symphonies*. New York: William Morrow and Company, Inc., 1971.

Brown, Slater, *The Heyday of Spiritualism*. New York: Pocket Books, 1972.

Burton, Jean, *Heyday of a Wizard*. New York: Alfred A. Knopf, 1944.

Capron, E.W., *Modern Spiritualism*. New York: Bela March, 1855.

Crowley, Aleister, *Magick in Theory and Practice*. New York: Dover Publications, Inc., 1976.

Cutten, George, *The Psychological Phenomena of Christianity*. New York: Charles Scribner's Sons, 1909.

Ebon, Martin, (ed.), *Exorcism: Fact not Fiction*. New York: New American Library, 1974.

Ebon, Martin, *The Devil's Bride*. New York: Harper & Row, 1974.

Erickson, Milton and Kubie, Lawrence, "The Permanent Relief of an Obsessional Phobia by Means of Communications with an Unsuspected Dual Personality." *Psychoanalytic Quarterly*, 8 (1939), 471–509.

Evans, Hilary, *Intrusions: Society and the Paranormal*. London: Routledge and Kegan Paul, 1982.

Flournoy, Theodore, *From India to the Planet Mars*. New York: Harper & Brothers, 1900.

Fortune, Dion, *Psychic Self-Defence*. Wellingborough, Northamptonshire: Aquarian Press, 1981.

Goodman, Felicitas, *The Exorcism of Anneliese Michel*. Garden City, New York: Doubleday & Company, Inc., 1981.

Gray, William, *Inner Traditions of Magic*. New York: Samuel Weiser, 1978.

Hamilton, Michael, (ed.) *The Charismatic Movement*. Grand Rapids: William B. Eerdmans Publishing Company, 1975.

Hartmann, Franz, *Magic, White and Black*. Wellingborough, Northamptonshire: Aquarian Press, 1969.

Hollenweger, W.J., *The Pentecostals*. Minneapolis: Augsburg Publishing House, 1972.

Home, Daniel D., *Incidents in my Life*. New York: Carleton, 1863.

Home, Mme. Dunglas, *D.D. Home, His Life and Mission*. London: Trubner & Co., 1888.

Hyslop, James H., *Borderland of Psychical Research*. Boston: Herbert Turner & Co., 1906.

——————— , "The Doris Case of Multiple Personality." *Proceedings of the American Society for Psychical Research*, 11 (1917) 5–866.

——————— , *Contact with the Other World*. New York: The Century Co., 1919.

Inglis, Brian, *Natural and Supernatural*. London: Hodder and Stoughton, 1977.

Kenny, Michael, "Multiple Personality and Spirit Possession." *Psychiatry* 44 (1981), 337–58.

Kittredge, George, *Witchcraft in Old and New England*. Cambridge: Harvard University Press, 1929.

Lang, Andrew, *Cock Lane and Common-Sense*. New York: AMS Press, 1970.

Langton, Edward, *Good and Evil Spirits*. London: SPCK, 1942.

Leadbeater, C.W., *The Astral Plane*. Madras, India: Theosophical Publishing House, Adyar, 1973.

Leek, Sybil, *Driving Out the Devils*. New York: G.P. Putnam's Sons, 1975.

Leonard, Gladys Osborne. *My Life in Two Worlds*. London: Cassell & Company Ltd., 1931.

Levi, Eliphas, *The Great Secret*. Wellingborough, Northamptonshire: Aquarian Press, 1981.

Lhermitte, Jean, *Diabolical Possession, True and False*. London: Burns & Oates, 1963.

Litvag, Irving, *Singer in the Shadows*. New York: Macmillan Company, 1972.

Manning, Matthew, *In the Minds of Millions*. London: W.H. Allen, 1977.

——————— , *The Link*. New York: Holt, Rinehart and Winston, 1975.

Maple, Eric, *The Domain of Devils*. London: Robert Hale Ltd., 1966.

Maquart, F.X., "Exorcism and Diabolical Manifestation" in *Satan* (ed. Charles Moeller). London: Sheed and Ward, 1951, 178–203.

Martin, Malachi, *Hostage to the Devil*. New York: Reader's Digest Press, 1976.

Masters, Anthony, *The Devil's Dominion*. New York: G.P. Putnam's Sons, 1978.

Matson, William, *The Adversary*. New York: Wilbur B. Ketcham, 1881.

Mayer, Edward, "A Case Illustrating So-Called Demon Possession." *Journal of Abnormal Psychology*, 6 (1911), 265–78.

McAll, R.K., "Demonosis or the Possession Syndrome." *International Journal of Social Psychiatry*, 17 (1971), 150–58.

——————— , *Healing the Family Tree*. London: Sheldon Press, 1982.

McGiffert, Arthur, *A History of Christianity*. New York: Charles Scribner's Sons, 1923.

Montgomery, John W., (ed.) *Demon Possession: A Medical, Historical, Anthropological and Theological Symposium*, Minneapolis: Bethany Fellowship, Inc., 1976.

Nicola, John, *Diabolical Possession and Exorcism*. Rockford, Illinois: Tan Books, 1974.

Norvell, *Exorcism: Overcome Black Magic with White Magic*. West Nyac, New York: Parker Publishing Company, Inc., 1974.

Oesterreich, Traugott, *Possession and Exorcism*. New York: Causeway Books, 1974.

Owen, A.R.G., "A Preliminary Report on Matthew Manning's Physical Phenomena." *New Horizons*, 1 (1974), 172–73.

Pearce-Higgins, J.D., "Dangers of Automatism." *Spiritual Frontiers*, 2 (Autumn, 1970), 213–23.

_____ , "Twentieth Century 'Exorcism'." *Spiritual Frontiers*, 1 (Winter, 1969), 43–48.

Pearce-Higgins, J.D. and Whitby, G. Stanley, *Life, Death and Psychical Research*. London: Rider and Company, 1973.

Peebles, J.M., *The Demonism of the Ages*. Battle Creek, Michigan: Peebles Medical Institute, 1904.

Pelton, Robert, *Confrontations with the Devil*. New York: Pocket Books, 1979.

_____ , *The Devil and Karen Kingston*. New York: Pocket Books, 1977.

Prince, Walter Franklin, *The Case of Patience Worth*. New Hyde Park, New York: University Books, 1964.

_____ , "The Doris Case of Multiple Personality." *Proceedings of the American Society for Psychical Research*, 9–10 (1915–1916), 9-1331.

Randall, Edward C., *Frontiers of the After Life*. New York: Alfred A. Knopf, 1922.

Rodewyk, Adolf, *Possessed by Satan*. Garden City, New York: Doubleday & Company, Inc., 1975.

Shepard, Leslie (ed.), *Encyclopedia of Occultism and Parapsychology*, 2 Vols. New York: Avon, 1978.

Shepard, Leslie, *How to Protect Yourself Against Black Magic and Witchcraft*. Secaucus, New Jersey: Citadel Press, 1978.

Smith, Susy, *The Mediumship of Mrs. Leonard*. New Hyde Park, New York: University Books, 1964.

Stevenson, Robert Louis, *Across the Plains, with Other Memories and Essays*. London: Chatto & Windus, 1915.

Strachan, Francoise, *Casting out the Devils*. New York: Samuel Weiser, Inc., 1972.

Summers, Montague, *The History of Witchcraft and Demonology*. New Hyde Park, New York: University Books, 1966.

Thomas, Charles Drayton, *Life Beyond Death with Evidence*. London: Wm. Collins Sons & Co. Ltd., 1930.

Troubridge, Lady Una, "The *Modus Operandi* in So-Called Mediumistic Trance." *Proceedings of the Society for Psychical Research*, 32 (1922), 344–78.

Tyrrell, G.N.M., *The Personality of Man*. Middlesex: Penguin Books, 1960.

Salter, W.H., *Trance Mediumship*. London: Society for Psychical Research, 1950.

Van Dusen, Wilson, *The Natural Depth in Man*. New York: Harper & Row, 1966.

——————, *The Presence of Other Worlds*. New York: Harper & Row, 1974.

——————, "The Presence of Spirits in Madness," *New Philosophy*, 70 (1967), 461–77.

Vogel, Carl, *Begone Satan!*, Published by Rev. Celestine Kapsner, St. John's Abbey, Collegeville, Minnesota, 1935.

Walker, Nea, *The Bridge*. London: Cassell & Company Ltd., 1927.

Whitton, Joel L., " 'Ramp Function' in EEG Power Spectra during actual or attempted Paranormal Events." *New Horizons*, 1 (1974), 174–183.

Wickland, Carl, *The Gateway of Understanding*. Los Angeles: National Psychological Institute, 1934.

——————, *Thirty Years Among the Dead*. London: Spiritualist Press, 1968.

Wilson, Colin, *The Occult*. New York: Random House, 1971.

——————, *Poltergeist*. London: New English Library, 1981.

Wolman, Benjamin, (ed.), *Handbook of Parapsychology*. New York: Van Nostrand Reinhold Company, 1977.

Yap, P.M., "The Possession Syndrome." *Journal of Mental Science*, 106 (1960), 114–37.

Part Three

Bull, Titus, *Analysis of Unusual Experience in Healing Relative to Diseased Minds*. New York: James H. Hyslop Foundation, Inc., 1932.

——————, *The Imperative Conquest*. New York: James H. Hyslop Foundation, Inc., 1936.

Canetti, Elias, *Crowds and Power*. New York: Seabury Press, 1978.

Fortune, Dion, *Applied Magic*. New York: Samuel Weiser, Inc., 1976.

——————, *Sane Occultism*. Wellingborough, Northamptonshire: Aquarian Press, 1972.

Freud, Sigmund, "Group Psychology," *The Complete Psychological Works of Sigmund Freud*, Vol. XVIII. London: Hogarth Press, 1964.

Jung, Carl G., *The Archetypes and the Collective Unconscious*. Princeton, New Jersey: Princeton University Press, 1980.

Le Bon, Gustave, *The Crowd*. London: Ernest Benn Ltd., 1952.

Kampman, Reima, "Hypnotically Induced Multiple Personality: An Experimental Study." *International Journal of Clinical and Experimental Hypnosis*, 24 (1976), 215–27.

Kampman, Reima and Hirvenoja, R., "Research of Latent Multiple Personality Phenomenon Using Hypnosis, Projective Tests and Clinical Interviews." *Hypnose Psychosom, Md.*, (1972), 106–109.

McDougall, William, *The Group Mind*. New York: G.P. Putnam's Sons, 1920.

Orzeck, A.Z., McGuire, C. and Longenecker, E.D., "Multiple Self-Concepts as Effected by Mood States." *American Journal of Psychiatry*, 115 (1948), 349–53.

PART FOUR

Brennan, J.H., *Astral Doorways*. London: Aquarian Press, 1972.

Bohm, David, *Wholeness and the Implicate Order*. London: Routledge & Kegan Paul, 1981.

Conway, David, *Ritual Magic*. New York: E.P. Dutton, 1978.

Du Prel, Carl, *The Philosophy of Mysticism*. 2 Vols. London: George Redway, 1889.

Flournoy, Theodore, *Spiritism and Psychology*. New York: Harper & Brothers Publishers, 1911.

Fortune, Dion, *Applied Magic*. New York: Samuel Weiser Inc., 1976.

Frey-Rohm, Liliane, *From Freud to Jung*. New York: G.P. Putnam's Sons, 1974.

Gurdjieff, G.I., *Views from the Real World*. New York: E.P. Dutton, 1975.

Jacobi, Jolande, *The Psychology of C.G. Jung*. New Haven: Yale University Press, 1977.

James, William, "Frederic Myers's Service to Psychology." *Proceedings of the Society for Psychical Research*, 17 (1901), 13–23.

——————, *The Principles of Psychology*. 2 Vols., New York: Dover Publications Inc., 1980.

Jung, Carl G., *Aion: Researches into the Phenomenology of the Self*. Princeton, New Jersey: Princeton University Press, 1975.

——————, *The Archetypes and the Collective Unconscious*. Princeton, New Jersey: Princeton University Press, 1980.

——————, *The Structure and Dynamics of the Psyche*. Princeton, New Jersey: Princeton University Press, 1980.

Kampman, Reima, "Hypnotically Induced Multiple Personality: An Experimental Study." *International Journal of Clinical and Experimental Hypnosis*, 24 (1976), 215–27.

Knight, Gareth, *A History of White Magic*. New York: Samuel Weiser, 1979.

——————, *The Occult*. London: Kahn & Averill, 1975.

Lewin, Kurt, *A Dynamic Theory of Personality: Selected Papers by Kurt Lewin*. New York: McGraw Hill, 1935.

Long, Max Freedom, *Recovering from the Ancient Magic*. Cape Girardeau, Missouri: Huna Press, 1978.

—————— , *The Secret Science at Work*. Marina del Rey, California: DeVorss & Company, 1953.

—————— , *The Secret Science Behind Miracles*. Marina del Rey, California: DeVorss & Company, 1954.

Orzeck, A.Z., McGuire, C. and Longenecker, E.D., "Multiple Self-Concepts as Effected by Mood States." *American Journal of Psychiatry*, 115 (1948), 349–53.

Ouspensky, P.D., *In Search of the Miraculous*. New York: Harcourt Brace & World, Inc., 1949.

Pope, Kenneth and Singer, Jerome (eds.), *The Stream of Consciousness*. New York: Plenum Press, 1978.

Singer, June, *Boundaries of the Soul: The Practice of Jung's Psychology*. Garden City, New York: Doubleday & Company, Inc., 1972.

Steiner, Rudolf, *An Outline of Occult Science*. Spring Valley, New York: Anthroposophic Press, Inc., 1972.

Tart, Charles, *States of Consciousness*. New York: E.P. Dutton, 1975.

Von Franz, Marie-Louise, *Projection and Re-Collection in Jungian Psychology*. La Salle: Open Court, 1980.

—————— , *Shadow and Evil in Fairy Tales*. Irving, Texas: Spring Publications, Inc., 1980.

Wilson, Colin, *Access to Inner Worlds*. London: Rider, 1983.

—————— , *Mysteries*. London: Hodder and Stoughton, 1978.

Acknowledgments

Permission to reprint the following material is gratefully acknowledged. Information that will enable the publishers to rectify an error or omission will be welcomed.

Chapter 2 Pp. 24–25: *The Psychology of Suggestion* by Boris Sidis. Appleton-Century-Croft; pp. 26–27; *Proceedings* of the Society for Psychical Research, Vol. IV. The Society of Psychical Research, 1984. ISSN 0037-1475; pp. 31–32: *Divided Consciousness: Multiple Controls in Human Thought and Action* by Ernest Hilgard. John Wiley & Sons. **Chapter 3** Pp. 36–37: *Outline of Abnormal Psychology* by William McDougall. Charles Scribner's Sons; pp. 45, 48: *I'm Eve* by Chris Sizemore & Elen Pittillo. © 1977 by Chris Costner Sizemore and Elen Sain Pittillo. Doubleday & Co., Inc.; pp. 51–52: *The Minds of Billy Milligan* by Daniel Keyes. Random House, Inc.; pp. 57–59: *The Dissociation of a Personality* by Morton Prince. Meridian Books. **Chapter 5** Pp. 67–68: *The Heyday of Spiritualism* by Slater Brown. Hawthorne Books; p. 71: *Heyday of a Wizard: Daniel Home, The Medium* by Jean Burton. Alfred A. Knopf, Inc.; p. 70: *The Encyclopedia of Occultism and Parapsychology*, ed. Leslie Shepard. Gale Research Co.; p. 72: *Proceedings* of the Society for Psychical Research, Vol. XXXV. The Society for Psychical Research, 1984. ISSN 0037-1475; p. 73: *Heyday of a Wizard: Daniel Home, The Medium* by Jean Burton. Alfred A. Knopf, Inc.; pp. 75–76: *Proceedings* of the Society for Psychical Research, Vol. XXXII. The Society for Psychical Research, 1984. ISSN 0037-1475; pp. 76–78: *The Mediumship of Mrs. Leonard* by Susy Smith. University Books, Inc.; p. 80: *Experimental Magic* by J.H. Brennan. The Aquarian Press Ltd., Denington Estate, Wellingborough, Northants., England; p. 81: *The Encyclopedia of Occultism and Parapsychology*, ed. Leslie Shepard. Gale Research Co.; pp. 82–83: *Unfinished Symphonies* by Rosemary Brown. Souvenir Press; p. 84: *Singer in the Shadows* by Irving Litvag. © 1972 by Irving Litvag. Macmillan Publishing Co.; pp. 85–86: *The Link* by Matthew Manning. © 1974 by Colin Smythe Ltd. Holt Rinehart and Winston, Publishers; p. 92: *Confrontations with the Devil* by Robert Pelton.

Portal Press, by arrangement with Writers' House Inc. **Chapter 6** Pp. 96–101: *Begone Satan!* by Carl Vogl. TAN Books & Pubs., Inc.; pp. 102–05: *The Devil and Karen Kingston* by Robert Pelton. Portals Press, by arrangement with Writers' House Inc.; pp. 106, 113: *Psychic Self-Defence* by Dion Fortune. The Aquarian Press Ltd., Denington Estate, Wellingborough, Northants., England; pp. 109–10: *The Gateway of Understanding* by Carl Wickland. National Psychological Institute. **Chapter 7** P. 118: "Dangers of Automatism" by Canon Pearce-Higgins. *Spiritual Frontiers* (Autumn 1970, II-4), Frank C. Tribbe, editor. © 1970 by Spiritual Frontiers Fellowship, 10819 Winner Rd., Independence, Mo. 64052, U.S.A.; pp. 119–20: "How to Guard against Possession" by Paul Beard. *Spiritual Frontiers* (Autumn 1970, II-4), Frank C. Tribbe, ed. © 1970 by Spiritual Frontiers Fellowship; pp. 125: *How to Protect Yourself against Black Magic and Witchcraft* by Leslie Shepard. Citadel Press. **Chapter 8** Pp. 131–32: "A Case Illustrating So-Called Demon Possession" by Edward Mayer. *Journal of Abnormal Psychology*, Vol. 6, 1911. The American Psychopathological Association. **Chapter 9** P. 144: "The Presence of Spirits in Madness" by Wilson Van Dusen. Swedenborg Foundation, Inc., 139 East 23rd Street, New York, N.Y. 10010. **Chapter 11** P. 176: *Analysis of Unusual Experiences in Healing Relative to Diseased Minds* by Titus Bull. James Hyslop Foundation. **Chapter 14** P. 217: *Analysis of Unusual Experiences in Healing Relative to Diseased Minds* by Titus Bull. James Hyslop Foundation. **Chapter 16** P. 247: *Views from the Real World* by G.I. Gurdjieff. © 1973. Triangle Editions, Inc.; p. 247: *In Search of the Miraculous* by P.D. Ouspensky, quoted with permission of Tatiana M. Nagro, copyright holder.

Index